COMPLIANCE: REGULATION AND ENVIRONMENT

BRIDGET M. HUTTER

CLARENDON PRESS · OXFORD
1997

Oxford University Press, Great Clarendon Street, Oxford OX2 6DP

Oxford New York
Athens Auckland Bangkok Bogota Bombay
Buenos Aires Calcutta Cape Town Dar es Salaam
Delhi Florence Hong Kong Istanbul Karachi
Kuala Lumpur Madras Madrid Melbourne
Mexico City Nairobi Paris Singapore
Taipei Tokyo Toronto
and associated companies in
Berlin Ibadan

Oxford is a trade mark of Oxford University Press

Published in the United States
by Oxford University Press Inc., New York

© Bridget M. Hutter 1997

British Library Cataloguing in Publication Data
Data available

Library of Congress Cataloging in Publication Data
Data available
ISBN 0-19-826475-5

1 3 5 7 9 10 8 6 4 2

Typeset by Hope Services (Abingdon) Ltd.
Printed in Great Britain
on acid-free paper by
Biddles Ltd., Guildford and King's Lynn

Oxford Socio-Legal Studies

Compliance: Regulation and Environment

OXFORD SOCIO-LEGAL STUDIES

General Editor: Keith Hawkins, Reader in Law and Society, and Fellow and Tutor in Law of Oriel College, Oxford

Editorial Board: John Baldwin, Director of the Institute of Judicial Administration, University of Birmingham; William L. F. Felstiner, Professor of Sociology, University of California-Santa Barbara; Denis Galligan, Professor of Socio-Legal Studies and Director of the Centre for Socio-Legal Studies, Oxford; Sally Lloyd-Bostock, Senior Research Fellow, Centre for Socio-Legal Studies, Oxford; Doreen McBarnet, Senior Research Fellow, Centre for Socio-Legal Studies, Oxford; Simon Roberts, Professor of Law, London School of Economics.

International Advisory Board: John Braithwaite (Australian National University); Robert Cooter (University of California-Berkeley); Bryant Garth (American Bar Foundation); Volkmar Gessner (University of Bremen); Vittorio Olgiati (University of Milan); Martin Partington (University of Bristol).

Oxford Socio-Legal Studies is a series of books exploring the role of law in society for both an academic and a wider readership. The series publishes theoretical and empirically-informed work, from the United Kingdom and elsewhere, by social scientists and lawyers which advances understanding of the social reality of law and legal processes.

To
Clive

General Editor's Introduction

This study deals with one of the key ideas for those interested in the law in action, though there is not much yet in the socio-legal literature that specifically addresses the notion of compliance. Bridget Hutter's book is particularly welcome, therefore, as one of the first to explore the practical meaning of the concept in any detail. It presents a fine-grained analysis, one firmly in the interactionist tradition.

As Dr Hutter observes, we tend to take compliance for granted as an uncomplicated matter denoting whether a state of conformity with a rule or requirement actually exists or not. What the author does, how-ever, is to show that this is much too simplistic an assumption. She focuses on the nature and scope of compliance by conducting an empir-ical analysis of the compliance-seeking activities of three different kinds of regulatory inspector, and in doing so exposes the many facets and complexities of the concept in practice. Each of the inspectorates stud-ied by the author (those for factories, industrial air pollution, and rail-ways) shared a common formal organisation in the Health and Safety Executive, but their officials typically set about their law enforcement tasks in very different ways indeed and in often very different settings. The author's socio-legal analysis shows that what is thought of as com-pliance is provisional, and is a matter constantly open to interpretative work, leading to processes of social control marked by flexibility, adap-tiveness, and reflexivity.

This book addresses a self-evidently important topic in the literature of social control, and is a welcome addition to a number of other works in the field of social regulation that have already appeared in *Oxford Socio-Legal Studies*.

Keith Hawkins

Preface

Compliance is a much referred-to concept but it is not one which has been subject to any sustained academic scrutiny. In many respects it is a concept the meaning of which is taken for granted. Compliance with laws, rules, and regulations is assumed to be a straightforward and uncomplicated matter which simply denotes whether or not individuals and organizations have fulfilled the demands of the law. In practice, things are not so simple.

This study considers the concept of compliance in relation to the regulation of economic activities by the use of the criminal law. In particular, it considers the regulation of occupational health and safety and the environment in England and Wales in the 1980s. Sociological analysis treats regulatory compliance both as a concept and as a process of interpretative understanding. Moreover, it focuses on the social environments within which regulation occurs. The meaning of compliance is thrashed out in a web of social, political, and economic contradictions. It is important to understand the broader structural factors which influence regulation and its definition at the everyday level.

My aim has been to focus on one part of the regulatory process, namely the enforcement of regulation by field-level inspectors from three different inspectorates, the Factory Inspectorate, the Industrial Air Pollution Inspectorate, and the Railway Inspectorate. This book presents a snapshot of regulatory compliance and its interpretation and construction at a particular moment in time and within a specific legal jurisdiction. There have been important changes to the organizations studied and the most significant of these are discussed in Chapter 2. But they do not change the basic argument and purpose of this book, to analyse and understand compliance, partly through the collection of in-depth, rich empirical data. These data, in combination with and by comparison to research undertaken elsewhere and in different jurisdictions, illuminate and further our understanding. Common patterns and themes do emerge.

These patterns and themes 'matter' in a pragmatic sense. Regulation touches upon areas of vital importance to our lives, in the case of this research as employees, as rail travellers, and as ordinary members of the public who could fall victim to pollution or poor standards of occupational health and safety. It is therefore in our interest to know more about the workings of this 'grey area' of criminal law and social control.

This research received the full support and co-operation of the regulatory agencies involved. Senior staff of the Health and Safety Executive exercised great vision and confidence in exposing their organization to a team of researchers, particularly during a period of intense scrutiny from a government which was critical of both the civil service and regulation. I owe a special thanks to all of the inspectors I accompanied during the research period. It cannot be easy being shadowed, and I was given a warm welcome and access to both the public and private thoughts of inspectors.

The research for this book was undertaken as part of a programme of research into the regulation of occupational health and safety at the Centre for Socio-Legal Studies in Oxford. Many of the ideas contained in the book were developed in discussion with other members of the research team. Moreover, joint papers arising from the research have been written with Keith Hawkins, Peter Manning, and Sally Lloyd-Bostock. The Centre was an exciting and supportive environment within which to work and the Director, Don Harris, was especially important in facilitating this. I am very grateful to all concerned for the intellectual environment provided while I first worked on the research for this book and later as I wrote and rewrote it. This work has also informed my subsequent research into the impact of occupational health and safety in the railway industry, the data for this also having been collected while I was member of the Centre.

Special mention should be made of Keith Hawkins. Keith has written extensively on the subject of social regulation and it was he who first emphasized to me the crucial importance of *compliance* in the study of regulation. I have benefited from numerous discussions of my work with Keith. Moreover, he has in characteristically generous fashion commented extensively on various drafts of this book. I am very grateful to him for his intellectual and personal support at all stages in this research. Likewise Paul Rock has been very supportive in discussing this research with me over the past decade. He made many detailed and constructive comments on an earlier draft of this book for which I am, as ever, very grateful. I should also thank Nigel Dodd for commenting on the final chapter and Jane Cottee for help with typing the manuscript. Needless to say I hold full responsibility for the final product.

This book is dedicated to Clive Briault who has endured living with me through the entire project. He has survived being the 'lay' reader

of all possible drafts of this work, never hesitating to pull me up for jar-
gon and ungrammatical sentences. Perhaps he learnt something too.

BMH
May 1996

Contents

List of Tables   xvii

List of Figures   xviii

Abbreviations   xix

Table of Statutes   xx

Table of Statutory Instruments, Cases and Tribunal   xxi

Part 1: Setting the Scene   1

1   Organizing Themes and Concepts   3

    Regulation   4
        Theories of Regulation   4
        Types and Forms of Regulation   6
        Regulatory Offences   7
        The Regulatory Process   9
        Participants in the Regulatory Process   10
    Compliance and Regulation   12
        Definition and Discretion   12
        Compliance as Process and Negotiation   13
        Compliance as an Enforcement Process   14
        Compliance and Variation   17
    Research Approach   19

2   The Health and Safety Executive   21

    The Health and Safety Executive   21
        Robens   21
        The Structure of HSE   23
    Selection of a Sample   28
        Principles of Selection   28
        The Pilot Study   29
    The Selected Inspectorates   30
        Historical Perspective   30
        The Inspectorates 1974–1989   35
        Organization   36
        The Inspectors   44
        Formalization and Organizational Control   50

Enforcement Approach 51
Postscript 56
Industrial Air Pollution Inspectorate 57
Railway Inspectorate 59
Health and Safety Executive 61
Conclusions 62

Part 2: Defining Compliance 65

3 The Legal and Administrative Framework 67

Legal Definitions of Compliance 67
The Health and Safety at Work etc. Act 1974 69
Environmental Regulation 70
Administrative Definitions of Compliance 72
Consistency and Uniformity 77
Conclusions 78

4 The Working Definition of Compliance 80

The Concept 80
The Field-Inspector's Perspective 85
Principles of Definition 85
Conclusions 102

Part 3: Monitoring Compliance 105

5 Inspectors Take the Initiative: Proactive Methods 107

Routine Inspections 107
Spot Checks 107
Inspection Programmes 109
Types of Inspection 112
Inspections: Structures and Content 113
Routine Inspection as a Method of Assessing Compliance 115
Sampling 120
Conclusions 126

6 Responding to Complaints and Accidents:
Reactive Enforcement Methods 127
Complaints 127
Complaints and Compliance 133
Accidents and Incidents 136
Accident Reporting 137

The Decision to Investigate 138
Accidents as a Means of Assessing Compliance 145
Proactive and Reactive Enforcement: Assessing the Balance 150
Self-regulation 151
Conclusions 153

**Part 4: Interactions Between Inspectors and the
Regulated** 155

7 Whose Compliance? 157

Industries 157
Companies 160
Organizations 166
Contact Persons 166
Managers and the Workforce 169
Management 173
The Workforce and Workforce Representatives 178
International Dimensions 180
Reasons for Compliance and Non-Compliance 182
Co-operation 187
Conclusions 193

8 Compliance as a Process of Enforcement 195

Enforcement Careers 195
Entering the Career 196
Regulatory Goals 205
Enforcement Strategies and Tactics 206
Enforcement Pyramids 206
Sanctions Pyramid: Research Findings 207
Pyramid of Enforcement Strategies: Research Findings 228
Leaving the Enforcement Career 232
Conclusions 233

Part 5: Conclusion 235

9 Conclusion 237

Theories of Social Control 238
Policy Implications 243
APPENDIX: THE ORGANIZATION OF DATA COLLECTION 249

xvi *Contents*

The Factory Inspectorate   249
Industrial Air Pollution Inspectorate   250
Railway Inspectorate   252
Common Points   253
The Research Environment   254

Bibliography   257
Author Index   269
Subject Index   271

List of Tables

1. The Sample: Basic Facts   31
2. The Number of Informations Laid by FI, IAPI, and RI
   1980–1985   53
3. The Number of Notices Served by FI, IAPI, and RI
   1980–1985   54
4. The Probability of a Site being Prosecuted by the
   Factory Inspectorate and Industrial Air Pollution
   Inspectorate 1983–1985   55
5. The Probability of a Site being Served with an
   Improvement Notice by the Factory Inspectorate and
   the Industrial Air Pollution Inspectorate   55
6. The Probability of Prosecutions by the Factory and the
   Railway Inspectorates in 1983 and 1984 Expressed as
   a Proportion of Employees in the Relevant Industries   56
7. Improvement Notices served by the Factory
   Inspectorate and Railway Inspectorate in 1983 and
   1984 Expressed as a Proportion of Employees in the
   Relevant Industries   56
8. Injuries to Employees Reported to the Factory and
   Railway Inspectorates April 1987–March 1988   137
9. Railway Accident Investigations 1983–1984   141
10. Comparison of FI and IAPI Resources 1980–1987   190
11. Comparison of FI and RI Resources 1980–1985   191
12. IAPI Prosecutions, 1978–1983   192
13. Infractions Declared by IAPI 1980–1989   219
14. Appeals Against Enforcement Notices (Improvement
    and Prohibition) Issued by HSE Inspectorates 1980
    and 1985   224

List of Figures

1. Health and Safety Commission—Health and Safety
   Executive Organization Chart   26
2. HM Factory Inspectorate—Organization Chart   37
3. Organizational Structure of the Industrial Air Pollution
   Inspectorate   41
4. The Sanctions Pyramid   227
5. Pyramid of Enforcement Strategies   229

Abbreviations

BISPA	British Independent Steel Producers Association
BPEO	Best Practical Environmental Option
BPM	Best Practicable Means
CBI	Confederation of British Industry
COSHH	Control of Substances Hazardous to Health Regulations 1988
EMAS	Employment Medical Advisory Service
FCG	Field Consultancy Group
FI	Factory Inspectorate/Inspector
HSC	Health and Safety Commission
HSE	Health and Safety Executive
HSW	Health and Safety at Work etc Act 1974
IAPI	Industrial Air Pollution Inspectorate/Inspector
LDA	Lead Development Association
NIG	National Industry Group
NGO	Non-governmental Organization
REI	Railway Employment Inspector
RIAC	Railway Industry Advisory Committee
RI	Railway Inspectorate
RLSD	Research and Laboratory Service Division
RSC	Railway Safety Case
TAPD	Technical and Air Pollution Division
TLV	Threshold Limit Value
TUC	Trade Union Congress

Table of Statutes

Alkali Act 1863...32, 33
Alkali Act 1874...33, 34
Alkali Act 1881 33
Alkali etc Works Regulation Act 1906...........................34, 70–1, 197
British Transport Commission Act 1957.............................197
Clean Air Act 1956...70, 71, 86
Control of Pollution Act 1974..........................53, 70, 71, 192
Deregulation and Contracting Out Bill 1994........................61
Environment Act 1995 58
Environmental Protection Act 1990....................34, 58, 134
Factories Act 1802..30
Factories Act 1833..30
Factories Act 1961.............................35, 71, 81–2, 196, 223
Health and Safety at Work etc. Act 1974.............23–5, 34, 35, 36, 43,
            52, 60, 69–70, 71, 72, 73, 75, 79, 115, 138, 140,
                  157, 169, 179, 185, 187, 204, 216, 223
Railways Act 1993..60
Regulation of Railways Act 1840 30
Regulation of Railways Act, 1842.................................33, 197
Regulation of Railways Act 1871.............33, 138–40, 143–5, 148, 252
The Road and Railway Traffic Act 1933 197

Table of Statutory Instruments, Cases and Tribunal

STATUTORY INSTRUMENTS

The Construction (Working Places) Regulations 1966 ....71, 73
Control of Substances Hazardous to Health Regulations
    1988 ....61, 151, 208
Environmental Protection (Applications, Appeals and Registers)
    Regulations 1991 134
Health and Safety (Emissions into the Atmosphere)
    Regulations 1983 ....53, 192
Notification of Accidents and Dangerous Occurrences Regulations
    1980...136
Notification of Accidents Order 1986...136
Railways (Notice of Accidents) Order 1986 136
Reporting of Injuries, Diseases and Dangerous Occurrences
    Regulations 1985..136, 137
The Railways (Safety Case) Regulations 1994 60
The Railways (Safety Critical Work) Regulations 1994.......................60
The Safety Representatives and Safety Cases Regulations, 1977 169
The Woodworking Machinery Special Regulations 1922; 1945........71
The Woodworking Machines Regulations 1974......................71–2, 82

CASES

Edwards v. *National Coal Board* [1949] 1 KB 704...................................86
Warner v. *Metropolitan Police Commissioner* [1968] 2 All ER 356..............8

INDUSTRIAL TRIBUNAL

National Smokeless Fuels Ltd v. *R. Perriman* 14 July, 11 & 12 October,
    1982. Case no. H/S 15896/82...100

PART 1

Setting the Scene

1 Organizing Themes and Concepts

This book has been inspired by and is devoted to an in-depth examination of a single concept, namely that of compliance. Taken at face value this concept may appear to be straightforward. The *Concise Oxford Dictionary* (1990) defines compliance as 'the act or an instance of complying; obedience to a request, command etc'. The definition offered of the word 'comply' appears similarly uncomplicated—'act in accordance (with a wish, command, etc)'. Compliance thus conjures up notions of conformity.

This research is concerned with compliance with the law, a matter which may also appear unproblematic. In a formal sense the concept of compliance is strictly tied to the law. But regulatory laws, more so than much other legislation, need interpretation by field-level officials. It is not always clear what the law means, and hence what compliance might look like and entail. Regulatory law is often vague, involving broad legal standards and the exercise of discretion by officials. A socio-legal perspective of compliance reveals it to be a complicated process of adaptation, flexibility, reflection, and, above all, interpretation. This is in stark contrast to the image given in some official publications.

If we take examples from the substantive areas most appropriate to this study, namely those of health and safety at work and environmental regulation, there is a tendency to refer to 'compliance rates' as if they are unproblematically constructed. A British Factory Inspectorate publication on *Managing Safety*, for instance, discusses legal compliance: '[L]egal compliance . . . reflects the extent to which a range of specified hazards have been eliminated' (HSE, 1981, p. 27) and it suggests that '[L]egal compliance can be quickly achieved by a determined and systematic approach' (*ibid.*). The earlier Robens Report into *Safety and Health at Work* had highlighted some of the drawbacks of such an interpretation: '[i]t is not enough to think in terms of "ensuring compliance" with minimum legal standards . . . the concept is too narrow and restrictive. . . . Inspectors should seek to raise standards above the minimum levels required by law' (1972, para. 211). The growing literature on regulation adds weight to the view that compliance is a much wider and more complicated concept than may at first be apparent.

Although compliance has emerged as a central feature of regulatory control it has received very little direct attention with respect to its nature and scope. Di Mento's (1986) study of environmental control in the United States is one major exception and Friedland's (1990) edited case studies is another, although the latter is very much preoccupied with the subject of gaining compliance. Manning (1988) notes that compliance may be left as an 'undefined sponge concept' which can be used to refer to a range of factors from accident rates to sanctioning strategies. Hence compliance is an unrefined concept, indeed some might argue it is an unrefinable concept. This study will investigate the nature and scope of compliance and attempt to map out what it actually means.

REGULATION

Before exploring the existing uses of the concept of compliance in the academic literature, we should set the scene for such a discussion. A prominent context here is that of *regulation*, an area of social and legal control where compliance appears to be of particular and primary importance. Regulation refers to the use of the law to constrain and organize the activities of business and industry. It is state activity and as such is contentious, most especially because it is at the heart of debates about the extent to which governments should adopt a 'laissez-faire' approach to markets and their activities and the extent to which they should intervene to protect particular groups (Hutter and Sorensen, 1993).

Theories of Regulation

Theories of regulation divide on the issue of whom governments intervene on behalf of. Accommodative or consensual theories regard regulatory policies as protective of 'public goods' (policies such as anti-pollution laws) or protective of specific populations (policies such as consumer, employee, or anti-discrimination laws) (Lowi, 1972). The activities of relatively powerful groups are thus regulated in favour of a less powerful majority. Not all commentators, however, accept that this is an accurate picture of what actually happens. Conflict theorists believe that regulatory laws and polices do nothing to curb seriously the activities of business and industry, which they believe to be both major players in the shaping of regulatory policies and players who are deemed to be favoured in the implementation process (Carson, 1974; 1980; Gunningham, 1974; Snider, 1987; Yeager, 1991).

These theories place very different interpretations upon the emergence, framing, and enforcement of regulatory legislation. Whilst they all recognize the tension between regulation and business interests and recognize the presence of conflicting interest groups they regard the resolution of these tensions in different ways. Accommodative theorists portray regulatory legislation as the result of an accommodation between interest groups. They adhere to a consensual, pluralist model of society and argue that the legislation is neither as interventionist as the reformers would want it to be nor as lax as business would prefer (Carson, 1974; Paulus, 1974). Conflict theorists, who tend to adopt a dominant power group model of society, regard economic interests as paramount. They argue that the dominant class has ensured that its interests are not seriously affected by regulation. For example, they argue that business and industry are well represented in government and are therefore significant in shaping the legislation (Gunningham, 1974; Yeager, 1991).

Different theories give varying interpretations of enforcement activity. Accommodative theorists regard low levels of prosecution as a rational response to limited agency resources, ambiguous legislation, and weak sanctions (Cranston, 1979; Hutter, 1988; Richardson, 1983). Conflict theorists, however, cite a reluctance to prosecute as evidence of ineffective legislation, the 'capture' of the regulatory agency by business and the power of business (Bernstein, 1955; Box, 1983; Clinard and Yeager, 1980; Gunningham, 1974; Yeager, 1991). Both groups agree that tactical manœuvres at the time of legislating weakened regulatory law, but whereas conflict theorists believe the law was weakened to the point of ineffectiveness, consensual theorists believe that improvements have been effected, albeit not on a scale the reformers would have wished.

Sociological theories of regulations are mirrored in other social science approaches to regulation, for example, by economic theory. Ogus (1994), in the most comprehensive and detailed discussion of law and economic theory to date, draws a distinction between two broad economic theories which in many respects mirror the sociological theories outlined above.

Ogus (1994, p. 1 ff.) identifies a tension between two systems of economic organization, namely the market system and the collectivist system. In the market system individuals and groups are largely free to pursue their own goals, whereas in the collectivist system the state seeks to correct deficiencies in the market system for the collective good. The market system gives rise to a private-interest theory of regulation which regards private interest groups as securing regulatory benefits for themselves through their use of the political and legal systems. A collectivist view of regulation gives rise to public-interest theory which regards regulation as a corrective to the operation of the market and as operating in pursuit of collective goals.

There also appear to be cultural differences in regulatory theory. American scholars tend to subscribe to rather more extreme theories than do, for example those in Britain and Australia. At one extreme the United States has given us 'capture' theory, that is the theory that regulatory agencies have been 'captured' by business. According to this theory 'captured' regulatory agencies share the world-view of business, partly because they are in close, co-operative, and possibly dependent relations with business and partly because the agency can only recruit specialist staff from the regulated community. The result, it is argued, is regulatory failure (Bernstein, 1955; Nader, 1980). At another extreme, a different form of regulatory failure is identified by American theorists, namely that of over-regulation or regulatory excess. Wilson (1985, p. 24) explains that this theory suggests, first, that regulations were laying onerous burdens on industry and, secondly, that they were sanctioning even the most trivial offences. This inflexibility, it is suggested, both alienated business and imposed unreasonable costs upon it (Bardach and Kagan, 1982).

British and Australian authors, in contrast to their American counterparts, tend to advocate the pluralist (Grabosky and Braithwaite, 1985; Carson, 1974) or occasionally the conflict (Gunningham, 1974; 1987) models of regulatory theory. These countries are very similar for two main reasons: first because they share very similar regulatory laws and structures, and, secondly, because there has been a coincidence of scholars (notably Carson and Gunningham). The differences between these theorists and those from the United States have largely been explained in cultural terms. For example, the American system is said to be more adversarial and litigious than the British and Australian systems (Hawkins, 1992; Kelman, 1981; Vogel, 1986).

Types and Forms of Regulation

The regulation literature often distinguishes between economic (or financial) regulation and social regulation (Hutter and Sorensen, 1993;

Snider, 1987; Ogus, 1994; Yeager, 1991). *Economic or financial regulation* generally refers to the regulation of financial markets, prices, and profits. *Social regulation* refers to laws protecting the environment, consumers, and employees. It concerns the regulation of industrial processes which may cause harm to workforces, the public, and the environment (Hawkins and Hutter, 1993).[1] Yeager (1991, p. 9) explains that such regulations 'restrict management autonomy at the point of production' and 'address the negative effects of production relations on consumers, workers, communities and the general environment' (*ibid.*, p. 24).

Governments can regulate business and industry in a variety of ways. They may establish *economic incentives* such as effluent charges or taxation policies. Alternatively they may opt for *legal* regulation either through civil litigation or criminal sanctions such as fines or imprisonment. *Administrative* measures, such as *licensing*, are another method which may be adopted, as are *self-regulation* or *self-audit*, where government seeks to establish the principle that businesses and industries regulate themselves.[2]

This research falls within the area of social regulation in its consideration of environmental and health and safety at work regulation. It is primarily concerned with the regulation of industries in Britain, in particular the use of criminal sanctions as a method of regulation. Nevertheless, other forms of regulation are not completely ignored, since self-regulation and administrative strategies are very much involved in the spheres of regulation under consideration.

Regulatory Offences

The use of the law to regulate the ill-effects of industrial and business activities has increased dramatically since the nineteenth century. New categories of criminal behaviour have been created and it is important to distinguish between different types of law and crime involving businesses. Snider (1987) identifies laws which regulate business (and the crimes of business—that is, corporate crime) and laws in the interest of business (and crimes against business—that is, white-collar crime). Regulatory offences fall most readily within the former category, that

---

[1] The distinction between economic and social regulation is not always so clearcut and this is largely a heuristic division. See Yeager, 1991, 24.

[2] See Gunningham, 1984, ch. 13; Grabosky and Braithwaite, 1986, ch. 14; Di Mento, 1986, ch. 3; and Ogus, 1994, pts. III and IV for a more detailed discussion of the various forms of regulation available to governments. See Cheit, 1990, for a discussion of private-standard setting by such bodies as trade associations and professional societies.

of corporate crime—although it should be remarked that this label here may be misleading for regulatory offences which may be committed by individuals and a wide range of businesses and industries, not just by corporations. Indeed regulatory laws pertain to a wide range of small businesses, such as corner shops, market traders, farms, and workshops, none of which fit easily our stereotypes of 'the corporate criminal' (Croall, 1988). For this reason, the term 'regulatory crime' may be more helpful.

The use of criminal sanctions to control regulatory behaviour is controversial. Some regard regulatory offences as different from traditional criminal offences and argue that they should be regarded as a separate phenomenon in academic study (Baucus and Dworkin, 1991). Some authors refer to regulatory offences as 'quasi-criminal' offences,[3] others distinguish between 'real crimes' and 'regulatory offences'.[4] Proponents of these views argue that regulatory offences are administratively and morally distinct from traditional crimes. It is considered significant that regulatory offences are often handled differently from traditionally criminal offences—by different enforcement agencies and by administrative (as well as criminal) procedures. Moreover, it is argued that regulatory offences do not tend to elicit the public outrage commonly evoked by traditional crimes and hence may not be regarded as immoral.

These arguments embrace a complexity of political and academic views which it is important to separate. Certainly there will be a substantial number of people who will regard many regulatory offences as immoral—not least because they may involve serious injury or even death. But the interesting question in this instance is why death and injury may be regarded as less offensive in certain circumstances than others. We should perhaps heed Tappan's (1947) warning against employing normative definitions of crime and maintain as research questions the nature of the relationship between the law and morality and the law and class. As Baucus and Dworkin (1991, p. 235) argue, we need to know the reasons for the differential handling of offences. For instance, we need to know whether or not large companies can (and do) use their power to manipulate the labelling process and minimize sanctions.[5] What are the complexities posed by regulating corpo-

[3] See, for example, Lord Reid in *Warner* v. *Metropolitan Police Commissioner* [1968] 2 All ER 356.

[4] Council of the Law Society, 1967; Jackson, 1967; Justice, 1980; Smith and Hogan, 1978.

[5] See generally, Hutter, 1988, ch. 2.

rations? How can regulatory responsibility be satisfactorily assigned within large corporate bodies? (Wells, 1992).

Moreover, is moral ambivalence encouraged by regulatory legislation? This legislation is notable for abandoning the concept of *mens rea* and accepting the principle of strict liability. Thus notions of individual guilt and moral culpability are not requirements for a criminal conviction under regulatory law. Arguably this dilutes the moral force of the legislation (Justice, 1980; Paulus, 1974). Ironically this seems to be the case despite increasing evidence that regulatory officials give the strict liability provisions at their disposal pragmatic value only in relation to serious offences. In other cases they reintroduce at the operational level the notion of *mens rea* (Hartung, 1950; Hawkins, 1984; Hutter, 1988; Richardson *et al.*, 1983).

Social scientists interpret the issue differently. Strict liability may be interpreted as a harsh measure which increases the ease and efficiency of enforcement and offers substantial protection to the public. But the consequences of a strict-liability regime may lead to a rather different interpretation. The inclusion of a strict-liability principle may result in a hesitancy to prosecute or sanction offenders. Thus it may reduce considerably the stigma attaching to regulatory offences (Carson, 1970; Ogus, 1994; Paulus, 1974). Strict liability may therefore be regarded either as an expedient means to an end or as a cynical move to weaken regulatory law and its enforcement. It may either facilitate prosecution, discourage it, or force an accommodation between two extremes.

The Regulatory Process

Once governments have decided which form of regulation to adopt they generally put into place some apparatus for its implementation.[6] The 'natural history' of regulation involves the enactment of legislation;[7] its implementation by the administrative bureaucracy charged with enforcement;[8] and the impact of the regulations upon those they seek to control and protect.[9] The focus of this study is on the

---

[6] The exceptions here would involve regulations which were purely nominal and 'without teeth'. The resources accompanying some early 19th Century protective legislation in Britain were quite meagre and these laws sometimes had a rudimentary administrative apparatus. This was the case, for example, with the early Factory Acts. See Ch. 2.

[7] See Carson, 1980; Gunningham, 1974; Paulus, 1974.

[8] See Carson, 1970; Hawkins, 1984; Hutter, 1988; Kagan, 1978; Richardson *et al.*, 1983.

[9] To date this is the least researched area. See Brittan, 1984; Genn, 1987, 1993.

implementation stage, most particularly the enforcement activities of field-level officials charged with applying the law and policy-making about the law. It is important to recognize that the implementation stage of regulation involves a division between policy-making and enforcement. The policy-making effort is very much directed to stand-ard-setting and organizational interpretations of the law,[10] whereas the enforcement aspect of implementation is focused on inspectors and their decision-making about the law and agency policies.[11] These offi-cials are in the front line of regulatory enforcement, and it is they who have the discretion (perhaps even sometimes create the discretion) to determine how government regulation is ultimately translated into action—they are the 'gatekeepers' to the regulatory process. But, as we will see, they do not work in a vacuum or free from constraints—they operate within varying political, social, legal, and organizational para-meters.

Participants in the Regulatory Process

The regulatory agency is but one participant in the regulatory process. Governments are to varying extents continuing participants in regula-tion. The regulatory bureaucracy will be part of the state apparatus and may well be accountable to government. Moreover, the government will always be in the background with the power to revoke existing legislation, enact new legislation, and control budgets. Individual Members of Parliament may become involved as 'moral crusaders' for particular legislation or causes. More likely, they will follow up queries or complaints from constituents.[12]

In the wider society there will be groups with a broad interest in the regulatory process. Health and safety issues, for example, will attract the interest of trade unions and employers associations. Environmental

[10] Very few studies of policy-making have been undertaken to date. Notable excep-tions include Mashaw and Harfst's (1990) study of motor-vehicle safety regulations in the United States; Cheit's (1990) comparison of setting safety standards in the public and pri-vate sectors; and in the criminal justice area, Rock's (1986) ethnographic study of policy-making in the Canadian Justice Ministry and his UK Home Office Study (1990).

[11] In contrast to the scarcity of studies of policy-making there is a long tradition of research into the activities of field-level officers. Early studies were about the police—see, for example, Banton, 1964; Bittner, 1967; Cain, 1973; Manning, 1977; Piliavin and Briar, 1964; Skolnick 1975. More recently, there have been similar studies of regulatory officials—see, for example, Cranston, 1979; Hawkins, 1984; Hutter, 1988; Jamieson, 1985; Richardson *et al.*, 1983.

[12] Such activity tends to be especially heightened at election time: see Hutter, 1988.

matters might concern trade associations and those particularly affected by particular environmental issues, such as a local community which is affected by a specific polluter. The press may also be involved in bringing public attention to pressure groups or particular problems. Indeed, the media may be quite significant in forming public and political attitudes (Cohen, 1980; Hutter and Manning, 1990 pp. 106–10). Companies will obviously be prominent players in the regulatory process, as may their suppliers. Within companies there will be a range of participants, namely owners, management, employees, and possibly a safety or environmental organization, comprising, for instance, specialist committees and personnel. The extent to which these groups work together to promote regulatory objectives or come into conflict about them is largely unknown, although there do seem to be cultural differences (Kelman, 1981).

Beyond individual companies there may be industry-based participation in the regulatory process through, for example, trade associations. There will be differences in financial and technical ability between members of these associations and hence differences in their ability to influence the regulatory process, either through the trade association or by more direct means. Likewise, there will be differences between trade associations (Cheit, 1990; Yeager, 1991).

Companies and industries all work within the wider economic context of the market. There will be local, national, and, increasingly, international markets, all of which may have varying impacts upon regulation and which may themselves be partly constituted by regulation. Ultimately, of course, the general economic climate of the local, national, or even international context within which regulation is enacted will influence the regulatory process, as will the political context of regulation. The regulatory process involves the interaction of all of the participants in regulation (Olsen, 1992). It also concerns the interaction between the economic, political, and bureaucratic contexts of regulation and the influence of these upon the participants in the process (Hutter and Manning, 1990).

The different sociological theories of regulation attribute these participants varying degrees of power within the regulatory process. Conflict theorists believe that business and industry generally hold a dominant position while consensual theorists see this group as one of a plurality of players, all of whom are competing for their interests to be taken into account. None of this should disguise the complexity of regulation. Different models of regulation undoubtedly 'fit' varying substantive examples, at varying time periods and in different cultures (Cotterell, 1992). Regulation is a complex and complicated process as the discussion of the single concept of compliance will reveal.

COMPLIANCE AND REGULATION

Definition and Discretion

Compliance is a concept relevant to all forms of enforcement, but it appears to take on particular importance in the regulatory context. The concept of compliance is used in a variety of ways in the regulation literature. Manning (1988) notes that compliance is what the agencies involved define it to be, 'a process of extended and endless negotiation'. A number of important themes are raised here. Manning immediately raises the significance of *definition*, since conformity with the law is not self-evident. Legal mandates are often unclear about what constitutes compliance. As Di Mento (1986, p. 25) notes '[l]awmakers often do not specify the meanings of words and phrases.' Sometimes this is intentional, sometimes an oversight, and sometimes impossible. Lawyers would immediately identify the issue of discretion here, that is the scope for interpretation of the law allocated to, or appropriated by, decision-makers in the legal process.[13]

The 'law in action' inevitably involves interpretation of the 'law in books' and in some systems, notably the regulatory systems which are the focus of this study (health and safety and environmental regulation in Britain), enforcement officials are allocated a good deal of *de jure* discretion (see Chapter 3). When legal mandates are unclear or unspecific then what constitutes compliance is, as Edelman *et al.*, remind us, largely dependent 'on the initiative and agenda of those persons within organizations who are charged with managing the compliance effort'

---

[13] Discretion is an important topic for legal scholars: see in particular Davis, 1969; Galligan, 1986; Hawkins, 1992; Jowell, 1973; Kadish and Kadish, 1973. Studies of discretionary decision-making comprise a significant part of the regulation literature. Some of these studies allocate discretion and its uses a central position: see Adler and Asquith, 1981; Baldwin, 1985; Jowell, 1975; Mashaw, 1983. Others take a broader focus and emphasize the general approach to decision-making taken by legal actors (whether or not this decision-making is *de jure* is in some respects irrelevant to some of these authors.) See Cranston, 1979; Hawkins, 1984; Hutter, 1988; Kaufman, 1960; Richardson *et al.*, 1983. A much more established tradition of this type of study exists with reference to the police, see Banton, 1964; Cain, 1973; Manning, 1977; Skolnick, 1975.

(1991, p. 73). Compliance is thus a complex process of defining responses to mandates that are often ambiguous (Edelman *et al.*, 1991, p. 75). This occurs at field-level and the level of policy-making which may involve both standard-setting and administrative guidance about how to comply with statutes and regulations and policy-making about how to enforce these. Indeed this may well be a reflexive process in which policy-makers, field-level inspectors, and even the regulated feed their expectations and practices into each other and adapt accordingly. As Di Mento notes, one consequence of this is that 'Compliance has no one definition. Non-compliance has no one explanation. . . . Recommendations aimed at achieving compliance must recognize the varying and at times contradictory perceptions of rule violations and must take into account the complex processes that make for non-compliance' (1986, p. 163).

Compliance as Process and Negotiation

A theme running through much regulation literature is that compliance with regulatory legislation should be regarded as much as a process as an event. Regulatory officials may regard compliance both as a matter of instant conformity and an open-ended and long-term process which may take several years to attain.[14] Edelman *et al.* (1991) seek to shift the emphasis to the *process* of compliance, particularly in view of their belief that compliance is a social and political process that evolves over time. Similarly Di Mento (1986, p. 34) argues that compliance should be seen as 'evolving from interaction among several groups, as occurring over time and as an outcome that is difficult to control by any single policy lever'. This is the case at both the level of standard-setting (Di Mento, 1986, pp. 26, 28) and the enforcement stage of the regulatory process (Bardach and Kagan, 1982, p. 63).

Implicit in the notion of compliance as a process and the product of the interaction of several participants in the regulatory process is Manning's earlier point that compliance is 'the process of extended and endless negotiation'. The view that conformity to the law may be a matter of negotiation between enforcement officials and those they control is not one that we would necessarily expect to command instant recognition. Yet it is an approach that some would argue is embedded in the history of law enforcement. Rock (1983), for example, has analysed the

---

[14] See generally Chs. 4 and 8 below. Also, Hawkins, 1984.

negotiated character of the criminal and social order in late seventeenth- and early eighteenth-century England, arguing that criminality was negotiated out of political necessity in a geographically and socially fragmented society (see also Winter, 1985). More recently Rock (1995) has suggested that a negotiated style of social control may be the major pattern of formal social control in Western society. This is a view which is lent credibility by a growing body of literature in the enforcement of regulatory legislation where negotiation has been identified by numerous studies as a distinctive feature of regulatory enforcement (Carson, 1970; Cranston, 1979; Hawkins, 1984; Hutter, 1988; Richardson *et al.*, 1983). Indeed, the tendency of regulatory officials to adopt enforcement strategies where they attempt to gain the compliance of the regulated through informal enforcement techniques which centre around negotiation has led some to use the term compliance to denote a whole enforcement system.

Compliance as an Enforcement Process

The question of how regulatory officials use the law and what they aim to achieve was the starting point of many of the early studies of regulatory enforcement. Authors such as Carson (1970); Cranston (1979); Hawkins (1984) and Richardson *et al.* (1983) all sought to understand how the law and criminal sanctions are used to control business and industrial activities. Each of these studies identified the adoption of common enforcement practices by officials from a variety of backgrounds. Enforcement of the law, it was argued, did not refer simply to legal action but to a wide array of informal enforcement techniques including education, advice, persuasion, and negotiation. These were used by all law enforcement officials, but came into particular prominence in the regulatory arena.

A binary model of enforcement styles has been adopted by some researchers to enhance our understanding of law enforcement. This model takes account of the methods and techniques used by enforcement officials and the objectives towards which they work. The enforcement style approximating to that often adopted by regulatory officials is variously referred to as the accommodative (Richardson, 1983) or compliance (Hawkins, 1984; Reiss, 1984) strategy of enforcement. Compliance is of central importance to this strategy since securing compliance is its main objective, through both the remedy of existing problems and, above all, the prevention of others. The preferred methods to achieve these ends are co-operative and conciliatory. So where compliance is less than complete then persuasion, negotiation, and education are the primary enforcement techniques. Thus compliance is not necessarily regarded as being achievable immediately, but may rather be seen as a long-term aim. The use of formal methods, especially prosecution, is regarded as a last resort, something to be avoided unless all else fails to secure compliance.

This model of enforcement is contrasted with another termed the sanctioning strategy by Hawkins (1984) and the deterrent model by Reiss (1984). This is a penal style of enforcement which accords prosecution an important role. Indeed, the number of prosecutions initiated may be regarded as both a sign of success and as an indicator of work undertaken. But while Hawkins and Reiss would agree that the methods preferred in such a model are penal and adversarial, they disagree about the objectives of such an approach. Reiss clearly regards both deterrence and compliance systems as 'oriented towards preventing the occurrence of violations' (1984, p. 24), whereas Hawkins would not attribute the sanctioning model such a narrow objective. Rather, he argues, the sanctioning model is primarily concerned with delivering punishment which may have a variety of objectives ranging from pure retribution to a variety of utilitarian aims (Hawkins, personal communication).

While studies generally associate regulatory enforcement with the accommodative style and the sanctioning style with the police, it was always emphasized that in reality all enforcement agencies would use both styles, albeit with differing levels of commitment. This is because the two broad strategies are analytical models or ideal types of enforcement strategy. This said, it remains the case that the majority of studies, especially the earliest ones, identified the accommodative style as characteristically a regulatory enforcement style. The first studies to document any significant deviation from this pattern were of American regulatory agencies in the 1970s. Kelman's (1981) study of OSHA and Shover *et al.*'s (1982) study of the Office of Surface Mining both describe regulatory agencies which adopted enforcement strategies closely approximating to the sanctioning style. My research into the law-enforcement procedures of Environmental Health Officers mapped out further evidence of variations in the enforcement strategies of regulatory officials. Indeed, these data led me to refine the binary model of enforcement to include two ideal-typical strategies, which can be used in the context of this research to describe and explain differences of approach among different regulatory inspectorates.

The Persuasive and Insistent Strategies

The persuasive and insistent strategies discussed in Hutter (1988) both approximate to the accommodative or compliance model of enforcement, as opposed to the deterrence or sanctioning model. Both strategies share the common objective of securing compliance, but they differ about the stringency of the means to this end. The *persuasive* strategy epitomizes the accommodative approach adopted by so many regulatory agencies. The range of tactics favoured by those adhering to such a strategy are informal. Officials educate, persuade, coax, and cajole offenders into complying with the law. They explain what the law demands and the reasons for legislative requirements, and they discuss how improvements can best be attained. Patience and understanding underpin the whole strategy, which is regarded as an open-ended and long-term venture. This strategy approximates Braithwaite, Walker, and Grabosky's notion of the Diagnostic Inspectorate (1987).

The *insistent* strategy is a less benevolent and less flexible approach than the persuasive strategy. There are fairly clearly-defined limits to the tolerance of officials adhering to this strategy. They are not prepared to spend a long time patiently cajoling offenders into compliance and they expect a fairly prompt response to their requests. When this is not forthcoming then officials will automatically increase the pressure to comply and will readily initiate legal action to achieve their objectives should they encounter overt resistance to their requests. However, it is important to stress that the ultimate objective of these enforcement moves is to gain compliance, not to effect retribution, and this is one of the major differences between the insistent and sanctioning strategies.

As Braithwaite, Walker, and Grabosky (1987) note, there is an important and empirically significant middle ground between the sanctioning and compliance models identified in the binary model of enforcement. The insistent strategy forms part of this middle ground, which includes the 'Token Enforcers' described by Braithwaite *et al.* and Bardach and Kagan's ideal of 'flexible enforcement', wherein officials are flexible both in their interpretation of the rules and in their readiness to use legal coercion. The differences between the persuasive and insistent strategies concerning rule-interpretation in many respects mirror their varying propensities to use legal coercion; those who are most flexible in their interpretation of the law are also more inclined to be flexible in their readiness to apply legal sanctions.

Circumstances Encouraging Negotiation

The circumstances which allow or even demand that compliance be a matter for discussion and negotiation vary. At one level the whole structure of regulatory law may be regarded as encouraging negotiation, this being particularly so in Britain where much regulatory legislation comprises duties rather than commands and where administrative discretion takes on central importance (see Chapter 3). At another level the nature of the activities controlled by regulatory officials may lead to negotiation. This has a number of facets, as Hawkins (1984) explains. He draws a distinction between forms of deviance which are 'continuing, repetitive, or episodic in character' and deviance which consists of isolated discrete and bounded incidents (1984, p. 6), his argument being that a negotiating strategy is more likely in the former. He contends that this is largely because the former type of deviance is 'amenable to strategies of correction or control in a way that most forms of isolated crime cannot be' (1984, p. 6) because they are unpredictable as to timing and location.[15]

The complexity of the problems encountered by enforcement officials may also be significant (Hawkins, 1984, p. 108). A technically complex situation may demand constant negotiation and renegotiation about the source of a problem and how it might be remedied. Enforcement officials dealing with these types of deviance are able to develop a social relationship with those they regulate. Hawkins (1984, p. 123) argues that the establishment of such relationships is more likely to cultivate the 'sense of mutual trust' which is 'important in sustaining the bargaining relationship'. Also of relevance is Galanter's (1974) distinction between 'one shotters' and 'repeat players', the point being that 'repeat players' are able to gain knowledge of each other's practices and expectations. Moreover, they have greater incentives to enter a cooperative relationship than do 'one-shotters' who may not meet again. This research will explore these themes, arguing that the development of social relationships between the regulated and those they control is primary in determining the enforcement approach adopted.

Compliance and Variation

Given the social complexity of the regulatory process, the range of participants it involves, and the breadth of many legal definitions, there is

[15] Again, these categories are best regarded as 'ideal-types' as some types of law breaking do not fall easily into one category or the other.

considerable scope for variation in the definitions and in turn the achievement of compliance. To quote Di Mento (1986, p. 135) '[c]ompliance is a human activity outcome. . . . To understand compliance one must understand variation among the individuals and groups involved in the regulatory process.' Definitions of compliance may vary according to a variety of criteria, for example, the technical and disciplinary backgrounds of those involved, and this may determine whether something is compliant or not (Cheit, 1990; Di Mento, 1986; Edelman *et al.*, 1991, p. 73; see generally Chapter 3).

But social activity is not random. It is patterned and structured and part of the sociological enterprise is devoted to identifying and explaining the patterns of social interaction. Existing studies of law enforcement have identified very different patterns of enforcement ranging from the co-operative to legalistic. Grabosky and Braithwaite (1986), for instance, constructed a typology of seven types of regulatory agencies according to their enforcement styles from their examination of ninety-six agencies involved in business regulation in Australia (see also Gunningham, 1987; Hutter, 1988, 1989; Kelman, 1981; Shover *et al.*, 1982).

Explanations of these variations range from an emphasis upon the regulated activity to the motives of the regulated firms (Rees, 1988); or more broadly upon the social, political, and organizational contexts of enforcement (Hutter, 1988, 1989). An important aim of the present research is to add to our knowledge of the variations that exist in the enforcement of the law, paying particular attention to the social influences upon the law in action. In turn we may come to understand better the limits of the law and the role, if any, of criminal sanctions in social regulation.

Compliance theory is still rudimentary. We still know very little about how regulatory officials regard compliance. What factors are relevant to the practical definition of compliance? More precisely, how is compliance defined by these officials in their routine work? How is compliance negotiated? Which situations are likely to render a more stringent definition than others? And what factors are likely to effect a change in definition? We need to explore how compliance may depend upon legal, political, and social structures; the sensitivity of the methods of monitoring compliance; and the settings within which enforcement takes place. In turn this may throw some light on regulatory theory. Is compliance the result of accommodation between a plurality of interests or is it defined, negotiated, and maintained by a dominant interest group of business interests?

This monograph is structured around three main issues. The first is the *definition* of compliance, in which particular attention will be paid to the everyday definitions employed by inspectors—what I term the working definition of compliance. How do inspectors construct a definition of compliance? What principles do they apply? How do these relate to the legal and administrative definitions of compliance?

The second main area of consideration is the *assessment* and monitoring of compliance, that is the methods inspectors employ to determine whether or not—or to what extent—their definition of compliance is being met and maintained. The third focus will consider *whose* compliance is being sought. Who are the regulated? Do regulatory officials differentiate categories of the regulated? If so, does this influence the way in which they define, achieve, and assess compliance? The relationship between regulatory agencies and regulated businesses may be regarded as reflexive, that is, as a continual process of adaptation and re-adaptation by one party and then the other according to the responses received (Hawkins and Hutter, 1993). It is important to consider what theories regulatory officials hold about why the regulated do or do not comply and how these theories are fed into the enforcement process. A subsidiary concern will be the ways in which compliance is *achieved* and maintained. Here we will consider the organization of enforcement and the legal and non-legal enforcement techniques employed by inspectors to achieve compliance. As Yeager (1991, p. 11) observes, rates of violation are the joint production of business and regulatory behaviour. It is thus to the law in interaction that we must turn our attention.

RESEARCH APPROACH

This research is in the interactionist tradition which has proven well suited to the examination of the law in action (e.g. Banton, 1964; Becker, 1963; Cain, 1973; Hawkins, 1984; Lemert, 1967; Manning, 1977; Richardson, 1983; Rock, 1973, 1986; Skolnick, 1975). This sociological tradition is specifically concerned with subjective meanings and experiences as constructed by participants in social situations (Burgess, 1984). Meidinger (1987) denotes the sociological approach 'a cultural perspective' which 'focuses on the understandings that are negotiated and enacted by actors in regulatory arenas' (*ibid.*, p. 356). Following Becker (1982), Meidinger defines culture as 'a set of shared understandings which makes it possible for a group of people to act in concert with each other' (*ibid.*, p. 359). This cultural approach focuses attention upon the rules of the regulatory 'game'; conflicting interpretations of the social world; the political resolution of these conflicts; and social change and the social processes whereby change occurs. Such a definition is important because it draws attention to the impact of broader social pressures and structures upon the regulatory process and its participants. As Yeager (1991, p. 43) reminds us, the structural biases of the law are reproduced in the microsociology of interactions between inspectors and companies. Meidinger (1987, pp. 369–73) identified five sources of regulatory culture, all of which will appear as significant influences in this monograph. These are general culture; social structure; law; regulatory tradition; and regulatory work.

Qualitative methodology undoubtedly offers the most appropriate and useful research tools for such a study. Qualitative methodology is peculiarly successful in this type of research for it is specifically designed to elucidate the meanings of social situations and focus upon the way in which different people experience, interpret, and structure their lives (Burgess, 1984). The next chapter will explain how these methods were used with reference to health and safety and environmental regulation in England and Wales, to research empirically the theoretical concerns discussed in this Chapter. The objective is not to provide an up-to-date account of how these areas of regulation are currently practised, but instead to take a detailed 'snapshot' of these regulatory activities over a three-year period, the purpose being to explore the nature and implications of compliance and hopefully further our understanding of some of the important theoretical issues raised so far.

2 The Health and Safety Executive

The focal point of the empirical work undertaken was the Health and Safety Executive (HSE), the largest regulatory body in Great Britain (Centre for Socio-Legal Studies, 1983) and thus especially attractive to students of 'social regulation'. This Chapter describes the origins, structure, and aims of HSE during the research period 1983–6, and explains how this study was organized. In particular, it details how and why the inspectorates, which form the basis of this research, were selected and how fieldwork with them was structured.

There have been changes to the organization and its inspectorates since the data for this study were collected. The most notable of these are discussed in a postscript towards the end of the Chapter. The main emphasis, however, is upon the fieldwork period, as this is the backdrop to the 'snapshot' provided by this study. The analysis is concerned primarily with generic features of the activities of the regulatory inspector.

THE HEALTH AND SAFETY EXECUTIVE

Robens

In order to understand the origins of HSE and its parent organization, the Health and Safety Commission (HSC), we need to go back to 1970. In May of that year the then Labour Secretary of State for Employment and Productivity, Mrs Barbara Castle, appointed a Committee of Inquiry to undertake a wide-ranging review of health and safety in Great Britain. The Committee was chaired by Lord Robens and its remit was to examine critically 'the provision made for the safety and health of persons in the course of their employment' (1972, p. xiv) and to consider whether changes were needed and, if so, of what type. Three main factors prompted this enquiry:

1. There had never been a comprehensive review of the subject as a whole (1972, para. 16);
2. There were disturbing levels of accident and disease at work which were felt to be in particular need of scrutiny (1972, paras. 17 and 18); and

3. the 'traditional regulatory approach', that is an approach based on an extensive system of detailed statutory provisions administered and enforced by government departments and local authorities, was considered to be in need of examination.

In its *Report*, presented to Parliament in 1972, the Committee was very critical of the then existing provisions for health and safety in the workplace and it proposed radical changes. The legislative changes proposed are discussed in Chapter 3, while this Chapter concentrates on the institutional reforms suggested by the Committee and on their effects. The main criticism levelled by the Committee was that administrative jurisdictions were too fragmented (1972, para. 32). It was felt that there were too many disparate agencies, responsible to too many government departments, enforcing too much legislation. In just England, for example, five different government departments and the local authorities were responsible for the administration and enforcement of nine separate groups of health and safety statutes (*ibid.*). The consequence, it was argued, was confusion in the individual workplace, amongst the inspectorates, and in policing and law-making (1972, paras. 34–9). It was proposed that a more unified and integrated system should be created 'to increase the effectiveness of the state's contribution to safety and health at work' (1972, para. 41). Moreover, it was argued that '[r]eform should be aimed at creating the conditions for more effective self-regulation by employers and workpeople jointly' (1972, para. 452), the intention being to make those involved understand that health and safety matters are their own concern and not just the remit of external agencies.

The reforms favoured by the Robens Committee were essentially unifying and centralizing. It was recommended that there should be 'A New Statutory Framework' (1972, ch. 4) and a central part of this would be the establishment of a National Authority for Safety and Health at Work. It was recommended that:

The Authority should have a distinct, separate identity with its own budget, and full operational autonomy under the broad policy directions of a departmental Minister. It should have a comprehensive range of executive powers, and functions. Statutory provisions formulated by the Authority should be laid before Parliament by the sponsoring Minister (1972, para. 467).

This Authority would incorporate six existing inspectorates, namely those concerned with factories, mines, agriculture, explosives, nuclear installations, and alkali works. The eventual objective would be the merger of these inspectorates and the creation of a 'unified inspectorate' (1972, para. 204ff). The Committee considered that there were:

very strong arguments for the creation of a single safety and health inspectorate as a matter of operational efficiency. A single inspectorate would bring together into a common pool the technical expertise which, although often concerned with similar types of problem, is at present dispersed between a number of separate organizations. . . . Unification would create the conditions for a more efficient deployment of inspection resources within a comprehensive framework of operational objectives and priorities spanning the whole field of safety and health at work (1972 para. 205).

Another concern of the Committee was that the members of the Managing Board of the Authority should be drawn from diverse backgrounds. The role of the Board would be to help formulate policy, make decisions, and generally direct the work of the Authority. The key point here is that members of the Board would *participate* in the work of the Authority and not just offer advice (1972, para. 17). The corporatist body proposed was thus in keeping with the desire of the Committee to create a culture in which employers and the workforce would work jointly to promote health and safety.

The aims of the organizational recommendations forwarded by the Robens Committee were essentially to simplify and streamline the administration of health and safety provisions in Great Britain. But, as Manning and I have argued elsewhere (1990), the proposals recommended by the Committee were not always as simple once enacted as it was intended they should be. A central problem is that a large, centralized institution such as that recommended by Robens can result in complicated bureaucratization through its attempts to achieve the coordination of its constituent parts.

The Structure of HSE

The Health and Safety at Work etc Act 1974 (HSW Act) adopted many of the recommendations of the Robens Committee. Indeed, the structure of the organization now responsible for health and safety at work throughout Britain approximates fairly closely to that advocated by the Committee. HSC stands at the apex of the organizational hierarchy and is accountable to the Secretary of State for Employment, to whom it reports annually. Following the wishes of the Robens Committee, HSC comprises a full-time Chairman, who is selected by the Secretary of State, and representatives from the employers' associations, trade unions, and local authorities. In 1985 there were three representatives appointed after consultation with the Trade Union Congress (TUC); three appointed after consultation with the Confederation of British Industry (CBI); and two appointed after consultation with local authority organizations.

The duties of the Commission, as outlined in section 11 of the HSW Act are to assist, encourage, and train those concerned with the promotion of health and safety; to secure and publish the results of research; to provide an information and advisory service for government departments, employers, employees, and others concerned; and to develop new health and safety regulations. In pursuance of these objectives the Commission is supported by an array of Advisory Committees and Working Parties which help it to develop law and policy. The work of these committees and of the Commission is reported upon annually to the Secretary of State for Employment and this Annual Report is publicly available as an HMSO publication.[1]

HSC has been described a perhaps 'the most corporatist body in Britain' and by the same author as one example of 'corporatism working in Britain' (Wilson, 1985, pp. 113, 168). This said, Wilson joins with others in identifying a number of biases inherent in corporatism which may, from the perspective of this study, influence how the issue of compliance is defined and implemented (Hawkins, 1992a; Wilson, 1985). HSC, it is argued, is dominated by the TUC and CBI, with the local authorities playing a subordinate role. Of the two main players the CBI appears to be the most powerful, partly because of its greater resources and consequent ability to devote more time, people, and money to the subject of occupational health and safety. However, the CBI itself has been criticized for being unrepresentative, particularly with regard to small firms whose interests appear to be unrepresented at the expense of larger and medium-sized firms. Finally, the consultative procedures involved in corporatism are prone to be lengthy and time-consuming with relatively few results. Gräbe (1991) notes that the experience of tripartism in West Germany—where the participation of employers and employees in state regulatory activity has a much longer history than in Britain—reveals a major disadvantage to be slow procedures.

HSE is essentially the operational arm of the HSC, and accordingly its functions are 'to exercise on behalf of the Commission such of the Commission's functions as the Commission directs it to exercise' (HSW

---

[1] This is in accordance with the HSW Act 1974, Sched. 2, para. 15.

Act 1974, s. 11(4)) and to take responsibility for the enforcement of the relevant legislation. The Executive comprises three persons, all of whom are appointed by HSC; one, with the approval of the Secretary of State for Employment, is the Director General of HSE. The other two Executive members are the Deputy Director General and the Director of the Resources and Planning Division. This Executive makes all formal decisions, in addition to overseeing major appointments in the organization, making final decisions about expenditure and the allocation of resources, and monitoring the general work of the organization. Under the general direction of the Director General and a Management Board, comprising the Directors of the main policy branches and Chief Inspectors of the relevant inspectorates, HSE at the time of this research comprised a tripartite structure centring on its policy, technical, and enforcement functions (see Figure 1).

The *policy branches* of HSE were involved with general issues concerning a range of industries, such as 'the conveyance of dangerous substances' or the policy regarding asbestos. Hence they examined hazards and problems which might have been common to a variety of workplaces. They co-ordinated information, research, and testing, and determined acceptable standards. Their primary task was to develop policies and regulations. Another function undertaken by the policy branches was liaison with other central-government departments, local-authority organizations, and international bodies. One of the policy branches, namely the Resources and Planning Division, dealt with the allocation of financial and manpower resources within the Executive and handled its information and publicity services.

The *technical* branches encompassed three main divisions, namely the Employment Medical Advisory Service (EMAS), the Research Laboratories and Services Division (RLSD), and the Technology and Air Pollution Division (TAPD). The latter, which was established in late 1985, was essentially specialist in orientation. TAPD comprised, for example, the Field Consultancy Groups (FCGs) of the Factory Inspectorate (FI) and, before its move to the Department of the Environment in 1986, the Industrial Air Pollution Inspectorate (IAPI). All of these (except IAPI) provided an advisory service to the rest of the organizations.

The *enforcement* functions of HSE were undertaken by the Inspectorates under its auspices. FI was the largest of these groups and was considered by some to be the dominant inspectorate, since by virtue of its greater numbers its inspectors were conspicuous in the

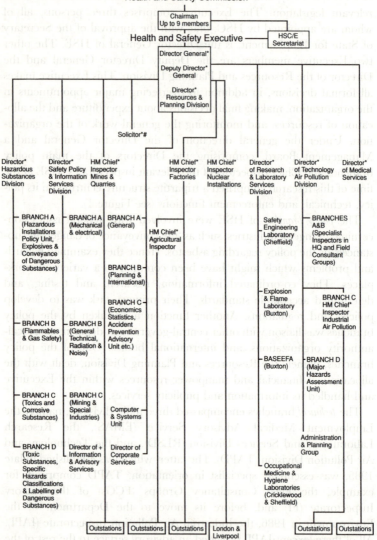

Health and Safety Commission

Chairman
Up to 9 members

Health and Safety Executive ——— HSC/E Secretariat

Director General*

Deputy Director* General

Director* Resources & Planning Division

Solicitor*#

| Director* Hazardous Substances Division | Director* Safety Policy & Information Services Division | HM Chief* Inspector Mines & Quarries | | HM Chief* Inspector Factories | HM Chief* Inspector Nuclear Installations | Director* of Research & Laboratory Services Division | Director* of Technology Air Pollution Division | Director* of Medical Services |

- BRANCH A (Hazardous Installations Policy Unit, Explosives & Conveyance of Dangerous Substances)

- BRANCH B (Flammables & Gas Safety)

- BRANCH C (Toxics and Corrosive Substances)

- BRANCH D (Toxic Substances, Specific Hazards Classifications & Labelling of Dangerous Substances)

- BRANCH A (Mechanical & electrical)

- BRANCH B (General Technical, Radiation & Noise)

- BRANCH C (Mining & Special Industries)

Director of + Information & Advisory Services

- BRANCH A (General)

HM Chief* Agricultural Inspector

- BRANCH B (Planning & International)

- BRANCH C (Economics Statistics, Accident Prevention Advisory Unit etc.)

Computer & Systems Unit

Director of Corporate Services

Safety Engineering Laboratory (Sheffield)

- Explosion & Flame Laboratory (Buxton)

- BASEEFA (Buxton)

- Occupational Medicine & Hygiene Laboratories (Cricklewood & Sheffield)

- BRANCHES A&B (Specialist Inspectors in HQ and Field Consultant Groups)

BRANCH C HM Chief* Inspector Industrial Air Pollution

- BRANCH D (Major Hazards Assessment Unit)

Administration & Planning Group

| Outstations | Outstations | Outstations | London & Liverpool | | | Outstations | Outstations |

* Members of Management Board of Health and Safety Executive
+ Has direct functional responsibilities to the Chairman of the HSC and the Director General of HSE
# Has direct functional responsibilities to the Chairman of the HSC

FIG. 1.   Health and Safety Commission—Health and Safety Executive Organization Chart

policy and administration branches and even dominated the union. This was not to deny the very distinct character of the other constituent inspectorates, namely the Explosives, Nuclear Installations, Agriculture, and the Mines and Quarries Inspectorates. These inspectorates and IAPI all undertook similar functions. These were the enforcement of the HSW Act and other related legislation; the inspection of workplaces; the investigation of accidents and complaints; and an advisory role with regard to the workforce, employers, and the public.

In addition to the above it should be mentioned that the Executive had made a number of formal agreements with other agencies to act on their behalf in a variety of areas. Two agencies which operated under such agreements were the Railway Inspectorate (RI) of the Department of Transport and the National Radiological Protection Board. The Robens Committee experienced difficulties in determining where to draw boundaries which would include or exclude various classes of workers, hazards, and legislation from the remit of the National Authority. On balance, for example, it decided that radioactive substances should fall outside the remit of the health and safety organization, but that there should be a close relationship between the Authority and the National Radiological Protection Board (1972, paras. 107 and 339). To some extent the remit of HSE was the outcome of political in-fighting. Carson (1982, p. 192) quotes Mr Michael Foot, the Secretary of State for Employment responsible for implementing the Robens Report, as saying that the Report started a 'first-class Whitehall row' which was 'a classic in Whitehall history'.

It is important to understand that the mandate of the HSE at the time of fieldwork was still relatively new and emergent, its establishment dating from only 1974. The Executive comprised a wide diversity of personnel, skills, traditions, and interests. There were, for instance, substantial differences between the inspectorates coming under the responsibility of HSE (see below). There was a great deal of mutual ignorance and suspicion about the activities of these inspectorates. Moreover, a number of central sources of stress and tension emerged within HSE during this transition period to a more centralized form (see Hutter and Manning, 1990). In essence the Executive was still in the process of being shaped during the research period.

SELECTION OF A SAMPLE

Principles of Selection

In deciding which of the inspectorates to include in the study, account was taken of their differences rather than their similarities. It was considered that such an approach would provide a rich variety of settings within which the concept of compliance could be explored. Six main lines of demarcation were employed when determining which inspectorates to select. First, in no order of priority, was *the size of the inspectorate* and the complexity of its organization. HSE inspectorates ranged in size from 622 in the FI to thirty-seven in the IAPI. Moreover, while some inspectorates operate a simple headquarters and district system, others had quite a complex internal structure. The relevance of these criteria centred upon the type of control system which was likely to accompany their organizations and the effects of this on the discretion of individual officers. It was postulated that the larger the inspectorate, the more formal and extensive would be the attempts to guide and control the activities and decisions of inspectors in the field.

The second consideration was *the range of activities subject to control*. Some inspectorates, such as the Agricultural, Mines and Quarries, Nuclear Installations, and Railway Inspectorates, dealt with a very specific and limited range of industries. Others, such as the FI and, to a lesser extent, the IAPI, were responsible for a wide range of activities. This could have interesting implications concerning the relationship between inspectors and the regulated which might, in turn, influence the meaning of compliance (see Hutter, 1989; Scholz, 1984; Shover *et al.*, 1982). Moreover, it could have some bearing on the abilities of inspectors to understand the problems they encountered and to communicate with the regulated (Hutter, 1989; Shover *et al.*, 1982). Indeed, the third criterion of selection addressed this point explicitly in taking *the expertise of inspectors* as its reference. The educational expertise of inspectors varied, as did their industrial experience. Whereas some were highly trained and specialized, holding doctorates or professional qualifications and having spent some considerable time in a profession, others were less educated and more generalist in orientation.

The *enforcement approach* adopted by inspectorates, as indicated by their apparent propensity to use formal-legal methods, was the fourth consideration when selecting the sample. Attention was therefore paid to basic agency statistics detailing the number of notices served and prosecutions initiated, the assumption being that variations in these statistics might be indicative of different enforcement strategies. So, a greater number of prosecutions and notices may reveal a more stringent approach to enforcement than would a low incidence of these. Note was also made of the rhetoric of each inspectorate concerning its views about legal action. Some studies suggested that regulatory agencies tend to adopt more conciliatory enforcement styles than, for example, the police (Hawkins, 1984; Reiss, 1984; Richardson *et al.*, 1983). But a number of researchers had discerned variations within the same or similar agencies. (Hutter, 1988; Shover *et al.*, 1982). Again this might have interesting implications for the meaning of compliance. The fifth line of demarcation centred upon the *degree of exposure* inspectorates were likely to have *to* the wider *general public*. Some regulatory agencies worked with companies and/or activities which had a highly public and visible profile, whereas others were operating in industries which might be, to all intents and purposes, 'hidden' from the public eye and knowledge. Other studies have shown that such factors can prove significant in explaining and understanding enforcement activity (Hutter, 1988; Hutter and Lloyd-Bostock, 1990). The sixth, and final, consideration was the amount of *inspectorate interaction with other regulatory agencies*. The reason for including this criterion centred upon evidence from past studies which indicated that regulatory officials may use the presence of other agencies in their own negotiations about compliance (Hawkins, 1984; Hutter, 1988).

The Pilot Study

From the beginning of the research two inspectorates were excluded from the study, namely the Nuclear Installations Inspectorate and the Mines and Quarries Inspectorate. Both were to receive the exclusive attention of colleagues, while it was felt that immediate obstacles would be put in my way, with respect to the Mines and Quarries Inspectorate, partly on account of my being female. The exclusion of these two inspectorates did remove one potentially interesting line of study, namely that of inspectorates which deal with one industry, and in large part with a monopoly employer—the Central Electricity Generating Board in the case of the Nuclear Installations Inspectorate and the National Coal Board with respect to the Mines Inspectors. It was for this reason that attention was paid to another inspectorate which was not at the time of this research part of HSE but which worked for it under an agency agreement, namely RI.

Time was devoted in 1983 to reading official publications about the inspectorates. More importantly, time was spent accompanying inspectors from each inspectorate in order to gain a clearer idea of the tasks and people they regulated and to gain some impressions about the inspectors themselves.[2] The significance of these visits was heightened by the fact that they injected meaning to official publications such as Annual Reports, which made little sense to the researcher at the very start of the study.

Following the pilot study, it was decided to include three inspectorates in the study. This was one more than had been the original intention but a wealth of data was at my disposal, providing an opportunity that could not easily be ignored. Those selected for the sample were the Factory, Industrial Air Pollution, and Railway Inspectorates. As we can see from Table 1, these three inspectorates differed from each other in a variety of ways, most especially with regard to their size, qualifications, enforcement strategies, and the range of industries they dealt with. But this Table identifies just the rudimentary lines of demarcation originally used to select the sample. In order to gain a more detailed understanding of the three inspectorates studied, the next section will be devoted to a resumé of their histories, mandates, organization, and approach. Further details about the organization of data collection can be found in Appendix One.

THE SELECTED INSPECTORATES

Historical Perspective

All of the inspectorates in this research were established in a period of increasing governmental regulation. FI is the oldest of the inspectorates. The first Factory Act dates from 1802 although it was not until the 1833 Act that any effective steps were taken to enforce the protective legislation enacted by Parliament. The first Inspecting Officers of Railways were appointed in 1840 under the Regulation of Railways Act 1840. These early officers worked for the Board of Trade on secondment from the Royal Engineers, a source of full-time recruitment of the

---

[2] Observation is an especially helpful method of investigation in the early stages of research. See Becker, 1958.

TABLE 1. The Sample: Basic Facts*

	Factory	Inspectorates Industrial Air Pollution	Railway
Number of Inspectors	622	37	15**
Number of regional Offices	20	12	8
Range of Industries controlled	Very wide	Restricted	Very Restricted
Qualifications required for entry to inspectorate	A degree or equivalent qualification and preferably relevant employment experience; or 3 years practical experience	Minimum: a degree; usually a higher degree and professional qualifications	A degree or equivalent. Most were chartered engineers
Previous Industrial Experience	Not essential	Essential	Essential
Notices served: Improvement (Crown and Non-Crown)	3321	1	0
Prohibition (Deferred and Immediate)	1801	0	7
Prosecutions	1855 (informations laid)	1	3
Interaction with the Public	Occasional	Common	Infrequent
Interaction with other regulatory agencies	Occasional	Occasional	Occasional
Local Authorities	Occasional	Frequent	Frequent

* 1984 figures. Source: HSC, 1985.

** RI comprised the Chief Inspector; 6 Inspecting Officers; 2 Assistants Inspecting Officers and 15 Railway Employment Inspectors. It is the latter whose task it is to enforce health and safety legislation (Dept. of Transport, 1985).

inspectorate until very recently. And the first move by central government to protect the atmosphere from pollution by noxious vapours was
the Alkali Act 1863. Central-government inspectors were appointed to
work under the Board of Trade, to take responsibility for alkali works
in the whole country. The work of the early factory inspectors has
attracted most academic interest from historians and sociologists
(Bartrip and Fenn, 1980, 1983; Carson, 1974; Martin, 1983). Environmental issues are of increasing interest, and accordingly there has been
a growing body of literature on environmental regulation. The regulation of air pollution has been the subject of several historical studies
(Ashby and Anderson, 1981; Brimblecombe, 1987) and also features in
the work of pressure groups (Frankel, 1974) and political scientists
(Vogel, 1986). It is perhaps surprising, given the immense interest
shown in the history of the railways, that so little has been written about
the history of the Railway Inspectorate, except for the occasional paper
written by Inspecting Officers. The closest one comes to a popular history of the Inspectorate is a history of railway disasters, namely Rolt's
Red for Danger which carries the subtitle 'The Classic History of British
Railway Disasters' and is regularly reprinted.[3] The most relevant academic study is the work of Parris (1965), *Government and the Railways in
the Nineteenth Century*.

The early history of all three inspectorates is characterized by tightly
limited mandates and restricted enforcement powers. It was some thirty
years before early factory legislation was supported by an effective
enforcement machinery. Even then it is arguable that the few inspectors appointed were insufficient to make any great impact (Bartrip and
Fenn, 1980), in particular because the inspectorate was then regarded
as a temporary rather than permanent agency (Martin, 1983, p. 12). In
the early days it was not only the resources of the administrative
machinery that were limited, but also the scope of the protective legislation, with the initial concern of the legislation being the working conditions of minors in the textile factories. During the course of the
nineteenth century the concern of the legislation extended to incorporate the whole workplace in manufacturing industry and to cover a
wide range of aspects of work (Bartrip and Fenn, 1983). The administrative resources also expanded so that by 1880 thirty-eight sub-
inspectors were employed in addition to the full inspectors, although

[3] This publication reveals much admiration for RIs who are referred to as 'those most
admirable guardians of the public safety' (1986, p. 17).

the inspectorate was reduced from four in 1833 to two in 1859 (Martin, 1983).

Early air-pollution legislation was also very restricted in its scope. The Alkali Act 1863 referred to just one pollutant, namely hydrogen chloride gas, from one process, the reaction between sodium chloride and sulphuric acid. Within its first year the Inspectorate managed to reduce this pollutant from 1000 tons a week to forty-three, but this did not apparently improve the atmosphere greatly. This was because the scope of the Act was so limited and did not allow for the regulation of the many other substances polluting the atmosphere (Ashby and Anderson, 1981; Frankel, 1974). Further air-pollution legislation was passed in 1874 and 1881 but neither Act widened the scope or powers of the inspectorate substantially.

In the early days of the railways numerous companies were setting up railways, so it is perhaps not surprising that one of the first tasks of the Inspecting Officers of Railways, as defined by the early legislation, was the inspection of new railways. Another important task was to be receiver of information about accidents. However, in common with the other inspectorates researched, the Inspecting Officers' powers were quite limited. It was not until the 1842 Regulation of Railways Act that Inspecting Officers had the power to postpone the opening of a railway that did not meet their satisfaction. Likewise, it was not until the Regulation of Railways Act 1871 that the holding of accident inquiries was legalized.[4] Prior to this the investigation of accidents took place solely on an informal basis and only with the agreement of the railway company involved.

Historical research into these inspectorates is both fascinating and important for the clues it may offer in explanation for present day practice. Much attention has been directed to the emergence of protective legislation, particularly its role in encouraging the development of specific forms of enforcement strategy. With reference to FI in the nineteenth century Bartrip and Fenn explain that: '[w]ithin the inspectorate there were those who favoured an enforcement policy weighted towards conflict and prosecution, and those who were sympathetic towards an approach emphasizing co-operation and persuasion' (1983, p. 213). These authors continue to describe how during the period 1859–78 these different views about enforcement practice came into conflict under the two joint Chief Inspectors. One, Alexander Redgrave,

---

[4] This legislation is still of central importance today. See Ch. 6.

regarded prosecution as a last resort while the other, Robert Baker, 'almost gloried in it' (Bartrip and Fenn, 1983, p. 215). The strategy which eventually came to dominate was that of Redgrave; his evidential requirements meant that he only prosecuted when there was a high chance of conviction. A similar enforcement strategy was adopted by the first Alkali Inspector, Dr Robert Angus Smith, a well-known sanitary chemist. He established a co-operative, persuasive approach, partly, it could be argued, because of shortcomings with the legislation (Ashby and Anderson, 1981). It has further been argued that the weak powers accorded to the early Inspecting Officers of Railways encouraged them to adopt the persuasive enforcement styles which historians associate with their early work (Alderman, 1973; Parris, 1965).

The historical development of these inspectorates explains other aspects of their approach to work. For instance, the history and philosophy of the RI is in many respects geared to accidents rather than safety, and to the public rather than the workforce. It was not until the 1974 HSW Act that the health and safety of the workforce became an integral part of the inspectorate's work. But Inspecting Officers had undertaken inquiries into accidents involving railway employees for many years before they were given the statutory authority to do so in 1900. They had also, even in the early years, taken an interest in the hours of work of railway employees, but this interest was partly stimulated by the ways in which this problem may have endangered the safety of the travelling public (Bartrip and Burman, 1983; Parris, 1965). Similarly the most notable feature of the 1874 Alkali Act was that it introduced the concept of 'best practicable means' to air pollution legislation (see Chapter 3). This concept was established as an integral part of the Alkali Inspectorate's approach to air pollution control by Robert Smith's successor as Chief Inspector, Alfred Fletcher, a central position it retained until the Environmental Protection Act 1990.

Historically it is the Alkali etc. Works Regulation Act 1906 which is of major importance. Indeed the 1906 Act, and additions of processes and gases from several Works Orders stretching from 1928 to 1971, formed the basis of industrial pollution control until 1975. Much of this Act has now been repealed and overtaken by other legislation, notably the HSW Act 1974 and its associated statutory instruments.

The Inspectorates 1974–89

The Factory Inspectorate

FI was the largest of HSE inspectorates, with some 627 generalist and 198 specialist inspectors working under its auspices in 1984 (HSCb, 1985, p. 8). Present-day FIs are responsible for enforcing health and safety legislation in manufacturing and services industries, including construction, shipyards, docks, the education and health services, and in transient activities such as the transportation of dangerous substances by road (see HSC, 1988, p. 48). Since 1974 the Inspectorate has worked with two major pieces of legislation, namely the Factories Act 1961 and the HSW Act 1974. This latter piece of legislation created a large number of 'new entrants' who were not previously covered by the law, but who are now the responsibility of FI.

The Industrial Air Pollution Inspectorate

This Inspectorate differed from the others in the study to the extent that it was not concerned with the health and safety of the workforce, but rather with the control of environmental pollution. In particular it was responsible for atmospheric emissions from specific industrial processes and works scheduled in law for control. Generally it was the most serious pollutants which were regulated by this inspectorate, with minor and less serious emissions falling within the remit of the local authorities.

In 1975, following the recommendation of the Robens Committee, the inspectorate became part of HSE. There followed considerable debate about under whose auspices the IAPI should come.[5] The general feeling within the inspectorate seemed to be that it should be part of the Department of Environment to which it had belonged before joining HSE. In April 1987, just twelve years after joining HSE, the inspectorate did return to this Department to form part of a new integrated pollution control inspectorate, namely HM Inspectorate of Pollution (see below).

Railway Inspectorate

RI was the smallest of the inspectorates included in this research and at the time of my fieldwork the only one never to have been part of

[5] For a full discussion of this see the *Fifth* and *Tenth Reports* of the Royal Commission on Environmental Pollution and a debate on environmental pollution reported in Hansard (HL) Cn. 354–404, 29 Oct. 1984.

HSE. Instead the inspectorate worked for the Executive on an agency basis, its main base and employer being the Department of Transport, in whose London offices the inspectorate's headquarters were then located.

Upon the enactment of the HSW Act the Department of Transport entered an agency agreement that the RI would enforce the Act on all statutory railways and tramways in Great Britain and non-statutory passenger-carrying railways and tramways having a track gauge of not less than 350mm. This agreement took effect on 1 April 1975 and it involved the inspectorate recruiting new staff (Railway Employment Inspectors (REIs)) to undertake the additional work.

While the existence of a multitude of railway companies was one of the main reasons for the creation of RI, one of its attractions as a subject for this research was the fact that, due to changes in the railway industry, this inspectorate was dealing predominately with a monopoly employer, namely British Railways. Inspectors did, of course, spend time with other smaller railways, such as London Transport, Tyne and Wear, the Glasgow Underground, and the numerous minor railways, such as the Severn Valley Railway and the Dart Valley Railway, but these were relatively small demands when compared to the national network under the control of British Rail.

Organization

Factory Inspectorate

This inspectorate had the most complex structure of those studied, partly as a function of its large size. The most basic division was between the headquarters and field-level organization.

In 1984 FI's headquarters were relocated to Bootle, where some twenty to thirty inspectors were employed in a variety of administrative and specialist divisions. As we can see from Figure 2 these divisions come under the direct responsibility of two Deputy Chief Inspectors and one Senior Area Director and under the ultimate responsibility of the Chief Inspector of Factories.

Supervision of the Inspectorate's field organization was divided between the two Deputy Chief Inspectors and the Senior Area Director, as was responsibility for the various divisions. These dealt with personnel matters such as training and staffing; technical problems which affected a cross-section of industries, such as those involving

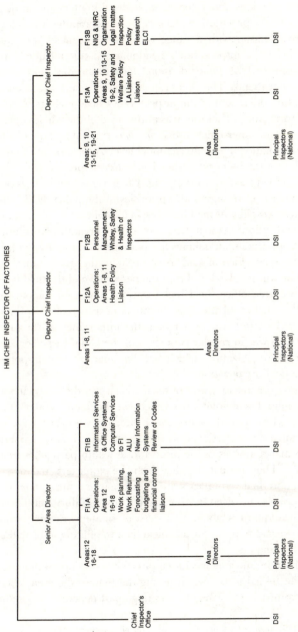

Fig. 2. HM Factory Inspectorate—Organization Chart

asbestos; policy decisions about, for example, legal matters and inspection practice; and the provision of services such as computer and information systems. Liaison with a range of 'outside' agencies was also co-ordinated from the inspectorate's headquarters: this included, for instance, liaison with HSE policy divisions, local authorities, and other government departments. The preparation of work plans and annual budgets was also undertaken at the inspectorate's headquarters.

The Chief Inspector of Factories was at the head of the whole organization and, as with other chief inspectors, was the public face of the inspectorate on a national and international level. A focal point of both publicity and accountability were the *Annual Reports* produced by the inspectorate, carrying a foreword by the Chief Inspector.[6] Decisions about the allocation of resources and priorities in the policy field were the ultimate responsibility of the Chief Inspector, who was accountable to the HSE for decisions made in these areas. The breadth and volume of the Chief Inspector's undertakings are perhaps indicated by the fact that he had his own office of staff to co-ordinate the many functions and activities he was involved in. From the perspective of the field-level inspector in the area office the Chief Inspector appeared remote. In part this was a function of the large numbers of inspectors employed by this agency. Its effect was to heighten the importance of the local area director who was in regular contact with the Chief Inspector and the headquarters organization, which had line-management responsibilities for the field organization.

The field-level organization was of most concern to the study. It was structured around twenty-one area offices in England, Wales, and Scotland, headed by area directors. Area directors were in charge of the administrative district assigned to them, and were hence responsible for the formal responses of the inspectorate within particular areas of the country. They mediated policy from headquarters and determined how it, and their resources, were to be organized throughout the year. They were also involved in structuring a flow of information from the field to headquarters about a variety of matters, ranging from responding to formal requests for technical data to offering information about personnel matters.

On a much more informal level area directors were more influential than one might be led to believe in setting the tone of the area office. The working atmosphere of the office in large part depended upon the

---

[6] HSC and HSE now publish one *Annual Report* for all constituent inspectorates.

attitude of the area director. This was specifically related to such factors as the amount of information area directors were willing to pass on from headquarters to their inspectors; the amount of control exercised over staff and discretion permitted to individual inspectors; and, at the most fundamental level, the interest shown by the area director in the careers of his or her staff. Not surprisingly these matters informed inspectors' choices about which offices they would prefer to work in or to avoid, should they be asked to move areas.[7]

Area directors commanded a structure of industry groups which came under the day-to-day charge of a principal inspector, who was directly accountable to the area director. These groups were responsible for specific industries across the whole of the area. The type of industries catered for and the resources allocated to each varied between areas according to locality. Industry groups were staffed by Class 1A and 1B inspectors, that is, those working at the basic grades of the organization. In addition to their industry responsibilities some of these groups also inspected small, miscellaneous factories and workshops falling within a particular geographical area.

Each area office also had responsibility for a National Industry Group (NIG), which served as the national focus for communications between an industry, unions, and the inspectorate. These groups investigated any particular problems concerning their industry and advised the rest of the inspectorate of the standards and methods they should be requiring across the country (see Chapter 4), in particular through formulating written guidance on health and safety standards (HSC, 1990b, p. 25).

Although not official policy, certain groups were regarded by inspectors as more prestigious than others, not least because experience in them was felt to enhance their chances of promotion: the NIGs and chemical groups were two notable examples here. Although a generally unpopular move, it was considered that time spent in a headquarters or policy branch of either FI or HSE was also an advantageous career move.[8] It was often the work with the larger and more technically complex industries that was highly regarded, while many inspectors preferred to avoid the work with the small workshops and factories. Working 'the rabbits', as inspectors often referred to these premises,

---

[7] Preference about geographical location was also important in inspectors' decisions about which area office they would like to work in.

[8] Reiner, 1991, p. 80 ff., found that experience in administration was also considered to be especially important as a career move within the police.

offers us clues to the reasons for this, namely that the inspectors regarded themselves as working (often against the odds) to raise the standards in an unknown maze of small premises. Moreover, this work was not regarded as especially demanding, and hence not so interesting for some inspectors. The majority of inspectors in the area office were generalists, who need not necessarily have had any specific training for the industry groups for which they worked. There were, however, seven specialist field-consultancy groups throughout the country, comprising specialist FIs who could provide detailed technical assistance when required by their generalist counterparts.

Industrial Air Pollution Inspectorate

Prior to its departure from HSE this inspectorate was part of the Technical and Air Pollution Division. Its inclusion in this, as opposed to the Enforcement Branch which comprised all of the other inspectorates in the Executive, was to the outsider, at least, rather peculiar.[9] The apparent rationale for this was that, compared to other inspectorates in HSE, this was a highly specialized agency (but so were others such as the Nuclear Installations Inspectorate). The Chief IAPI, whilst remaining on the Management Board of the Executive, was technically subject to the Director of the Technical and Air Pollution Division. But in practice, the Chief Inspector remained the key figure for inspectors and it was to the inspectorate's headquarters, still located in the London buildings of the Department of Environment, that they continued to turn for guidance and information.

IAPI's headquarters organization was simple and compact (see Figure 3). The Chief Inspector traditionally played a vital role in promoting environmental standards and issues. He represented the 'public' face of the inspectorate at a national level and assumed an important consultative role with industry. Liaising with, and providing information for, other governmental and international agencies was also an important part of the job. The Chief Inspector was ultimately responsible for major policy decisions, including future planning, and for the activities of his staff throughout the country. As such, it was he who was accountable to both the Executive and the public for the Inspectorate's work.

---

[9] In this respect it is perhaps telling that the HSC's *Annual Report 1984–5* noted assurances to the Secretary of State for the Environment that the increasing integration of IAPI and its sampling teams into HSE would not threaten the inspectorate's specialism and distinctiveness (HSC, 1985b, p. 20).

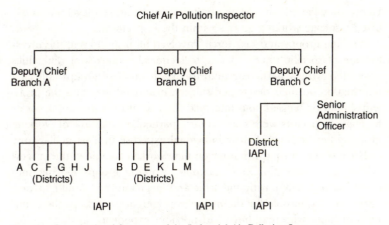

Fig. 3. Organizational Structure of the Industrial Air Pollution Inspectorate

The work of the headquarters staff was very much orientated to supporting the Chief Inspector in his role. The Deputy Chief of Branch C co-ordinated the collection and dissemination of information. For example, he was responsible for the co-ordination and issue of 'best practicable means' notes and guidance notes; for the preparation of the *Annual Report* and plan of work; and for the co-ordination of research and training programmes. He also took an interest in legal matters such as overseeing enforcement practice and legislative proposals. The organization of the three major task forces on arrestment, dispersion, and monitoring (see below) fell within the remit of this Deputy, as did the inspectorate's relations with external agencies such as Parliament, other government departments, and other sections of HSE. It should also be noted that European matters were taking up an increasing proportion of this Deputy's time.

The other two Deputy Chief Inspectors divided a variety of similar tasks between them. They each took responsibility for half of the inspectorate's field-staff throughout the country. This involved them in overseeing the work of district inspectors, by means of telephone calls; reports on scheduled processes in each district; copies of any correspondence between the local inspectors and industry; and by the occasional visit to the districts for which they were responsible. In addition to their line-management role these two Deputy Chiefs were responsible for the review of best practicable means requirements and general policy development for air pollution control from scheduled processes.

Hence they liaised with related industries at a national level and organized associate working groups within the inspectorate.

Working groups and task forces involved all inspectors in the investigation of specific topics relating to technical problems or difficulties associated with a particular industry. Each of these groups collected information on their designated subject, examined how best the problem should be tackled, and informed the rest of the inspectorate of its findings. Inspectors were selected for a particular task force or working group either because of their individual expertise in a particular area or because the district within which they worked contained the process subject to examination. For example, working groups looking into problems associated with the iron and steel industry would involve inspectors responsible for the major iron and steel works in the country and those who may have had previous experience in these industries.

The large majority of inspectors worked in one of the inspectorate's twelve districts in England and Wales.[10] Each district had one district inspector, who was normally in charge of two inspectors, although this varied according to staffing levels, with some districts having only one district and one other inspector. The district inspector was responsible to a Deputy Chief for the work of the inspectorate in the district and hence for organizing the supervision of all registered works within the area. He oversaw the work of the inspectors working for him and was responsible for communication with headquarters. He also undertook some of the same work as the inspectors working for him. Essentially this involved inspecting works, enforcing the law, and investigating complaints. Another important aspect of the field force's work was liaison with local Environmental Health Officers and the public. This inspectorate was organized much more informally than FI. There was less reliance on the written word, both in relations with industry and between inspectors. Instead, greater use was made of telephone calls and personal interaction.[11] In part this was a function of the small numbers of IAPIs and of the premises they controlled. But it was also symptomatic of an organization which accorded individual inspectors a good deal of discretion in the organization of workloads.

---

[10] Scotland had its own Chief IAPI and organization, which operated separately from its English and Welsh counterpart.

[11] The National Audit Office (1991, paras. 3.11–3.14) criticized the inspectorate for its lack of documentation.

Railway Inspectorate

At the time of my research RI was organized around its three main functions, with inspecting officers taking exclusive responsibility for the inspectorate's 'traditional' or historical role and REIs enforcing the provisions of the HSW Act.

The inspection and statutory approval of new works was the responsibility of Branch 1 of the inspectorate's headquarters staff. The inspecting officers in this Branch checked new signalling and electrification schemes and undertook the inspection of new works. They also took responsibility for approving any changes to level-crossings and for holding public inquiries concerning any modifications. The latter could occupy a lot of time, not least because it tended to attract considerable public interest, including Parliamentary questions.[12]

Branch 2 was concerned with accident investigation and policy. Accident investigation was, as already indicated, an important aspect of the inspectorate's work. This Branch was responsible for reporting procedures, collating trends and statistics, dealing with accident inquiries, and publishing accident investigation reports. The bulk of this work was undertaken by an Assistant Inspecting Officer of Railways to whom all accidents were initially reported for processing. This Branch also undertook safety policy functions and provided advice to other sections of the Department of Transport. A less prominent task undertaken by Branch 2 was handling foreign agency agreements such as that between the RI and the Government of Hong Kong.

Branch 3 was perhaps the most relevant for the purposes of this study, as its remit covered the HSE agency agreement work. This Branch was headed by an Inspecting Officer of Railways who undertook many of the day-to-day dealings with the national or managing Executive of the railways. This officer was also responsible for a district organization of REIs who were engaged in inspecting local stations, signal boxes, and transient work sites. This district organization comprised three Principal Railway Employment Inspectors and eleven REIs, who covered England, Scotland, and Wales from eight regional offices. In addition one REI was responsible for all minor railways. As with IAPI, control within RI tended to be informal, and not many guidelines were issued to REIs. The inspectorate was small and it was argued that since these inspectors were professional and experienced they should not need to be closely controlled.

---

[12] All of this work was undertaken under the auspices of the Department of Transport.

The Chief Inspecting Officer of Railways stood at the apex of the inspectorate's hierarchy. As was the case with the Chief Inspectors of the Factory and Industrial Air Pollution Inspectorates, the Chief Inspector was an important symbolic figure who also undertook a significant substantive role within the inspectorate. The Chief Inspector at the time of my research estimated that HSE Agency work occupied approximately 12 per cent of his time, involving him in such things as attending HSE Management Board meetings and chairing the Railway Industry Advisory Committee (RIAC). But the majority of the Chief Inspector's time was devoted to the inspectorate's 'traditional' activities.[13] The ultimate decision about whether or not to inspect and approve new works was his and he also had delegated powers from the Minister to decide what type of accident inquiry to initiate. Ministerial correspondence and Parliamentary questions went through his office. In addition, he undertook personally some of the talks inspectors were requested to give, for example to railway societies.

The Inspectors

Differences in the size, complexity, specialization, and training of the inspectorates had implications for the responsibilities allocated to individual inspectors, the nature of their jobs, and ways in which inspectors experienced their work, for example the sources of job satisfaction and concern amongst inspectors.

Factory Inspectorate

Unlike the other inspectorates in the sample, FI was not exclusively male, although it was predominantly so. A few women had graduated through the ranks to senior positions,[14] but they were the exception rather than the rule.

It was not an essential requirement that generalist FIs had either a degree or previous industrial experience. Nevertheless many of those accompanied during the course of this research were graduates and some had previous working experience. In contrast to the image of field

---

[13] This involved him in regular meetings with the management of the railways, his contact with British Railways Board being the most frequent. Proposals to build a Channel Tunnel were also taking up much of the inspectorate's time.

[14] At the time of this research only two out of twenty-one area directors were women. In 1995 a woman was appointed as Director General of HSE. She was not however an ex-inspector but a career civil servant.

inspectors, suggested to me by some members of the other inspectorates and those subject to their control, FIs were not all 'classic graduates' who 'are green about the gills'. Jamieson (1985, p. 53) confirms that many moved into this inspectorate from other jobs, over half of her sample having had industrial experience prior to joining the agency. Moreover, she notes that there had been an increasing tendency to recruit science graduates. This inspectorate nevertheless included a higher number of 'young' inspectors than did the other inspectorates studied by me. One reason for the brash caricatures of FIs was undoubtedly their more legalistic approach and the zealousness with which many of them pursued their objectives. While the inspectors I accompanied, like their predecessors described by Carson (1970), considered their role to be advisory and educative there was an underlying cynicism about the intentions of many of those they regulated. FIs were certainly less inclined to see things from industry's point of view than either IAPIs or RIs.

At the time of my fieldwork there were variable levels of job satisfaction among FIs. Most seemed to have been attracted to the job by virtue of the variety it offered and a feeling that they would be taking a socially worthwhile job (Jamieson, 1985 p. 56). The drawbacks centred upon matters which affected individuals, such as poor promotion prospects and the threat of being moved to another area office. These were both matters which directly affected domestic circumstances in terms of standards of living and the upheaval accompanying geographical mobility, hence it was not surprising that they concerned married inspectors most directly, especially those with children (Hutter and Manning, 1990). Other sources of dissatisfaction centred upon the status of the inspectorate as a corporate body. The main worry here was that the inspectorate was undervalued by the government and wider society, in particular that the work of field-level inspectors was so regarded. There were two dominant concerns here: one centred upon the general lowering of morale in the Civil Service, resulting from the attacks upon it by the Conservative Government in the early 1980s. This took the form of communications by Ministers concerning a need for maintaining budget-control, efficiency, and effectiveness; governmental attempts to reduce the 'regulatory burden' on industry; and a philosophy of 'less government' (see Butler, 1993; Hutter and Manning, 1990; Stewart and Walsh, 1992). The other was a feeling among field inspectors that the nature of their job was changing, in particular that less and less emphasis was being placed upon inspections and more and more attention was paid to giving field-level inspectors a data-collecting and bureaucratic role.[15]

It has already been noted that one of the attractions of the inspectorate was the variety of the work it offered. Certainly this was not a routine office job and inspectors tended to visit a wide range of premises during the course of the working day. Much of their time was spent out of the office—usually several days a week—inspecting premises, checking that improvements had been effected following previous visits, and investigating accidents. Like other enforcement officials, they valued their time out in the 'field' and, as with other officials, this time was essentially solitary. Although they met a variety of people during the course of such a day this was in an 'official' capacity, as the lone representative of the HSE.[16] During these encounters the inspectors' workload was intense. They could encounter a wide range of sites, processes, machinery, and activity which needed to be understood and critically assessed. Some of these would be familiar to them already but others would be new or unknown, especially at the beginning of a career or in the initial period of time in a new industry group.[17] In addition, inspectors came into contact with a cross-section of people and organizations who were also assessed in terms of their technical abilities and commitment to health and safety.

The job of an inspector was not only intellectually demanding but also physically tiring, involving the physical inspection of plant and, on occasions, several hours' driving per day.[18] Indeed, given the inspectorate's policy of not announcing visits beforehand it was quite possible that long journeys could be undertaken, only for the inspector to discover that access to the site was not possible because work was not in progress or the 'contact' person or manager was not available.[19]

[15] It is not uncommon for enforcement officials to perceive office work as boring and as a diversion from their main job. See Hawkins, 1984, p. 47; Hutter, 1988, p. 89.

[16] The fact that these encounters were regarded as official and not necessarily relaxing is perhaps indicated by those inspectors who told the researcher that they preferred to spend their lunch breaks alone so that they had a 'break', lunch with the regulated being regarded as 'work'. Some FIs refused lunch because they considered that accepting could lead to too great a familiarity between them and the regulated. See Ch. 7.

[17] It should be remembered these inspectors were not specialists and were regularly moved between groups.

[18] These inspectors covered large geographical areas. For example, inspectors in the South-West Area covered the counties of Avon, Cornwall, Devon, Gloucestershire, Somerset, and the Isles of Scilly. Within these areas their work was functionally organized.

[19] While inspectors hoped to visit other premises in the area, this was not always possible. See Ch. 7 for discussion of contact persons.

Needless to say this was not a career which could easily be pursued by those lacking in confidence (see also Jamieson, 1985, p. 60). HSE Area Offices were dominated numerically by field inspectors so the individual inspector had plenty of regular contact with colleagues.

Industrial Air Pollution Inspectorate

IAPIs were, on average, older than their counterparts in the generalist sections of the FI. In part this was because recruits to this inspectorate were required to have both professional qualifications and industrial experience, and indeed they were expected to have held managerial positions prior to joining the agency. These requirements were making it increasingly difficult to find suitable recruits, especially as Civil Service rates of pay had not kept pace with those in the private sector[20] (Hutter and Manning, 1990; National Audit Office, 1991, para. 6.17). These requirements also contributed to the male dominance of the inspectorate, since industry appointed very few women to managerial positions, especially those with the appropriate scientific background for joining the inspectorate.

Newly-recruited staff to the inspectorate were expected to take on considerable responsibility very quickly. 'Learning the job' was not so much a matter of formal training in the classroom as being allocated a workload and being told to get on with the job. This was done under the supervision of the District Inspector who offered advice if it was requested or if he considered it necessary. New inspectors were expected to cope with the full range of problems immediately they joined the inspectorate. One recently appointed inspector I accompanied was dealing with one of the most difficult works in the district, to which he had been assigned within months of joining the agency. While some younger inspectors admitted that this introduction to the inspectorate was tough they generally agreed with senior members of the agency that those appointed should be of such a standing and calibre that extensive training should not be necessary. Such a view reveals the emphasis placed upon previous experience.

IAPIs were very proud of their qualifications and industrial experience. They valued the insights which previous managerial experience had given them into the workings of business and the regulatory process. Moreover, they argued that this placed them on an 'equal footing' with those they regulated. The image they tried to convey was very

---

[20] HSE and RI also experienced considerable difficulties in recruiting and retaining staff in the early 1980s. See, for example, HSC 1988, pp. 37, 48–9.

much that of the 'gentleman inspector', commanding respect and compliance by virtue of their technical and interpersonal skills. Another strong image was that of the 'poacher turned gamekeeper', again a projection which focused on prior experience and which also indicated professionalism as part of the total identity.[21] The use of professional skills to improve the environment was the main source of job-satisfaction for inspectors. The variety of work encountered and the independence and freedom expected of the individual also figured prominently in the attractions of the job. Like the other officials studied, these inspectors normally worked alone but, unlike FIs, they had little daily contact with their colleagues. As noted above, there were usually just two inspectors in a district, and given the size of districts it was not unusual for some inspectors not to visit the local office for days.[22] Nevertheless there were opportunities to meet colleagues from other districts, including at the inspectorate's annual meeting, training courses, and the meetings of the task forces and working groups.

For much of the period of my field work there were substantial areas of dissatisfaction amongst inspectors. These centred largely upon uncertainty about the institutional location of the inspectorate. Inspectors feared that their best interests were not being met within the HSE and there was a general feeling that a return to the Department of Environment would be the only 'salvation' of the inspectorate as they knew it: whether or not this proved to be the case is now in some doubt. What is certain is that this inspectorate had an especially strong sense of corporate identity, despite the dispersal of its inspectors throughout England and Wales. While it is likely that this was strengthened by the perceived threat of 'outside' attack through part of the duration of my fieldwork, this inspectorate has in the past held a reputation of insularity and secretiveness (Frankel, 1974), and this doubtless proved significant in the economic, political, and regulatory climates pertaining at the time of this research.

---

[21] The concern here is how inspectors saw themselves, not how accurately this measured up to the perceptions of the regulated. See Di Mento, 1986, p. 140, for a discussion of the importance of inspector professionalism to agency reputation and efficacy of enforcement.

[22] Like FIs, IAPIs covered large geographical areas. Two inspectors were responsible for the area from Bristol to Land's End. Similarly two inspectors were responsible for the whole of East Anglia, whilst three covered Greater Manchester, Lancashire, and Cumbria.

Railway Inspectorate

The basic division within the inspectorate was between Inspecting Officers and REIs. This was partly a consequence of Inspecting Officers holding the most senior positions in the organization, but there were also differences in training and background. These divisions were symbolized spatially in the inspectorate's headquarters, where Inspecting Officers all had offices along one side of a corridor and other staff were situated elsewhere: indeed this was the subject of some jokes among REIs, the route to upward mobility being regarded as a move across the corridor.

Inspecting Officers of Railways were traditionally ex-Royal Engineers officers. They retained their army titles and were respected and regarded as especially suited to the job because of their impartiality. More recently, however, the Royal Engineers had ceased to be a ready source of applicants to the inspectorate and this led in 1985 to the appointment of the first Inspecting Officer with no career military background. This officer started his career in the inspectorate as an REI and it seems likely that this will become a regular career route, as other REIs have been promoted into Assistant Inspecting Officer posts. In 1988 there was another departure from tradition when the first person without a railway background was appointed as Chief Inspecting Officer of Railways.

REIs have been recruited since 1975, when the agency agreement with the HSE came into effect. They were recruited almost exclusively from British Railways. All were chartered engineers who had ten to twenty years' experience on the railways, and all had held managerial positions. Their role centred exclusively on enforcing health and safety legislation and, as noted above, they comprised the regional organization of the inspectorate.

The majority of those in this inspectorate undertook a lot of travelling. Inspecting Officers, especially those concerned with the approval of new works and the inspection of level-crossing sites, had to travel nationwide and, in connection with their foreign agency agreements, internationally. This constant travelling doubtless proved strenuous, especially as these officers, like other regulatory officials, tended to travel alone and undertook an intensive workload once they reached their destinations. However, the travelling was not continuous and part of each week was normally spent in their headquarters offices where their colleagues were based.

REIs also travelled extensively within their regional jurisdictions. The work could be very solitary for these inspectors, as not all of them were based in offices with their colleagues. For example, there was just one inspector based in Scotland, and his nearest colleague was based in Newcastle. While these inspectors could be in regular telephone contact with their colleagues, they were, nevertheless, much more isolated than their colleagues in FI and IAPI. Accordingly, it was not surprising that they tended to be self-confident, independent people who were given considerable discretion in the way they handled their workloads.

One dominant impression from accompanying Inspecting Officers and REIs was that they enjoyed their work. They conveyed a strong sense of commitment and communicated a feeling of pride in their work. The main point of dissatisfaction within the inspectorate centred on salaries which, as with the other two inspectorates in the sample, had become increasingly unattractive when compared with those offered by industry. Consequently this inspectorate had also encountered problems in recruiting new staff.[23]

Formalization and Organizational Control

The degree to which procedures were formalized and the organization attempted to control the discretion of individual inspectors varied between inspectorates. All inspectors were expected to write reports of their visits for the files. These noted the date and type of visit and who was interviewed. A detailed summary was then given of the main points covered, including information about any future plans which could be relevant to health and safety or the environment. The reports noted any action taken and any action proposed, alongside the inspector's assessment of when the site should be revisited and what type of visit this should be. Any letters sent following an inspection were kept on file, and in some cases—particularly IAPI and REI—could also serve as a report of the inspection.

Inspectorates varied in their readiness to commit matters to paper. FIs and REIs were much more likely than IAPIs to write a letter detailing matters they expected to be remedied. In comparison to the other inspectorates in the sample FI was quite reliant upon the written word and its visits could generate a lot of paperwork. It tended to send

---

[23] The King's Cross and Clapham inquiries had not taken place at the time of this research, hence the criticisms they contained of the inspectorate were not at issue during this study.

letters following visits and it also had to complete several report forms on premises and on details of how it had allocated its time. IAPIs varied in their inclination to write letters and the tendency not to commit a great deal to paper was explained largely by the frequency with which these inspectors visited premises subject to their control. Those sites visited relatively infrequently tended to receive letters and important and serious matters were written about—in part as a precaution in case of formal legal action.

Other sources of control over inspectors are by now familiar. The formal and informal culture of the office can either reward or discourage legal action according to the strategy adopted. Recruitment and promotion policies will favour those adhering to a preferred policy. Moreover, the inspector's peer group can exercise a strong pressure to conform, although it should be pointed out that within this sample only FIs worked in any close proximity to significant numbers of their colleagues.[24]

Interestingly the degree of formalization of the prosecution process presented a mirror image of the controls exercised over routine workloads. In IAPI and RI, which tended to initiate legal action less readily than FI, the selection of cases for legal action was controlled through hierarchical review by progressively senior officers. In both of these inspectorates the decision to prosecute or serve an improvement notice had to be referred to and confirmed by the inspectorate's headquarters. FI did not exercise such controls over its inspectors. Rather, the individual inspector was responsible for taking the prosecution and the main role of any overseeing by more senior officers was to ensure that there was a case to answer. This was in contrast to the monitoring of routine work, where FI kept a much closer eye on the work of its inspectors than did IAPI and RI. This fully accords with the findings of my previous research into Environmental Health Officers (1989), namely that those areas which operated a more decentralized system for handling legal action prosecuted more frequently than those where legal action was more closely monitored by a central organization.

Enforcement Approach

The enforcement approach adopted by inspectors was one of the criteria used in the selection of the sample for this research. The basic

---

[24] See Blau, 1963; Hawkins, 1984; Hill, 1972; Hutter, 1984, 1989; Kaufman, 1960; and Richardson *et al.*, 1983 for further discussion of the organizational controls which may be exercised over enforcement officials.

indicator of enforcement approach was the apparent propensity to use formal-legal methods in the event of non-compliance.

Legal Tools

The HSW Act 1974 provides for three main legal moves in the event of non-compliance, namely improvement notices, prohibition notices and prosecutions. Section 21 of the HSW Act 1974 provides for the service of an improvement notice:

if an inspector is of the opinion that a person—
(a) is contravening one or more of the relevant statutory provisions, or
(b) has contravened one or more of those provisions
in circumstances that make it likely that the contravention will continue or be repeated.

The notice should specify the provisions concerned, why the inspector believes they are contravened, the remedy required, and the period within which this remedy should be effected. An improvement notice in effect sanctions a temporary state of non-compliance, hence it pertains to less serious and less risky problems (see Chapter 3). This is in contrast to the circumstances which section 22 of the HSW Act 1974 is designed to meet. Prohibition notices are for use in those cases where inspectors are of the opinion 'that the risk of serious personal injury is or, as the case may be, will be *imminent*' (s. 22(4)—my emphasis). It is not necessary that there is a legal contravention before such a notice may be imposed and it is perhaps worth underlining that a prohibition notice can refer to a prospective hazard. Given the need to establish an imminent risk of serious personal injury, prohibition notices tended to be inappropriate for the activities and processes regulated by the IAPI.[25]

Section 23 of the HSW Act 1974 permits inspectors to withdraw notices and to extend the period of a notice. If the recipient of a notice considers that it should not have been served then section 24 of the Act specifies a right of appeal to an industrial tribunal which may cancel, affirm, or modify the terms of the notice.

The ultimate legal tool available to inspectors in the event of non-compliance is prosecution. Under the terms of the HSW Act legal proceedings may be instituted either by inspectors or by the Director of Public Prosecutions (section 38). Inspectors are empowered to conduct

---

[25] This inspectorate used prohibition notices only twice between 1974 and 1986, against a smelting of lead scrap and a chemical incineration. See HSC, 1987.

cases in Magistrates Court proceedings in England and Wales, although this is of course not possible in cases which are taken to the Crown Court. Penalties of £420 (1989) may be imposed for summary cases. On conviction an indictment or fine may be imposed and in some cases the penalty may be 'imprisonment for a term not exceeding two years or a fine, or both' (section 33(3)(b)).

The Use of Legal Action

The following Tables give us a broad view of the use FI, IAPI, and RI made of legal enforcement methods in the early to mid 1980s.

A number of points arising from these data are of particular interest.

TABLE 2. The Number of Informations Laid by FI, IAPI, and RI 1980–1985

Year	Inspectorate		
	FI	IAPI	RI
1980	2,438	10	0
1981	1,537	17	0
1982	1,999	20	0
1983	1,974	17	2
1984	1,855	1	3
1985	1,780	1	10

Source: HSC/HSE Annual Reports; Health and Safety Statistics; Department Of Transport Railway Safety Reports.[26]

The first is the fall in the number of IAPI prosecutions after 1983, which was accounted for by legal changes[27] which ended IAPI's responsibility for itinerant cable business. The relatively high number of prosecutions IAPI initiated against this group, as opposed to others, highlights the seriousness which the inspectorate attached to non-registration and blatantly operating without pollution arrestment equipment (see Hutter, 1989; chapter 8 below). Secondly, the abnormally high number of improvement notices served by IAPI in 1980 was largely explained by the fact that fourteen of these were on the phurnacite plant of National Smokeless Fuels Ltd in South Wales, a case

[26] The data in Tables 2 and 3 were compiled by Michelle Bunn, Research Assistant at the Centre for Socio-Legal Studies, 1993.

[27] Amendments made to s. 78 of the Control of Pollution Act by the Health and Safety (Emissions into the Atmosphere) Regulations 1983.

TABLE 3. The Number of Notices Served by FI, IAPI and RI 1980–1985

| Year | Inspectorate | | | | | |
| | FI | | IAPI | | RI | |
	Imp*	Proh**	Imp	Proh	Imp	Proh
1980	2,922	1,178	17	0	0	0
1981	3,758	1,179	4	0	0	0
1982	3,800	1,471	4	0	0	0
1983	3,405	1,673	2	0	4	0
1984	3,322	1,805	1	0	0	7
1985	2,993	1,662	1	1	1	2

Source: HSC/HSE Annual Reports; Health and Safety Statistics; Department Of Transport Railway Safety Reports

* Improvement Notice.
** Prohibition Notice—includes deferred and immediate prohibition notices.

which is discussed in detail in Chapter 8.

There are problems in comparing the data available from the different inspectorates. For example, there are variations in the prosecution figures, where some of them cite figures for cases heard while others refer to informations laid.[28] Taking all of this into account, Tables 2 and 3 seem to suggest that the FI was much more inclined to use legal action than the other inspectorates. But data detailing the number of prosecutions and notices initiated by the inspectorates can offer us only crude indications of the propensity to avoid or to favour legal enforcement methods. To some extent, for example, these figures reflect the size of the agency's jurisdiction and the potential number of prosecutable offences coming to light.

In an attempt to gain a more detailed impression of how likely these inspectorates were to use the legal tools available to them, Tables 4 and 5 consider in greater detail the legal action initiated by the sample inspectorates. Table 4 relates the number of prosecutions initiated by FI and IAPI to the number of premises they were responsible for regulating.[29] Table 5 relates the number of improvement notices served by

[28] Moreover, there has been a tendency in recent years for *Annual Reports* to give figures for the whole of HSE legal activity rather than provide a breakdown according to inspectorate. There are also difficulties created in comparing data according to the time frame employed. For example, pre-1986 Factory inspectorate *Annual Reports* referred to calendar years, whereas after this date they referred to fiscal years.

TABLE 4. The Probability of a Site being Prosecuted by the Factory Inspectorate and Industrial Air Pollution Inspectorate 1983–1985

Inspectorate	Probability of Prosecution		
	1983	1984	1985
Factory	1:326	1:351	1:364
Industrial Air Pollution	1:975	1:1975	1:1978

Source: Agency Records (cited in Hutter, 1989)

TABLE 5. The Probability of a Site being Served with an Improvement Notice by the Factory Inspectorate and the Industrial Air Pollution Inspectorate

Inspectorate	Probability of Prosecution		
	1983	1984	1985
Factory	1:117	1:120	1:134
Industrial Air Pollution	1:975	1:975	1:1978

Source: Annual Reports

each inspectorate to the numbers of premises regulated.

Despite the difficulties in comparing RI with the other inspectorates by looking at the number of prosecutions and improvement notices served in relation to the number of premises regulated let us consider their and FI's legal action in relation to the number of employees regulated.[30]

Table 6 relates the number of prosecutions (cases heard) in 1983 and 1984 to the number of employees in the industries regulated by FI and RI. Table 7 gives similar calculations for improvement notices.

All of these data suggest that there may be variations between the enforcement practices of these inspectorates: FI was much more likely to prosecute than either IAPI or RI. Moreover, it was also more likely to serve an improvement notice than either of the other inspectorates.

[29] It is not possible to include RI in this comparison because it regulates the whole of the operating railway rather than a finite number of identifiable sites. It should be noted of course that the transitory construction sites which come under the ægis of FI cannot be included in this analysis because again their number is indeterminate. Similar limitations apply to the illegal cable burners prosecuted by IAPI.

[30] This criterion is not of relevance to IAPI which is not responsible for the health and safety of the workforce.

TABLE 6. The Probability of Prosecutions by the Factory and the Railway Inspectorates in 1983 and 1984 expressed as a proportion of employees in the relevant industries

	Year	
Inspectorate	1983	1984
Factory	1:12,225	1:13,158
Railway	1:109,000	1:69,667

Source: Annual Reports

TABLE 7. Improvement Notices served by the Factory Inspectorate and Railway Inspectorate in 1983 and 1984 expressed as a proportion of employees in the relevant industries

	Year	
Inspectorate	1983	1984
Factory	1:4,405	1:4,515
Railway	1:109,000	1:209,000

Source: Annual Reports

But none of the data seem to suggest that the legal tools available are used routinely by any of the inspectorates in this study. This is, of course, in keeping with many other studies of British regulatory agencies (see Chapter 1). Some of the reasons for these variations between inspectorates relate, as we will see, to the definition of compliance and the social settings within which compliance is negotiated and monitored.

POSTSCRIPT

Although the core functions and administration of HSE are much the same now as they were during the fieldwork period there have been a number of changes worthy of comment. Two such changes relate to two of the sample inspectorates. While the position of FI has remained the same as it was in the early 1980s the situations of IAPI and RI have changed.

Industrial Air Pollution Inspectorate

IAPI ceased to be part of HSE in 1987 when it returned to the Department of Environment, where it had been located prior to joining HSE. It also ceased to operate as a distinct inspectorate, becoming part of a generic pollution inspectorate, HM Inspectorate of Pollution.[31] The decision to create this new inspectorate was announced by the Government in August 1986 and it was charged with undertaking the work of IAPI, the Hazardous Waste Inspectorate, HM Radiochemical Inspectorate, and a Water Pollution Inspectorate. The powers and duties of these inspectorates were to remain the same as before, with the exception of the Water Pollution Inspectorate, which was to be newly created. HM Inspectorate of Pollution came into existence on 1 April 1987, one of its objectives being to develop a more integrated approach to pollution control. Once again inspectors were faced with being part of a larger organization comprising inspectorates with different cultures, expertise, pay structures, and statutory powers. Indications that the move from HSE back to the Department of Environment might not be the panacea inspectors had hoped for were not long in materializing. Morale among the inspectors remained low, culminating in the resignation of several inspectors, including the former Chief Industrial Air Pollution Inspector. This move to engender a more wide-ranging and integrated pollution control in Britain included proposals for the introduction of the concept of 'best practicable environmental option' (BPEO) instead of best practicable means. The concept was first referred to in the *Fifth Report of the Royal Commission on Environmental Pollution* in 1976. A former Director of HM Inspectorate of Pollution, Brian Ponsford, described BPEO as an 'elusive concept' which, while 'clear enough in general terms', had proved more difficult to define precisely (1988, pp. 268–9). Basically it requires a consideration of the wider implications of controlling specific emissions, taking into account the wider environmental impact. So in controlling, for example, air pollution, inspectors would try to ensure that this did not mean that industry simply transferred the pollution to another area, for example water. Mr Ponsford clearly felt that these problems were not insurmountable and saw the concept of BPEO as an important step forward in the move to provide integrated pollution control in Britain.

[31] It should be noted that the importance of the inspectorate maintaining links with HSC and HSE after its return to the Department of Environment were stressed. These agencies now work in fairly close collaboration. See HSC, 1990a, p. 52.

The concepts of integrated pollution control and best practicable environmental option were incorporated into the 1990 Environmental Protection Act. Provisions were made for the Secretary of State to draw up regulations of proscribed processes and proscribed substances and to make regulations for specifying emission limits and quality objectives (sections 2 and 3). Authorization is required for the operation of proscribed processes, requiring the use of the best available techniques not entailing excessive cost (section 7(2)(a)). Where the process is centrally controlled and is likely to involve the release of substances into more than one environmental medium regard must be taken of the best practicable environmental option available (section 7(7)).

The future of HM Inspectorate of Pollution remained uncertain as successive Conservative governments in the late 1980s and early 1990s discussed a variety of possible institutional arrangements for pollution control in Britain. In October 1994 the Department of the Environment published the Environment Agencies Bill, the main feature of which was the creation of a new Environment Agency. The objective was to create a central body which could take an integrated approach to protecting the environment from pollution and other hazards. Under the retitled Environment Act 1995 a new Environment Agency came into legal existence in August 1995 and began work in April 1996. It merged the responsibilities of HM Inspectorate of Pollution, the National Rivers Authority, and the local authority water authorities. The agency's income is provided by a government grant, fees, and charges, and it is responsible for integrated pollution control for most industrial processes, the regulation of waste disposal, and the control of the main river watercourses.

The setting up of the new Environment Agency has not been without controversy. There have been charges that the new environmental legislation weakens environmental protection. This has involved particularly harsh criticism of the duty upon the agency to take greater account of the costs and benefits of compliance. The majority of senior posts in this new organization went to former National Rivers Authority staff, including the post of Chief Executive. This has led to concerns that National Rivers Authority culture would 'swamp' the new organization (ENDS Report 1995, 247, p. 3). Clearly the concerns of former IAPIs about regulatory culture and enforcement have been far from eradicated.

Railway Inspectorate

In December 1990 RI became part of HSE and thus one of its constituent inspectorates. RIs were moved out of the Department of Transport to HSE buildings in another part of London (HSC, 1990b, pp. 32–3). Prior to this there had been a movement towards appointing non-railway personnel as Chief Inspecting Officers of Railway for the first time in RI's history. But the role of RI has also been heightened and changed by two major events which have caused the railway industry to be the subject of a wide-ranging review of its health and safety arrangements in recent years. More important is the privatization of British Railways. The other, occurring in the run-up to privatization but completely unconnected with it, is the aftermath of two major accidents, one involving a fire on the London Underground and the second a collision at Clapham Junction in 1988. These two accidents brought the subject of railway safety firmly and dramatically into the public arena. The King's Cross Underground fire involved multiple fatalities, massive publicity, suspicion of a breakdown in systems for safety, technical problems, and a clear need for public reassurance. Hence a formal court of inquiry was set up which undertook a deep and searching public examination of the accident and the railway company involved. This had much wider and deeper reverberations throughout the railway industry. It caused railway managers across Britain to ask themselves how their own procedures and standards would stand up to such public scrutiny. In the case of British Railways the test was not far away. In the wake of the publication of the King's Cross Inquiry Report and at a time when a number of high-profile transport accidents had caused transport to be the subject of much political and media attention, there was a major collision at Clapham Junction in South London. The Secretary of State for Transport came under great pressure and criticism, and accordingly announced the setting up of another court of inquiry to investigate this accident (Hutter, 1992). The inquiry and subsequent report led British Railways to initiate a major review of safety on the railways—encompassing both passenger safety and the health and safety of the workforce. On the basis of this review the British Railways Board implemented changes to improve its health and safety record. These changes were introduced in a period of great change for the railway industry, changes which potentially have major implications for all aspects of the railway industry in Great Britain, including its health and safety arrangements.

The Railways Act 1993 paved the way for the privatization of an industry which had been a unified nationalized industry since 1948. A complicated structure of some sixty independent businesses contracting with each other is intended to replace a unified vertical command structure. Complex new arrangements have been outlined both within the 1993 legislation and the discussions preceding it. The state regulation of health and safety at work remains much the same as before at an organizational level, remaining the responsibility of HSE, and most specifically RI. Under the 1993 Act HSE is one of the rail regulators, but what is unclear at the moment—and is thus a matter for further research—is the implications of the current changes for the role of HSE. Also of relevance is HSE's role in setting safety standards and implementing new regulations made under the HSW Act 1974, to meet the major changes now being institutionalized (The Railways (Safety Case) Regulations 1994; The Railways (Safety Critical Work) Regulations 1994).

Railtrack, a separate government-owned company which was set up in April 1994, will occupy a central position in this new structure. This company owns and manages the track, signalling, and other operational infrastructure of the railways. Under the legislation Railtrack will 'oversee the safety of the operational network under the supervision of HSE', such that the *Railway Gazette International* has referred to Railtrack as the 'safety regulator'. Thus this company will not only be directly responsible for the health and safety of its own workforce of some 12,000 employees but will also have indirect responsibilities involving all users of the railway network. For example, it will be responsible for ensuring that franchisees, the track renewal and infrastructure maintenance companies and rolling-stock lease companies have a properly validated safety case. HSE's principal relationship will therefore be with Railtrack. Whether or not this denotes a changing role for HSE remains to be seen. Clearly these are all matters for investigation.

The railway safety case (RSC) is a key tool in health and safety on the new railways. The Railways (Safety Case) Regulations 1994 outline the requirements and status of a safety case. The Schedules to these Regulations explain what should be covered, including consideration of safety policy, risk assessment, safety management systems, and safety standards. Railtrack's RSC will be subject to validation by HSE, while the RSCs of train and station operators must be validated by Railtrack. This raises complex questions about the responsibilities for health and safety within the new system and the place of health and safety requirements in the contractual relations between the different parts of the railway. The contractual relations are especially important, given that each contract may be separately negotiated. Indeed, the role of the Rail Regulator, the Franchising Director, and the Secretary of State all merit consideration, as each has responsibilities for health and safety-related issues. What does seem certain is that HSE will face a considerably more complex task in its dealings with some sixty independent companies than one complex yet unified company (see Hutter, forthcoming).

Health and Safety Executive

There have been a variety of other changes affecting HSE, many of which were emerging at the time of the research. The question of who should be responsible for Offshore Safety has been a matter of long-standing controversy (Carson, 1982). In 1990 HSE took over responsibility for this area. HSC and HSE have increasingly become concerned with health-related issues, for example the Control of Substances Hazardous to Health Regulations 1988. Likewise their responsibilities to the public as well as employees have increased with a greater emphasis, for instance, on preventing major hazards. Also the international aspects of health and safety regulation have gained in prominence, especially those related to Europe. For example, January 1993 saw the introduction of the so-called 'six-pack' of health and safety regulations which implemented previously agreed European directives.

At a domestic level, HSE (in common with the rest of the Civil Service) has continued to be subject to the 'open government' policies of successive governments committed to reducing the role of the state. The scope, depth, and character of regulatory activities have increasingly been the subject of critical examination; the development of the 'new managerial state' has subjected the civil service to effectiveness and efficiency studies (Butler, 1993); and questions of accountability have moved beyond their traditional remit and have become linked to performance indicators and assessment (Stewart and Walsh, 1992). Moreover, specific government policies have been designed to reduce regulation. For example the government paper *Lifting the Burden* (Minister Without Portfolio, 1986), which was presented to Parliament in 1986 (during the research period), has its successor and expression in the 1994 Deregulation and Contracting Out Bill.

The organizational priorities and arrangements within HSE change with the times, but the underlying tensions of regulation remain the same as they did over a century ago. In this respect much of what follows has contemporary significance.

CONCLUSIONS

The differences between the inspectorates in this study related to particular aspects of *regulatory work*. There were, for instance, differences in professional expertise and the importance attributed to technical knowledge, with both of these figuring more prominently in the work of IAPI and RI than FI (see Hutter and Manning, 1990). This is partly related to the nature of the activities regulated. Risk and uncertainty underpin all regulatory work, but to a greater extent in some areas than others. IAPI generally dealt with activities which could have an impact on national and even transnational air quality. FI and RI, however, tended to regulate more localized activities, which, while potentially life-threatening, had a narrower focus. In part this was because these inspectorates were more concerned with safety issues than with those involving health. And safety problems were typically more visible and tangible than those involving health and air quality. All of these factors have implications for the definition, assessment, and achievement of compliance. The inspectorates have traditionally differed in their responses to risk, with IAPI typically being more proactive than either FI or RI. A wider mandate, such as that relating to health risks and air quality, generally increases the difficulties of enforcement. The more precisely defined the enforcement task and the more tangible and visible the activity subject to control, the more precisely one can assess compliance and the easier it is to satisfy evidential requirements and proceed with legal action (Hutter and Manning, 1990).

Regulatory tradition is another important parameter of regulatory behaviour and a source of regulatory culture which permeates the definition, assessment, and achievement of compliance. HSE incorporates a diversity of inspectorates of different sizes, capabilities, and traditions. At the time of this research these inspectorates were generally clinging to their 'parent' traditions and customs, and there was resistance to the creation of the unified inspectorate envisaged by the Robens Committee (1972, paras. 204 ff.). The numerically small inspectorates felt threatened by FIs who, through their sheer numbers, occupied positions in Executive policy divisions and even the unions. It was feared that these inspectors would impose their more legalistic and sanctioning approach upon the whole organization. There was also concern that HSE would try to create a generalist inspectorate which would enter a site and be responsible for enforcing all HSE related legislation.

Whether or not any of these worries were well-founded is difficult to determine. Regulatory traditions do of course change over time, and they may also be changed by organizational measures such as recruitment procedures, promotion policies, reward structures, and policy changes. The creation of a unified inspectorate could necessitate detailed written rules and procedures, largely in recognition of the inability of any one inspector to be familiar with all aspects of the job. It could also create the need for a larger bureaucracy to generate these rules and procedures; to facilitate communication between the generalists and the specialists; and to control and co-ordinate the activities of these. An unintended consequence of the Robens Committee proposals could therefore be to complicate the very system they were attempting to simplify. On the other hand it is important to understand that there is much common ground between the various HSE inspectorates. The legal and political parameters of regulation are broadly similar for each inspectorate. Moreover, their definitions of compliance and the range of methods they use to assess compliance are broadly similar, as are the overall methods they use to achieve compliance.

PART 2

Defining Compliance

3 The Legal and Administrative Framework

At the most basic level compliance means a desired state of conformity with the law, a regulation, or a demand. Defining compliance may therefore appear to be simply a matter of 'measuring up' whether or not a given state of affairs or an act accords with the demands encoded in law. In practice this 'measuring up' may not be so simple, since interpreting the meaning of rules and applying them to real-life situations is not always straightforward. Indeed, cynics might point out that it is the fact that the law is not always clear and unambiguously applied that keeps solicitors, barristers, and other members of the legal profession in a job. This is not simply a case of dealing with those who seek to evade the law, but also relates to the fact that what happens in the 'real world' does not, indeed cannot, be reduced to the classificatory scheme of the law. Hence there is necessarily scope for interpretation in the enforcement of the law.

The scope of interpretation in implementing the law may be structured by a variety of factors, such as the way in which the law is framed and worded; enforcement agency directives about legal interpretation; the application of these interpretations by individual enforcement officials; and, in a number of matters, consideration of case law. In this Chapter a variety of definitions of compliance will be considered, starting with the legal definition and finishing with the subject of the next chapter, the working definition employed by those at the 'sharp end' of the enforcement process, the field-level officials.

LEGAL DEFINITIONS OF COMPLIANCE

The question of how precisely the law should be written is one that has occupied many a legal mind, not least because it is related to the issue of the scope which should be given to the enforcement official to determine what may be defined as an offence—how much *de jure* discretion officials should be accorded (Baldwin and Hawkins, 1984; Davis, 1969; Jowell, 1973). Pre-Robens, health and safety legislation tended to be very precisely defined. This may have left less scope for inspector interpretation, but in the view of the Robens Committee it created a host of other problems. In its final report the Committee made a number of major criticisms of the legislation it had examined. The fundamental defect identified was that there was 'too much law' (1972, para. 28). This had come about partly because of the piecemeal way in which certain health and safety problems had come into prominence and been responded to by Parliament (*ibid.*, p. 181) but it was also a consequence of the precision of the resultant laws—what the Robens Committee referred to as 'detailed prescriptions for innumerable day-to-day circumstances' (*ibid.*, para. 28). One effect of such rules is inflexibility and the need to create new laws to cope with changing circumstances and technology (1972, para. 23). This leads to a proliferation of new legislation and renders much existing legislation outdated and very often unrepealed. Not surprisingly the result is confusion and a body of law which, in the words of the Committee, is 'intrinsically unsatisfactory'. Moreover, the Committee found much of the law to be 'written in a language and style that renders it largely unintelligible to those whose actions it is intended to influence' (1972, para. 29).

The legislative changes proposed by the Robens Committee were as radical as the organizational changes it had suggested for the administration of health and safety legislation. And in some respects they were parallel to them. For example, the centralizing tendency proposed on an organizational basis was further advocated in respect of the law. The Committee recommended that the existing legislation be replaced, as far as possible, by a single 'enabling Act' which would comprise, among other things, a statement of general principles and a co-ordinated set of provisions which would be readily intelligible (1972, chs. 4 and 5). The aim would be to replace detailed statutory regulations with broad requirements, supported by voluntary standards and codes of practice which could be easily revised as necessary. Such a system, it was hoped, would combine the advantages of broad guidance with detail incorporated in precise rules. The Committee understood the pitfalls of both approaches, as it indicated when discussing the type of supporting instruments that should accompany the 'enabling Act':

Regulations which lay down precise methods of compliance have an intrinsic rigidity, and their details may be quickly overtaken by new technological developments. On the other hand, lack of precision creates uncertainty. . . . The need is to reconcile flexibility with precision. We believe that, whenever practicable, regulations should be confined to statements of broad requirements in terms of the objectives to be achieved. Methods of meeting the requirements may often be highly technical and subject to frequent change in the light of new knowledge. They should, therefore, appear separately in a form which enables them to be readily modified (1972, para. 138).

The Health and Safety at Work etc. Act 1974

The HSW Act 1974 is to all intents and purposes the 'enabling Act' the Robens Committee outlined. Accordingly the legal definitions of compliance it presents to inspectors take the form of general duties and broad statutory standards. The Act places a variety of duties upon employers and employees. The most general of these is stated in section 2, which places upon an employer a general duty 'to ensure, so far as is reasonably practicable, the health, safety and welfare at work of all his employees' (section 2(1)). This section of the Act goes on to specify some broad areas of concern in this respect, namely that attention should be paid to such matters as plant and systems of work; the handling, storage, and transport of articles and substances; and the provision of information, instructions, training, and supervision for employees. It is also the duty of employers to provide a written statement of policy regarding health and safety, including the organization and administration of this policy. This statement should be brought to the notice of employees and revised as necessary (section 2(3)). Duties are also imposed regarding the relations of employers with employee-safety representatives, who should be both recognized and consulted (section 2(61)). An employer also has responsibilities towards people not in their employment 'to ensure, so far as reasonably practicable, that persons not in his employment who may be affected are not, thereby, exposed to risks to their health and safety' (section 3).

Although employers and management carry the overall responsibility for health and safety, the Act also places duties upon employees. Section 7 obliges employees to 'take reasonable care' for the health and safety of themselves and others and to co-operate with employers in the discharge of their duties. Section 8 places a duty on employees not to interfere intentionally or recklessly with anything provided for their health, safety, or welfare. In addition, the legislation places duties upon 'persons in control of certain premises in relation to harmful emissions into the atmosphere' (section 5)[1] and manufacturers, designers, importers and suppliers 'as regards articles and substances for use at

[1] S. 5 is derived from the former Alkali Acts which are discussed in more detail below.

work' (section 6). Section 6, for instance, imposes the duty 'to ensure, so far as is reasonably practicable, that the article is . . . safe and without risks to health when properly used'; to carry out testing and examinations; to provide information about safe use; and to undertake research to eliminate or minimize risks to health and safety.

The duties imposed by the HSW Act are couched in very general terms. In particular, some of the standards are very broadly framed, a notable example being the phrase 'so far as is reasonably practicable'. These broad standards may have been incorporated for pragmatic reasons, for example, to try to ensure that the legislation is generally inclusive, that is, applicable to a wide range of health and safety hazards. But the HSW Act is not without its critics. The term 'so far as is reasonably practicable', for example, may be regarded as falling short of the absolute standards which could have been included by the legislature. The term 'practicable' involves the determination of technical feasibility while the more contentious word is 'reasonably', which is generally taken to refer to the cost of the improvement (Dawson *et al.*, 1988, p. 15). Hence the term 'reasonably practicable' involves 'a weighing of the risks against the measures necessary to eliminate the risk' (notes to section 2, HSW Act). This phrase, like so much regulatory legislation in Great Britain, follows the long tradition of accommodation between competing interest groups (see Bugler, 1972; Carson, 1974; Gunningham, 1974; Hutter, 1988; Paulus, 1974). From the point of view of industry it is only fair to take account of the cost of any duties imposed, but from the workers' perspective it is unjust to expect them to bear the health and safety costs of any lack of provision for their health and safety at work.

Environmental Regulation

Such a flexible legislative approach was not new to one of the inspectorates in my sample, namely IAPI. In fact the Robens Committee based its recommendations upon one of the central legislative concepts in the field of environmental control, namely that of 'best practicable means' (1972, para. 139). The term 'best practicable means' appears in several Acts of Parliament, including the Clean Air Act 1956; Control of Pollution Act 1974; and the various Alkali Acts. Section 7 of the Alkali Act 1906, for instance, requires that the owner of any work specified in the first Schedule to the Act :

shall use the best practicable means for preventing the escape of noxious or offensive gases by the exit flue of any apparatus used in any process carried on in the work, and for preventing the discharge, whether directly or indirectly, of such gases into the atmosphere and for rendering such gases where discharged harmless and inoffensive.

The Alkali Acts do not define what is meant by the term 'best practicable means', unlike the Clean Air Act 1956, section 34, which offers the following broad interpretation of practicability:

'practicable' means reasonably practicable having regard, amongst other things, to local conditions and circumstances, to the current state of technical knowledge, and 'practicable means' includes the provision and maintenance of plant and proper use thereof.

And the Control of Pollution Act 1974, section 72, adds: '[t]he means to be employed include the design, installation, maintenance and manner and periods of operation of plant and machinery, and the design, construction and maintenance of buildings'.

Central to these definitions is the notion that the standards set should be sufficiently flexible to be adapted to individual works and, moreover, that they should be subject to constant revision should there be any changes either in technical ability or in environmental needs (Schneider, 1992). Responsibility for determining these matters lies with the administrative agency.

This environmental legislation and the HSW Act pose practical problems to many employers, namely those of interpretation. The flexibility offered by broad statutory standards carries with it the difficulty of ascertaining precisely how they should be applied to particular circumstances. There are a number of ways in which employers can determine how to apply these standards. Trade associations or the HSE may offer leaflets and advice on how to apply the law to some circumstances. Alternatively there may be other legislation which applies, for example the Factories Act 1961, the Construction (Working Places) Regulations 1966, or the Woodworking Machines Regulations 1974.

Section 15 of the HSW Act gives the Secretary of State power to make *regulations*, and once passed they should have the full force of law. Hence regulations can impose mandatory duties, their purpose being to vary or specify the law. The Woodworking Machines Regulations 1974, for example, not only replace the Woodworking Machinery Special Regulations 1922 to 1945 but also specify the standards to be accepted by the HSE as being in compliance with the HSW Act. In contrast to the Act, the regulations indicate very detailed requirements. Regulation 12, for instance, specifies the precise minimum temperatures for rooms or other places where woodworking machinery is used. HSC takes a major role in drafting such regulations. All of this guidance may be accompanied by administrative definitions of compliance, none of which hold the same legal status as either statutes or regulations.[2]

ADMINISTRATIVE DEFINITIONS OF COMPLIANCE

Health and safety and environmental legislation places much emphasis and reliance upon the determination of administrative definitions of compliance. So it is left to the enforcement agency (and ultimately the courts) to decide what constitutes 'best practicable means' or 'reasonably practicable steps' at any time. But it does not make these decisions in isolation, and consultation with the affected parties is an integral part of the construction of an administrative definition of compliance.

Each of the inspectorates in this study had its own form of administrative definition. The most authoritative of the administrative definitions specified under the HSW Act are *Approved Codes of Practice*. Section 16 of the HSW Act provides for these 'for the purpose of providing practical guidance' with respect to the relevant legislation and regulations. Approved Codes of Practice give practical guidance about how to comply with statutes and regulations. They are more flexible than regulations, are less formally written, and are likely to be more technical than the legislation.

Theoretically these definitions hold purely administrative—non-statutory—status and are open to challenge in the courts. In practice few cases reach this stage, but for those that do there seems to be a presumption that these definitions may be accepted by the courts as evidence of a contravention of the law. The Introduction to the Approved Code of Practice, *Work with Asbestos Insulation and Asbestos Coating*, explains the legal situation as follows:

Although failure to comply with any provision of this code is not in itself an offence, that failure may be used in criminal proceedings as evidence that a person has failed to discharge his duty under a section of the Health and Safety at Work etc Act 1974 or had contravened a regulation, if the provision of the code relates to that section of the Act or to that regulation. In such a case however

---

[2] See Baldwin, 1995, chs. 5 and 6, for a detailed discussion of regulatory rules in the sphere of health and safety.

it will be open to the person charged to satisfy the court that he has discharged his duty or complied with the regulation in some other way (HSC, 1985a, p. 1).

The onus of proof is thus upon the defendant to demonstrate that he or she has been employing standards and methods equivalent to those specified in the Approved Code of Practice, not upon the agency to prove that an offence has been committed. The use of these administrative documents in this way may be regarded by some as tantamount to a legal definition of compliance.

Fieldwork observations revealed that whenever inspectors found that companies were deviating from Codes of Practice they subjected the alternatives adopted to considerable scrutiny—it was emphasized that Codes of Practice had been put together after a great deal of thought and that there were 'good reasons' for complying with their demands.

Guidance Notes are the other major form of administrative device provided by HSE. Again, these do not have the force of law, but they are authoritative to the extent that they indicate the requirements of the law. Paragraph 4 of the Guidance Note on *General Access to Scaffolds* GS 15 explains: '[t]he Note does not seek to interpret the law but the information is based on the legal requirements contained in the Health and Safety at Work etc Act 1974 (HSW Act) and the Construction (Working Places) Regulations 1966' (HSE, 1985, para. 4).

IAPI outlined its requirements arising from the law in 'BPM Notes' which were published for the different classes of works it regulated. These Notes used to be published as appendices to the Chief Inspector's *Annual Report* but after 1979 were published separately as a series of Notes on individual processes. The HSE publication BPM1/79 explains the purpose of the Notes:

'Notes on Best Practicable Means' are for the guidance both of the industry and the inspectorates concerned. The diversity of industrial plant is such that the Notes cannot be fully comprehensive. They are intended to cover the broad features of the process, leaving matters of detail and the many variations of specific processes to be dealt with by inspectors. A basis is thus provided for consultation between the inspectorates and works managements, with sufficient flexibility to meet the needs of local circumstances (HSE, 1979, para. 3).

The inspectorate aimed to review the Notes for each process approximately every five years. Some inspectors described 'best practicable means' as 'an ever-tightening noose', increasing the standard as it became practicable to do so. The development of new knowledge about the dangers of a given process would lead to earlier review. The notes were, as BPM/82 paragraphs 13–16 explain, primarily applicable to new works, including replacement plant. The exceptions to this were plants where a public health hazard was deemed to exist and those works subject to a great deal of complaint. If, for example, carcinogens are involved, then changes in knowledge may mean that improved arrestment equipment is required retrospectively.

RI used Approved Codes of Practice and Guidance Notes; and issued *Railway Construction and Operation Requirements* for new works. These were not mandatory, but if the railways do not comply with the requirements then the inspectorate may not pass new works as fit for passenger traffic. The requirements have been produced since the nineteenth century and, as with some of the other administrative definitions we have discussed, they seem to assume a quasi-legal status in practice, if not in law.

These administrative definitions usually comprised two parts. The first part identified minimum control limits should they be appropriate, and the second part recommended the way these limits might be met and the way in which substances and equipment should be handled and maintained. Control limits are possible only for certain types of substances and process, and are part of the effort to identify how compliance with the law can best be achieved. Approved Codes of Practice and Guidance Notes usually express limits in terms of 'threshold limit values' (TLVs) whereas BPM Notes typically refer to 'presumptive limits'. These limits are presumptive to the extent that, if works fail to meet them, then they are presumed not to be in compliance with the law. Quantitative limits are set where possible but when this is impracticable the administrative definition will be qualitative. BPM/82 (Best Practicable Means: An Introduction) explains:

Where quantitative emission limits would be impracticable, for example for uncontained sources, the requirements of best practicable means may be framed as qualitative assessments or as operational procedures, process control conditions, working practices or design principles, as is most appropriate (HSE, 1982, para. 18).

These definitions are not static. Indeed their whole rationale is that they should be changed in response to changing circumstances. The control limits are therefore those determined in light of the information currently available, and it is readily admitted—indeed it is emphasized—that these limits may not be safe and should be improved upon where possible. Guidance Note EH10 on Asbestos warns that: '[e]xposure to all forms of asbestos should be reduced to the minimum reasonably practicable . . . The control limits do not represent safe levels which once attained make further improvements in dust control unnecessary' (HSE, 1984, paras. 8 and 9).

Similarly Guidance Note MS8 on Isocyanates warns that '[s]ensitised workers may develop asthma at atmospheric levels of isocyanate below the control limit' (HSE, 1983, para. 6). The Guidance Note also explains that the effects of these chemicals are not fully understood: '[t]he mechanisms of action of isocyanates have not been fully elucidated, but there appears to be irritant, pharmacological and immunological effects' (HSE, 1983a, para. 2).

This, of course, highlights the degree of uncertainty involved in regulatory work and offers some indication of the difficulty in formulating rules (see Chapter 4; also Jasanoff, 1986; Reiss, 1992; Short, 1992). Administrative definitions of compliance can, as we might expect, be quite specific in their guidance. The *Railway Construction and Operation Requirements*, for example, set out the general requirements, and then go into greater detail about how to comply with them. The *Requirements for Level Crossings* (Department of Transport, 1981a), for example, incorporate both general phrases such as 'reasonable period' (2:2), 'where practicable' (2:2), 'satisfactory crossing surface' and 'adequate approaches' (2:4), and more precise standards. Section 5, for instance, details the conditions for suitability for automatic half-barriers, stating that the maximum speed of trains shall not exceed 160km/h, and what to do in the event of equipment failure and work affecting the crossing. Section 11 specifies the necessary traffic signals, carriageway markings, telephones, and audible warning devices.

Regulations, Approved Codes of Practice, and Best Practicable Means are all the result of a consultation process between the inspectorates, industry, and unions in accordance with the tripartite ethos of the HSW Act 1974. Although it is not the intention of this Chapter to discuss these issues in any depth it might help to illustrate the way in which the administrative definition is achieved with reference to the revision of the BPM Note on Lead, the revised version of which was published in 1985 (HSE, 1985b).

The revision of the BPM Notes on Lead was prompted by the fact that the technology of control had outstripped the former BPM Notes. In 1981 IAPI undertook preliminary studies in preparation for a revision of the existing BPM Notes on Lead. The inspectorate sought greater knowledge of best practicable practices, so a group of inspectors was asked to look at this with particular reference to low-level emissions and to identify priorities for action. A summary of this group's report appeared in the 1982 *Annual Report* where it was publicly stated that the industry's co-operation had been secured and that the group's findings would inform revision of the BPM Notes.[3] In 1983 a working party of inspectors from five districts where there was a concentration of lead works was set up to consider revision of the Notes and was charged to report by the end of the year. This move was partly informed by the *Ninth Report of the Royal Commission on Environmental Pollution* (April 1983). Paragraphs 6.4 and 6.41 and Recommendation 21 suggested that IAPI should consider the scope for decreasing the BPM emission limits currently applicable to scheduled lead processes. The working party met on seven occasions, and after the fifth meeting produced a consultative document which was sent to industry and the Department of the Environment for comment.[4]

Representatives from all of the inspectorates researched spoke of consultations at this stage as 'game-like'. One inspector described the consultation process as 'playing with words'. Very often, it was alleged, the final draft was not very different from the first draft but 'honour is preserved' and each side felt it had contributed to the decision. Basically industry needed convincing that the proposed demands were reasonable and, in the case of BPM Notes, may have needed reassurance that instant compliance was not demanded in the absence of new evidence of the dangers attached to emissions.

The lead industry is a well-organized one. Most users in the country are represented by the Lead Development Association (LDA). In the revision of the BPM Notes 'a lot of hard bargaining' took place, the result being a word-for-word agreement which comprised the new BPM Notes. The inspectorate was satisfied that the new Notes contained everything it wanted and the revised Notes were published in 1985. A major change was introduced into the revised Notes, namely a single concentration limit for all direct process emissions rather than various classifications of different sized works.[5]

---

[3] It should be noted that the revision of BPM Notes is rarely news to industry. IAPI (like the other inspectorates in this study) would have prepared the ground beforehand and industry would be expecting the proposed revisions.

[4] A draft document was previously circulated around the inspectorate for comment.

[5] Apparently many lead works were already meeting the limit of 10 mg/m3.

Consistency and Uniformity

Administrative definitions of compliance offer guidance for the implementation of broadly framed laws. Discretion is built into the regulatory system, providing a potential tension between discretion and consistency. Administrative definitions are intended to reduce discretion, but they are not designed to eliminate it. While not losing sight of the merits of uniformity (that is, apparent agency fairness and assurance for businesses that they will be regulated in the same way as their competitors), Bardach and Kagan warn of the dangers of equal treatment. They argue that strict, uniform laws can lead to over inclusiveness and unreasonableness:

Regulators are well aware of many mismatches between uniform rules and diverse circumstances. . . . But friction persists, especially when enforcement officials are denied discretion to adjust the rules or to overlook deviations. The results are unreasonableness (the imposition of uniform regulatory requirements in situations where they do not make sense) and unresponsiveness (1982, p. 58).

These dangers are fully recognized by the legislature in Great Britain, hence the broadly framed legislation relating to the environment and health and safety at work. The administrative definitions, it is stressed, are meant to be guidance rather than dictates. BPM/82, paragraph 19, for example, emphasizes that BPM requirements should be applied consistently between companies, but that local circumstances may require some variation on details. This is not to claim that the inspectorate was not sensitive to the need for consistency. HQ inspectors co-ordinated the agreements negotiated by the districts and thus attempted to minimize serious discrepancies. They were concerned when dealing with national companies that agreements reached on one site were in line with those reached elsewhere. All inspectors were aware that companies were very sensitive to uniformity but they felt that this was difficult to achieve as each plant was different. But where situations were comparable then it was considered that the same requirements should be applied.

Attempts to eliminate discretion and impose uniformity can never be fully successful, not least because inspectors visiting sites alone have ample opportunity to create their own discretion. Certainly individual inspectors tended to have their own 'hobby horses' when inspecting premises, so different inspectors visiting the same premises would pay particular attention to different aspects of health and safety or the environment. Very often these 'hobby horses' were related to the inspectors' training or occupation prior to their joining the inspectorates. Indeed, the professional expertise of those involved in regulation has been found to be one broad explanatory factor for differences in approach. Cheit (1990), for example, found that those responsible for private and public regulatory standard-setting in the United States had distinct ways of thinking about problems. This he partly related to the professional ethics of the personnel employed in each sector, although he cautions against too broad a generalization, such as the claim that all members of a profession adhere to the same ethic. The investigation of particularly unpleasant accidents could also cause inspectors to pay particular attention to machinery, substances, or activities involved in the accident. These differences are extremely difficult, if not impossible, to eliminate, and some would argue that this is in itself an undesirable goal.

Whether or not the array of 'supporting instruments' referred to in this Chapter as the administrative definition of compliance represents a simplification of the pre-Robens situation is a matter for debate. To many the growing number of administrative responses must prove very confusing. While laws do not need to be repealed in response to changing circumstances and technologies, lengthy consultation procedures do need to be followed before a new administrative response can be confirmed. Obviously this takes time and may not take priority, particularly when there are some areas and subjects not yet covered by Approved Codes of Practice and Guidance Notes.

In practice, of course, these administrative definitions—themselves refinements of the legal definition of compliance—have to be applied to particular circumstances. Hence they will be subject to interpretation (and possibly redefinition) by enforcement officials during the course of their routine work—for what is 'reasonable' and 'practicable' will vary not just over time but according to the company and the workplace concerned. It is this definition that I refer to as the *working* definition of compliance, a definition which is both legally encouraged and administratively sanctioned.

CONCLUSIONS

The law, itself a product of competing tensions and interest groups, is an important framework of regulation. As with much regulatory law, health and safety and environmental legislation in Britain is ambivalent. For example, it accords regulatory officials considerable powers of entry, inspection (of premises and documents), and even of the seizure or destruction of items which it is considered may cause a danger (HSW Act, section 20), while at the same time it provides relatively weak sanctions for non-compliance. The broad statutory standards which characterize regulatory legislation grant broad discretion to the regulatory agency. Health and safety and environmental legislation places much emphasis and reliance upon the determination of administrative definitions of compliance. These administrative definitions offer guidance for the implementation of broadly framed laws. They reduce discretion but are not designed to eliminate it. Thus both the legislative and the administrative definitions of compliance convey legitimacy to the working definition of compliance, that is, a definition ascribed meaning by front-line officials.

4 The Working Definition of Compliance

Inherent in the legal and administrative definitions of compliance is the assumption that no one definition is necessarily sufficient to cover all situations. Some discretion will inevitably be available to field-level officials, since full enforcement of the law is an impossibility: judgements always have to be made about both the meaning of the legal rule and its applicability to the problems encountered by officials. The resulting working definition of compliance is therefore not static, but is a fluid concept which comprises a variety of dimensions.

Inspectors operate with a variety of notions of compliance. *Full compliance* is a standard set of conditions which they are aiming towards: this will usually be at least the legal or administrative definition of compliance, and it may represent a standard above the legal minimum. Inspectors may also operate with *temporary definitions of compliance*, that is a state of affairs which is less than full compliance but which is tolerated for a fixed period, until such time as they consider it reasonable for a state of full compliance to have been achieved. Both of these are positive definitions, to the extent that they emphasize the degree to which something measures up to the required standard. When inspectors were wanting to emphasize the negative aspects of a situation they talked in terms of *non-compliance*.

Inextricably related to these terms are notions of acceptability. Compliant behaviour may be regarded as acceptable and non-compliance may be regarded as unacceptable, but this is not invariably the case. While inspectors do not refer explicitly to unacceptable compliance or acceptable non-compliance, both of these terms are relevant to the discussion. *Unacceptable compliance* existed when the minimum standards laid down in the legal and administrative definitions were met but the inspector felt that a particular company could easily achieve more. A business could be asked to exceed the legal and administrative definitions of compliance for a variety of reasons. In some cases the risks posed by a particular process or site could lead to extreme caution and to the imposition of standards which well exceeded the legal/administrative minimum. IAPIs dealing with an asbestos-stripping firm were particularly stringent in their demands. Indeed, they demanded that all types of asbestos be treated with equal caution, despite the fact that the most stringent standards and procedures applied only to blue asbestos. In other cases, inspectors considered that higher standards could be achieved with a minimum effort. IAPIs visiting a smelting works felt that, although sampling of emissions from the stack was within legal/administrative limits, the arrestment equipment could—and should—be used more efficiently to achieve improved results. The inspector argued that, although the presumptive limits were being met, best practicable means were not. He therefore considered it reasonable to ask for improvements. In a letter to the firm he wrote '[a]lthough this result [of sampling] is within the Inspectorate's requirements, experience with similar venturi scrubbing equipment installed elsewhere leads me to believe that a lower figure should be obtainable, if the equipment is operating efficiently.'

The term 'unacceptable compliance' could also refer to circumstances when the letter of the law but not the 'spirit of the law' is adhered to. A typical example of this is the case where a FI visited a small metal finishers which had been required to obtain a cyanide antidote kit. This had been done but no-one at the site knew how to use the kit. In this case the inspector arranged for a nurse from the Employment Medical Advisory Service (EMAS) to visit the site and instruct staff. In some cases ignorance is not the sole cause of unacceptable compliance. A visit to an engine manufacturer is illustrative. A FI on a routine inspection of the factory asked to inspect the examination certificates of machines which in law must be regularly examined. The inspector soon discovered that the same faults were reported on successive reports. Hence the company was complying with the requirement that it have the machines examined but did not then act upon the reports when faults were discovered, so was not complying with the spirit of the law.

Acceptable non-compliance refers to cases which do not meet the legal definition of compliance but which are nevertheless acceptable to inspectors, or even to the agency, in which case some inspectors prefer the term '*sanctioned non-compliance*'. Temporary definitions of compliance clearly fall into this category, but there are a variety of other circumstances which lead to sanctioned non-compliance. For example, strict adherence to the law could render certain common equipment or processes inoperative. This was the case, for example, when FIs overlooked the everyday use of meat-cutting band-saws, which were in breach of section 14 of the Factories Act 1961. The strictures of section

14 of the Factories Act could also be overcome legally. The Woodworking Machines Regulations 1974 could be regarded as sanctioning non-compliance with the high demands of section 14 to the extent that they validated a lower standard of protection.

Section 14 of the Factories Act specifies that:

(1) Every dangerous part of any machinery, other than prime movers and transmission machinery, shall be securely fenced unless it is in such a position or of such construction as to be as safe to every person employed or working on the premises as it would be if securely fenced.

(2) In so far as the safety of a dangerous part of any machinery cannot by reason of the nature of the operation be secured by means of a fixed guard, the requirements of subsection (1) of this section shall be deemed to have been complied with if a device is provided which automatically prevents the operator from coming into contact with that part.

Section 9 of the Woodworking Machines Regulations 1974 qualifies this:

Without prejudice to the other provision of these Regulations, the cutters of every woodworking machine shall be enclosed by a guard or guards to *the greatest extent that is practicable* having regard to the work being done thereat, unless the cutters are in such position as to be as safe to every person employed as they would be if so enclosed. [My emphasis.]

Another reason for acceptable non-compliance may be that the legislation is felt to be outdated or out of step with public opinion; some local authorities in England and Wales, for example, overlooked laws which permitted some shops to open for Sunday trading and not others partly because the legislation was felt to be out-dated and invidious in the distinctions made between those shops which were permitted or not permitted to trade on a Sunday. In such cases officials have not been accorded *de jure* discretion, but rather they have created their own scope for interpretation. In practice, inspectors will need to take account of matters over the course of a period of time. There may be persistent non-compliance or absolute full compliance, but it is more likely that there will be occasional non-compliance and occasional compliance. In such cases inspectors will look at the total situation and their definitions of compliance and enforcement approach will be determined by a business's general approach and response to health and safety or environmental matters. So their approach will be determined by an *aggregation* of a site's performance across the full range of health and safety or environmental requirements. For example, a FI on a check visit to a packaging company found that many of the improvements requested by the inspectorate had been met, but one or two matters were still outstanding. The inspector's response was advisory and educational because the improvements to date had been well done and signalled progress. In another example FIs found an entirely different situation, when a check visit to a foundry revealed that, while there had been substantial capital expenditure on additional machinery, few of the inspectorate's requests had been met. This general non-compliance with the inspector's demands led to a stringent response, namely an improvement notice. Improvement notices were served for particularly noticeable and serious instances of non-compliance, for example, a failure to provide guarding for power presses, and the inspector warned the company that prosecution had been seriously considered.

A definition of aggregate compliance may also be derived from a number of sites under common ownership or management. IAPIs in one of the areas I researched considered the state of compliance across three mineral works owned by the same company when determining how to respond to any one of them. The file notes reveal that the inspectorate pushed for new equipment to be installed on one site, and when this was achieved and exit emissions were reduced, it targeted the next site. The three sites were clearly taken in aggregate rather than isolation.

In all of the examples above a balance had to be struck between competing demands and principles. Temporary definitions of compliance highlight this tension. Typically inspectors would allow a temporary definition in the case of minor and the least threatening cases of non-compliance. For example, a FI visiting a small struggling business set up by two people using their redundancy money gave them time to 'get organized' before pushing them 'too hard' to improve 'non-vital matters' such as redecoration. This does not mean that these matters would never be improved, but clearly one of the dangers associated with temporary definitions of compliance is that lengthy—some might think unnecessarily lengthy—periods of non-compliance are tolerated. The Baryugil Report (Report of the House of Representatives Standing Committee on Aboriginal Affairs, 1984, para. 6.9) illustrates an extreme case of this where the Mines Inspectorate in Australia worked to a temporary definition of compliance from 1952–60 on the promise of the construction of a new mill. But this is a somewhat unusual case, as there was evidence of a serious hazard: the Baryugil Mine was an asbestos works (Gunningham, 1987).

Definitions of compliance are inextricably related to the degree of tolerance inspectors are either prepared or able to display towards a business. In some cases a temporary definition is not an option and inspectors will have to demand instant compliance. A distinction may be made here between *initial compliance* and *compliance-maintenance*. *Initial compliance* refers, for example, to the installation of equipment to meet requirements or the introduction of training schemes or company rules to effect changes in, for instance, operator practice. *Compliance-maintenance* refers to the ongoing adoption of capital equipment or work-force practices once they have been installed or initiated.

Initial compliance may be immediate or may take considerable time. Immediate compliance was only achievable in a proportion of cases, for example on construction sites where quick and inexpensive remedies were usually readily available. But immediate compliance was also possible elsewhere, as was revealed by the FI who requested that the new owners of a small factory immediately cut off sub-standard electrical plugs. Sometimes inspectors personally effected immediate compliance, such as the inspector who broke in two a dangerous, split wooden ladder. Typically full compliance could take some time to achieve so a temporary definition would initially be put in place, which again could take some time to achieve. This was for a variety of reasons. For instance, a technically complex situation could demand constant negotiation and renegotiation about the source of a problem and how it might be remedied. For instance, it might prove difficult to detect the source of a nasty smell in an industrial area, and even when the source had been established its cause might not be readily identifiable because of the complexity of many manufacturing processes. Even if the source could be detected negotiation might be required to reach a solution. In less dramatic cases it could simply be the time it took to effect a remedy which led officials to give offenders some leeway to comply with their demands. For example, it might take a factory owner some time to replace a non-standard guard for a machine, so the FI would negotiate with the owner about whether the machine could be used in the meantime and, if so, what sort of precaution should be taken.

The distinction between initial compliance and compliance-maintenance draws further attention to the fact that the construction of a working definition is dependent upon the particular situations and contexts within which inspectors operate. So are the methods they used to attain compliance. Which of the paths they followed depended upon a variety of factors such as the way in which non-compliance was discovered (Part 3), who is being regulated (Part 4), and the principles underlying the construction of a working definition of compliance.

The definition, achievement, and maintenance of compliance is a process which continues for as long as a business is in operation and known about by the regulatory authorities. But while the activities regulated by inspectors are continuous, inspectors' visits to these sites are 'momentary' and sometimes infrequent. They therefore make decisions from 'snapshots' of activity, and with the benefit of varying levels of training, guidance, and experience. Issues of compliance therefore emerge in different contexts and settings and the meanings they take on are moulded accordingly.

During the course of a working day inspectors may visit several sites and over time they recognize patterns of behaviour and clues and symbols upon which they classify and describe the regulatory activity they have to assess. In turn, they build up expectations on the basis of these categories and gain some sense of what they may or may not be able reasonably to expect a site to achieve. Most of this activity takes place in response to, and within the structures of, the legal and administrative categories discussed in the previous chapter. Indeed, the inspectors in this research constructed a working definition of compliance according to a variety of principles, most of which can be traced back to the legal and administrative definition and to the tensions surrounding and inherent in regulatory activity.

Principles of Definition

Compliance Costs

One of the central dilemmas of regulating industrial and commercial activity is the balance that should be achieved between the purpose of regulation—for instance, the protection of health and safety or the environment—and the financial demands this incurs. The precise balance between these factors is a matter left largely to the discretion of the enforcement agency or official. The main message of the legislation is that officials should be 'reasonable'. What is reasonable may of course vary according to whose perspective one views the situation from. Some commentators argue that the employer's or polluter's arguments will always look most reasonable to enforcement officials (Box, 1983; Bugler, 1972). This may reflect a belief that business is always more powerful and able to define compliance than are either the victims of offences or indeed regulatory officials (Yeager, 1991). Alternatively, such views may arise from a strong anti-business position which leads to criticism on largely ideological grounds (Pearce and Tombs, 1990; see also Hawkins, 1990). Others, however, criticize officials for being over-zealous or unreasonable. This includes the work of Bardach and Kagan (1982) which takes a strong pro-business stance in its emphasis on the negative consequences of regulation (see also Posner, 1981). Whatever the situation and from wherever it is viewed, officials are normally expected to take account of the *monetary costs* their demands would impose on a business. In some cases this is dictated by the legislation. Vogel (1986, p. 163) points out that the concept of 'best practicable means' implicitly takes account of the costs of compliance. For example, the definition of 'practicable' offered in the Clean Air Act 1956, section 34(1) indicates that account should be taken of the 'financial implications' of demands: ' "practicable" means reasonably practicable having regard, amongst other things, to local conditions and circumstances, to the financial implications and to the current state of technical knowledge, and "practicable means" includes the provision and maintenance of plant and the proper use thereof.'

Likewise the concept of 'reasonably practicable' entails consideration of cost, namely that the costs of improvement must not be disproportionate to the benefits to be gained. The judgement in *Edwards* v. *National Coal Board* is taken as a general definition:

'Reasonably practicable' is a narrower term than 'physically possible' and seems to me to imply that a computation must be made by the owner in which the *quantum* of risk is placed on one scale and the sacrifice involved in the measures necessary for averting the risk (whether in money, time or trouble) is placed on the other and that, if it be shown that there is a gross disproportion between them—the risk being insignificant in relation to the sacrifice—the defendants discharge the onus on them [quoted in Dawson *et al.*, 1988, pp. 14–15].

But as Ireland and Bryce argue 'the relation between the costs of pollution abatement and its benefits cannot easily be established' (1979, p. 627). This is underlined by the Director General of HSE in the 1979–80 *Annual Report* to HSC: '[a]ction must be available to reduce the chances of injury at a cost proportionate to the improvement in the situation. Here . . . we badly need more and better information about both the benefits secured and the costs involved' (HSE, 1980). This *Report* emphasizes that these issues affect the Commission in setting standards (see also Cheit, 1990) and individual inspectors in their every-day work.

The working definition typically took account of a variety of aspects of compliance costs. The *general economic climate* of the country was one component of this definition. A recurring theme of the fieldwork period was the recession. Annual Reports frequently referred to the general economic climate. The 1981 *Report of the Chief IAPI*, for instance, noted that '[t]he industrial scene continues to be both depressed and depressing with pictures of declining output and closures of long-established plants and works. If the latter were part of a process of renewal it would be welcome, but proposals for new registrations are few' (HSEb, 1982). The HSC's *Plan of Work 1983–4* addressed directly the problems this created for the promotion of health and safety—at its starkest the priority which should be accorded to health and safety relative to the objective of economic survival. This document concluded that 'the pressures of recession and worsening economic conditions' cannot 'lead us to the facile solution of relaxing safeguards and requirements in the mistaken view that we also reduce costs and thereby help industry' (1983, p. 1). This said, it was acknowledged that inspectors needed to seek compliance 'within the constraints of economic viability' (*ibid.*, p. 2). In 1975 the Chief Industrial Air Pollution Inspector had placed rather more emphasis upon this point: '[t]he quality of life is important to us, but it is not at the top of the list when the country is struggling to earn its bread and butter' (HSE, 1977, p. 1). This does not represent an abandonment of air pollution control nor a reduction in standards but rather a slowing down in the rate of improvement.

Individual inspectors were rather more aware of the economic climate at regional and industrial level. IAPIs in one of the offices I visited were the only inspectors during the period of fieldwork not to have experienced a high level of closures and the virtual abandonment of prior-approval work. Those inspectors who pointed out areas of flat-tened buildings where thriving industries had once stood and those who visited small businesses in serious financial difficulty were much more the norm at the time of fieldwork for this study. Standards were said to vary between different regions of the country, and some FIs felt that the term 'reasonably practicable' involved taking account of the state of the industry and locality.

Related to the regional variations in the recession was the impact of the general economic climate upon specific *industries*, some industries being affected much more than others by the adverse economic conditions. IAPI *Annual Reports* noted these developments. For example, they gave regular updates about the state of the iron and steel industry. The 1976 Report (HSE, 1978, p. 20) noted delays in improvements because of the economic circumstances of this industry. The 1977 Report (HSE, 1979a) again noted 'the parlous state of the iron and steel industry' but also made it clear that HSE would not accept an absence of progress in air pollution control. In the following year's report works closures were reported, as were tripartite talks between the industry, IAPI, and FI to discuss how best to secure compliance in the prevailing economic conditions.

Field-level inspectors were, of course, most concerned with the financial state of the *companies* they regulated, and most particularly the cost of the improvements they required. It was difficult for individual inspectors to assess the state of the businesses they regulated, with the possible exception of those responsible for nationalized industries. Members of RI, for example, had a fair idea of the financial state of British Railways, whose accounts are public. They had less knowledge of the financial state of some of the other railways they regulated, although they did know that many of the minor railways they oversaw were run by volunteers and were in a very poor financial state.

Individual FIs and IAPIs used a variety of indicators and methods to ascertain the financial state of the companies they were responsible for. Some of this information was 'hard' data, some was 'softer' and more impressionistic. The 'hardest' data inspectors had were financial reports such as the company's annual report and also newspaper reports (although it should be recognized that reports in both the national and local press may be based on rumour). In particular, inspectors paid attention to staffing levels (for instance, was the company recruiting staff or making them redundant?). Staff morale was also of significance, in particular whether there was a major reorganization pending or whether there had been wage rises, a wage freeze, or cuts in wages. Changes to the site were also taken into account. Of relevance here were the existence of improvements and additions to the sites or closures (such changes would be taken into account with respect to the particular site in question and the company's other sites, on a nationwide level if appropriate). Standards of housekeeping and maintenance were also felt to be significant clues to a business's financial condition, tending to slip when financial circumstances were tight. 'Soft' impressionistic indicators included an assessment of the types of cars in the car park, especially those belonging to managers and directors, the quality of managerial accommodation, and the number and quality of canteens on site.

Inspectors would always ask questions about how business was doing and what the company's future plans were. Vitally important here was the amount of trust inspectors had in their respondents. This was an interactive process. Inspectors assessed the quality of information they were given against their judgements of the persons giving them this information. They also judged the persons against their perceptions of the accuracy of the information, for example, how the information related to other indicators of the financial state of the business (see Chapter 7).

Inspectors tried to build up a picture of a company's financial state in order to determine what improvements they felt they could reasonably ask for. In particular they were concerned with the costs of these improvements. Two aspects of the working definition of compliance were especially significant here. The first was the *absolute cost* of the improvement or remedy being sought. Clearly there were wide differences in the costs of the improvements or remedies being sought across inspectorates and between premises—compare, for example, the cost of fixing a guard to a piece of machinery with the major capital expenditure which may be involved in the installation of air pollution equipment. Secondly, account was taken of how *widespread* the changes being sought were. The costs of an improvement being sought with respect to one machine or even one workplace would be significantly different from a situation where nationwide changes were being sought. Inspectors usually took account of this when deciding upon the flexibility they should display in the working definition.

These factors differed between inspectorates. IAPIs were generally asking for much costlier improvements than the other sample inspectorates and RIs were often asking for more widespread improvements. The extent to which IAPIs were asking for costly improvements was indicated by their tendency to cost improvements they had effected. Cost was prominent in IAPI discussions and descriptions of their work. This inspectorate's *1985 Annual Report*, for instance, noted the cost of control measures achieved. The discussion of past achievements and current standards in the iron and steel industry, for example, states that:

British Steel Corporation has estimated that the capital investment in air pollution control equipment on a new integrated steel works providing 2½ million tonnes per annum of liquid steel would be £76 million. The annual cost of operating and maintaining that equipment together with capital charges, would be around £20 million or £8 per tonne of liquid steel produced (HSE, 1986a, pp. 7–8).

Individual IAPIs also costed improvements. An inspector I had accompanied to a power station told me that the improvement just asked for would cost £10,000 to install; another visiting a chemical works proudly informed me that the works had spent £17,000 on pollution-control equipment for a problem which occurs only a few times a year in particular weather conditions. This amount of money, it was pointed out, was equivalent to the cost of paying a chemical engineer for a year and the inspector was clearly pleased that he and his colleagues had managed to persuade the company to spend the money on pollution-control equipment.

All inspectors were sensitive to economic difficulties which, provided the inspector judged the difficulties to be genuine, could lead to some flexibility in the definition of compliance. But this was only the case if the non-compliance detected was not too serious. Whenever and wherever inspectors discovered major offences they would offer no leeway, even if compliance posed a significant cost and threatened the existence of the business. Even if a works was scheduled for closure there would be no leniency if serious problems arose, although a slight deterioration in standards was tolerated and in such circumstances inspectors would not seek further improvements.

In the case of less serious non-compliance inspectors would judge how able the company was to effect improvements. They would be unsympathetic if they considered the company to be financially healthy, particularly if new works were proposed and the company was liable to make a large profit from any proposed development. IAPI, for example, would not relax any of its definitions of compliance in the case of new works. But if genuine difficulties were detected then inspectors would be more willing to construct a temporary definition of compliance and possibly to negotiate a programme of work (see Chapter 8). Sometimes this was formalized in the form of an improvement notice. A FI visiting a mill where there were many problems served several improvement notices upon the mill owner, with the file note accompanying the notices stating '[f]or economic reasons I am prepared to let there be an 18/24 month period for Improvement Notices'.

Inspectors were well aware that much of the expenditure they might be requesting was 'dead money', to the extent that it would not generate any financial return. An IAPI was careful to explain to me that arrestment equipment he had been trying to persuade a smelting works to install was very costly. It would have cost £20,000 to install, in addition to employing someone to work with the equipment full time. The cost of keeping the fan on the equipment in operation was also considerable, and all of this would be for the sole purpose of pollution control—none of the equipment would increase production. In other cases pollution-control equipment can save money for a company. In the case of health and safety the costs of improvements should be offset against the costs of the lost time which could be incurred by accidents and the effects of this on the morale of fellow workers. An REI makes such a point in a letter to a maintenance depot where he had discovered problems: '[a]n impact with vehicles on the wheel lathe, apart from being potentially dangerous to the operators, would be exceedingly costly to you. Does this not warrant a very comprehensive insurance, ie. a very safe and positive system of work?'

While inspectors acknowledged economic problems and were willing in many circumstances to take account of them they were also quick to point out improvements which could be introduced without great expenditure. In some cases compliance did not require new equipment—the maintenance of existing equipment was all that was required. The FI emphasized this in its 1975–8 *Report on Foundries*:

although some improvements involve capital expenditure in the short term, this is not true of all. It is nothing short of disgraceful that more than half of the pedestal grinding machines provided with exhaust ventilation were, during the 1978 survey, found to be operating below the design standard . . . In many cases, therefore, what is required is not so much vast expenditure as a fundamental change of attitude [HSE, 1980, p. 5].

Inspectors were of course fully aware of the tensions that might exist between cost and other pressures, such as production levels. One health and safety inspector explained that, as a former site-manager himself, he fully understood that they are expected to get things done as cheaply as possible and that this may mean cutting corners with respect to health and safety. REIs were especially aware that railway employees could be compromised by the pressures of running the trains on time, and as a consequence health and safety concerns could be overlooked. One REI noted a glossy brochure on business objectives and successes which had been produced by a major railway company. He was struck by the fact that health and safety had not been mentioned once.

In some cases inspectors could use their expertise to save a business unnecessary expense. This was the case when an IAPI visited a lead works which had unacceptable levels of emission. The bag filters in use were proving inadequate, so the works manager suggested a number of alternatives, including an electrostatic precipitator. The inspector advised that this would be expensive and too sophisticated and suggested a variety of cheaper alternatives. In some cases the inspector's advice was ignored and firms could install much more sophisticated systems than were strictly necessary. This happened in the case of a di-isocyanate works applying to IAPI for registration. The inspectorate required that the height of the chimney be raised. The works suggested that they put in scrubbers instead, but the inspector informed them that the chimney height was not negotiable. He further explained that the scrubbers would be expensive and unhelpful. A year later, however, the company had both raised the height of the stack and installed the scrubbers. Where the methods of achieving compliance were simply not acceptable to the inspectorate there was no scope for negotiations. Inspectors could, however, offer to help the regulated to find an adequate solution, as did a REI who would not accept as compliant the scaffolding which engineers were using to undertake some bridge repairs. It was agreed that the ideal solution would not be viable, largely because of its costs. But from the outset the inspector made it clear that they would have to agree a compromise, since he would force the issue and make sure something was done to improve the situation. Several options were discussed but none was agreed upon. Some were rejected because it was felt that it would be very difficult to ensure workforce compliance, others because they did not suit the peculiar circumstances involved. Eventually the inspector said that he would consult with FIs in the Building Industry Group of the local HSE offices to see if they could suggest a solution.[1]

Principles of cost also influenced the vigour with which inspectors were prepared to pursue the achievement of full compliance with their

---

[1] Inspectors were careful not to be too specific in their advice for fear of being held liable if something did not work out, since it was the responsibility of the regulated to comply. Inspectors might refer the regulated to a trade association or to another business which had had similar environmental problems in order for them to make up their own minds.

demands. Underlying all inspectorate considerations about whether or not to prosecute was a crude estimate of the relative costs and benefits of legal action. In some cases this was clearly articulated by the inspectors involved. One FI I accompanied explained why he was not considering prosecution following an explosion at a dairy which had seriously injured a worker. After the initial investigation the inspector did not have sufficient evidence of the cause of the accident to take the case to court. While further resources could have been directed to collecting this evidence the inspector was not inclined to do so. This was because the inspector did not consider that much would be achieved by prosecuting. In elaborating upon this point it was noted that it was likely that the explosion was caused by the worker who had been injured. This, together with the fact that the management had to close the dairy for several days to effect repairs, was interpreted by the inspector as both parties having already 'learnt their lesson', so further punishment was not warranted, especially in light of the extra resources required to assemble a case. A crude rule-of-thumb therefore was that where the costs of preparing a case were greater than the benefits to be achieved, prosecution was unlikely.

Yeager (1991), in his examination of environmental regulation in the United States, notes that the relationship between the economy and the law is dynamic, and that sectors of business vary in their ability to comply and to influence the implementation of legislation. So compliance and its definition are a continuing process. But regulatory definitions are not just the result of tension between costs and regulatory objectives. Other principles are also significant. Indeed, cost-benefit analyses explicitly take account of this and, as Cheit (1990) and Mashaw and Harfst (1990) explain, can be used by industry to fight regulation and be manipulated to produce desired outcomes. One of the most commonly identified pressures is that between cost and risk.

Risk and Uncertainty

An integral part of any definition of compliance was an assessment of the risks of injury and the dangers to health or the environment associated with a given site or activity. Risk is often distinguished from uncertainty. Whereas risks are calculable in terms of probability, uncertainties cannot be calculated (Reiss, 1992). However, the distinction between risk and uncertainty often becomes blurred in everyday risk analysis (Short, 1992). Inspectors continually operated with notions of risk and uncertainty; and while some of the risks were theoretically calculable, they were not necessarily calculated (Hutter and Lloyd-Bostock, 1992). Nor was it only implicit notions of risk that informed inspectors' decisions, they also operated with implicit notions of risk (*ibid.*). An important point to recognize is that the social construction of risk is continual. As Reiss explains: '[r]isk is not a simple construction which decision-makers use to guide decisions. Rather, given the uncertainty of outcome and organizational contingencies for review, decision makers engage in a continual process of social construction of risk' (1992, p. 301).

Inspectors encountered widely varying levels of risk. At one level they had to deal with hazards. HSC (1980, p. 16) categorized these into three main groups, namely events which, although rare, have potentially disastrous results when they do occur, that is major catastrophes; hazards resulting in premature death or permanent damage to health; and hazards leading to immediate physical injury. But the large majority of situations encountered by these inspectors did not involve immediate risks to health and safety or the environment and did not pose major risks to health. Such variation in the levels of risk encountered by inspectors was recognized by legislation. For example, two types of legal notice were available to inspectors, namely the improvement notice and the prohibition notice. Prohibition notices provided for the prohibition of machinery or activities that were an *immediate* danger to health. Improvement notices, however, pertained to less dangerous activity and provided for improvement within a specified period of time, or, looked at in a slightly different way, allowed non-compliance with the full standard until that date.

Possible levels of control vary. It may be possible to eliminate a particular risk, to minimize it, or to ignore it altogether. In practice it is usually accepted that risks cannot be completely eliminated. Bardach and Kagan, for example, write 'since a totally risk free society is not feasible, some lines must be drawn at lower levels of protection' (1982, p. 27). HSE makes a similar point: '[r]isks will always exist. It is not possible to construct a working environment entirely free from risk' (1981, p. 8). HSE was here referring specifically to the possibilities of reducing hazards through design: 'hazards may be reduced, but rarely eliminated entirely, at the design stage. Design is not an exact science and for any given problem there may be no ideal and entirely reliable solution' (1981, p. 8). But as it points out later in its report, the level of risk tolerated is dependent upon a number of factors: 'levels of acceptable risk have often been influenced by political, ethical and emotional factors as much as by rational allocation of preventative resources' (HSE, 1981a, p. 9).

There is considerable debate about the level of risk that should be accepted. At a scientific level there is debate about the evidence and its interpretation, and whether there may be a lack of adequate information (Douglas and Wildavsky, 1982). And at a political level different interest groups may be prepared to tolerate different levels of risk (Douglas and Wildavsky, 1982). Administrative considerations are also important, especially in a system where standard-setting is an agency rather than legislative task. The outcomes of these definitions are determined by the interactions between scientific, political, cultural, and administrative influences (Jasanoff, 1986), with the precise weight given to each varying between issues (Cheit, 1990).

These assessments of risk were complex and comprised a number of dimensions. This was true not only of the legislative and policy levels of decision-making, but also of the way in which field-level inspectors assessed risks and incorporated them into a definition of compliance. These inspectors assessed risks according to two types of knowledge, which might broadly be described as 'objective' and 'subjective'. 'Objective' knowledge included calculations of the dangers associated with a given substance, machine, or activity, in particular the seriousness of the consequences of any mishap (both actual and potential).[2] It also took into account the probability of something going wrong. These assessments were made with reference to such data as accident statistics or so-called scientific knowledge, where these were available. 'Subjective' knowledge refers to inspectors' own judgements about a particular site, referring to both its 'hardware', namely its machinery, processes, and equipment, and its 'software', namely its employers, managers, and employees (see Chapter 7). These are not calculable risks but uncertainties, that is, unquantifiable judgements based on experience and training.

Inspectors' perceptions of risk are influenced by many factors. Their pre-inspectorate experience and specialisms may be influential. These may determine their understanding of the available 'objective' knowledge. Those least familiar with the details of the 'objective' information would tend simply to implement the threshold limit values and recommendations contained in guidance notes and other administrative

---

[2] It should be noted that there may be widespread disagreement about the scientific basis of risk assessment and the proper standards of protection that should be sought. See Nelkin, 1992; Short, 1992.

documents, on the basis that these had been drawn up by people much more experienced and knowledgeable in the subject than themselves. Where inspectors had previous knowledge of a process, activity, or substance—for example, by virtue of having worked in that industry prior to joining the inspectorate or because they had academic or professional qualifications of direct relevance to the situation—then they might have brought with them their own theories about what was dangerous. For instance, some inspectors urged that care be taken in the handling of all mineral fibres despite the fact that only some, such as asbestos, had been scientifically proven and politically accepted as dangerous. Alternatively inspectors' investigations of particularly unpleasant accidents could lead them to treat certain machines or activities with more than usual caution. Indeed, inspectors' perceptions of risk were often greatly affected by accidents, both by their personal experience of accident investigation and through their reading of accident reports (Hutter and Lloyd-Bostock, 1992).

Assessments of risk also took account of what was being regulated and why. The regulations enforced by the inspectors in this sample related to a variety of matters, some of which were concerned directly with health and safety and others pertained to less risky matters such as welfare and amenity. It was invariably the case—from my observations—that inspectors accorded higher priority to health and safety matters than they did to welfare and amenity shortcomings. This is not to claim that they ignored the less risky problems, but rather that they were prepared to tolerate non-compliance until such time as more pressing matters were attended to, that is those perceived to involve more substantial dangers to health and safety.

There were also differences in the visibility and tangibility of the various problems inspectors encountered, which could also influence perceptions of risk. Safety matters, for example, were often more visible and more tangible than those concerning health (Hawkins, 1992a). While it may be fairly easy to understand and explain that an unguarded machine could lead to a finger being chopped off, it may be more difficult to explain that sustained exposure to high levels of noise could, over a period of time, cause deafness. Likewise, asbestos fibres, rubber fumes, mercury, and microbiological hazards could all be less obvious hazards. Certainly FI was concerned that industry could be influenced by such factors: '[o]ccupational health is a topic which should be as important to management and employees as safety, but it is frequently not recognized as a problem with any immediacy when the insidious effects of exposure, for example to toxic substances or noise, are slow to manifest themselves' (HSE, 1987, Foreword). Not only might this affect the ease with which compliance may be attained, it could—albeit on an unconscious level—influence inspectors during their daily routines. Indeed the tangibility of health and safety measures could itself be at issue. A FI, for instance, claimed that FIs tended to prefer mechanical guards to photosensitive guards because they were more tangible: it was easier to see if they were working and they could be much easier to correct.

In response to a significant risk to health and safety or to the environment there would be no relaxation of the definition of compliance and full compliance would be sought immediately. But where the possibility of something going wrong was perceived to be low and its effects were unlikely to be major then inspectors would usually be prepared to consider some leeway and would offer a temporary definition of compliance, giving the business time to attain a state of full compliance.

It should be emphasized that field-level inspectors' definitions of risk and the ways in which these informed their definition of compliance took place against a formal legislative and administrative background which already specified some of the principles and criteria of definition. The very regulation of activities by these inspectorates denoted that they had been considered sufficiently risky to warrant protection, in part because they represented an involuntary risk as opposed to a voluntary risk, such as smoking. A relatively high risk tended to be associated with emissions overseen by IAPI since they were responsible for regulating the most serious atmospheric emissions (see Chapter 2). The 1985 Annual Report explains this with reference to di-isocyanate works: '[t]his class is scheduled because of the toxic nature of these chemicals. They can induce asthmatic response in some individuals at very low concentrations, and also have the potential to sensitise some people who then react to very much lower concentrations on subsequent occasions' (HSE, 1986a, p. 20).

The frequency with which inspectors visited premises was related to the risks they associated with each site. IAPI monitored those sites with the most dangerous emissions most frequently. So, for example, lead works, coke ovens, and asbestos works were all frequently visited. Likewise premises with a potential for great harm in the event of failure were visited more than the average (see Chapter 6). Perceptions of risk also influenced the enforcement approach adopted, with non-compliance involving high-risk activities evoking a more immedi-ate and perhaps more severe response than activities involving lower-level risks. The severity of an offence was an important determinant in deciding whether or not to initiate legal action and, if so, what sort of legal action to initiate. If immediate action was required then a prohi-bition notice would be appropriate. For example, if a machine or situ-ation was believed to pose a risk of serious personal injury a prohibition notice would enable the inspector to stop the use of the machine or stop the activities straight away. Prohibition notices were seldom suitable for IAPI, given the need to prove imminent danger to health, but this does not mean that these inspectors never used them. The Chief Inspector's Report for 1985 notes the 'rare event' of an IAPI issuing a prohibition notice when he discovered the owner of a chemical waste incinerator attempting to dispose of waste pharmaceuticals in an unacceptable manner: '[t]he inspector decided there was a risk that the practice would result in harmful substances being emitted from the chimney in an uncontrolled way and so took this immediate step to stop the oper-ation' (HSE: 1986, p. 3).

Prosecution could also be prompted by a serious offence, measured in terms of either the actual harm caused or the severity of the risk posed by a particular transgression. FIs cited accidents as a reason for prosecution. This was probably because the evidence was readily at hand, and, as one RI explained, he did not have to prove that some-thing was reasonably foreseeable because it had already happened. Inspectors certainly considered that they could not afford to overlook examples of serious non-compliance.

The crucial point in the above discussion of cost and risk is that any relaxation in the definition of compliance was temporary. Full compliance was expected, indeed demanded, in the long term. There were many cir-cumstances which influenced the construction of the definition of com-pliance, only some of which related to cost and risk. The *physical location* of a site or its *surrounding topography* could be significant. For example, the geography of an area could influence how damaging an emission to the atmosphere was. The impact of emissions could be exacerbated because factories were in a valley, while hills next to a site could influence the direction of an emission. These were all matters which needed to be taken into account when defining compliance. Factories situated in these sorts of locations might need to install higher stacks to take their emissions higher into the atmosphere for their dispersal.

The *proximity of housing* to sites could also pose problems. In the case of environmental pollution it could lead to a higher level of complaint about health-related concerns or loss of amenity. Similarly the use or storage of dangerous chemicals near main roads or housing could cause great concern, leading to less flexibility in the definition and achievement of compliance and a greater frequency of monitoring.

Public concern or involvement could also influence the definition of compliance. The involvement of the local community in the level-crossing inquiries held by the RI was considered to be of the utmost importance. Those most likely to be influenced by any proposed change in arrangements had the changes explained to them and were consulted about them (see Chapter 5). IAPIs kept in close contact with sites about which there was particular public concern. Indeed, all of the inspectorates in the sample would be especially aware of any issue that was attracting high levels of public, and very possibly political, concern. Indeed this could well lead to some inflexibility in the definition of compliance. Not surprisingly a dramatic incident either nationally or internationally could lead to a tightening of the definition of compliance, especially if it was suspected that new evidence might have come to light. In turn, a great deal of public scrutiny could lead to stricter enforcement of a full definition of compliance. One of the factors precipitating prosecution was public concern about an incident. Examples of this could be IAPI dealing with an emission which had seriously affected public health or FI handling a case which received a lot of publicity, such as accidents involving children (for example, fairground accidents) or cases involving multiple fatalities. Indeed public or potential pressure could in its own right increase the probability of prosecution. The reasons for this centred in part on public accountability. The agency could be placed under scrutiny because of publicity and would be anxious to be seen to be doing something to control the situation (Black, 1971; Hutter and Lloyd-Bostock, 1990). Indeed, HSE was generally very sensitive to public reactions to health and safety and environmental matters falling within its remit. For example, the Chairman's Foreword to the *1987–8 Annual Report* stated: '[w]e attach considerable importance to our statutory responsibility to inform the public . . . we see it as an important part of our role to ensure that on . . . sensitive issues affecting the public, its concerns can be fully voiced and considered, alongside the expertise of the professionals' (1988, p. 4). There was also a feeling that public interest was increasing: '[p]ublic interest . . . has never been so great. A part of the reason lies in the increasing public awareness, intensified by a number of accidents, of the possible consequences to both man and the environment of modern industrial developments' (1990, p. iv).[3]

The *age* of a site was another factor influencing compliance, especially in environmental regulation. Generally IAPI accepted that existing works were designed to less stringent standards: 'it has long been Inspectorate policy that they are allowed to continue to operate to those standards if no public health hazard and no justifiable complaint exists' (HSE, 1986a, p. 9). At a time of recession this matter was of special concern to Inspectors. The Foreword to the *1977 Annual Report*, for example, states: '[t]here are limits to how far ageing plant, which in normal circumstances would have been replaced, can be maintained and there are already signs that some companies are having a struggle to prevent adverse environmental effects' (1979a, p. 1).

Indeed, 'best practicable means' could render IAPI impotent to improve conditions where works had outlived themselves but were still in operation. In such circumstances inspectors endeavoured to keep pollution to a minimum under the existing conditions, a task which could prove quite demoralizing. The case of the phurnacite plant at Abercrwmboi is a notable example. This plant was described in 1978–9 as 'the Inspectorate's most difficult registration in its class' and it presented the inspectorate with particularly difficult problems which were 'aggravated by its increasing age' (HSC, 1980, p. 23). In effect this meant that the plant could only be made environmentally acceptable by being redesigned and rebuilt, something which was not considered 'reasonably practicable' on grounds of cost. This was indeed the decision of an Industrial Tribunal which upheld an appeal by the plant's owners against an improvement notice issued in 1982 relating to a discharge of smoke.[4] Such an example illustrates how the best practicable means test could work against the improvement of environmental standards in the interests of costs. As such it is the sort of case which causes some to view the law as being 'too reasonable' to business interests.

Plans for new sites and buildings could lead to some flexibility of definition for all inspectorates. Hence they would be prepared to tolerate poorer standards temporarily in older, existing plant even though they

---

[3] See also Hutter and Manning, 1990; but particularly Yeager, 1991 for an extensive discussion of the environmental movement and mobilization of the law in the USA.

[4] Industrial Tribunals between National Smokeless Fuels Ltd and R. Perriman, 14 July and 11 and 12 Oct. 1982, Case H/S15896/82. See Ch. 7 for further discussion of the attempts to regulate this phurnacite plant.

may have wanted some indication that the improvements were imminent. A REI who had been told that office accommodation he was unhappy with during an inspection would soon be replaced subsequently wrote to the company on the subject: '[m]y attitude to the above . . . items will depend upon the length of time that the office is to remain in its present building'.

A *temporary change in circumstances* could also influence the definition of compliance and bring into play a temporary definition. For example, a strike could subsequently adversely affect air pollution control standards because equipment may have deteriorated during the strike. Until such time as inspectors considered it reasonable for such equipment to be restored to full working order they would be prepared to accept emissions which fell below the usual levels of compliance. In turn this could lead to higher levels of complaint, as the extract below, from IAPI's *1985 Annual Report*, reveals:

the return to production after the end of the NUM strike was accompanied by a revival of complaint. The refractory brickwork of coke ovens invariably deteriorates when normal operating temperatures and production schedules cannot be maintained. Cracks develop in the walls between ovens and flues allowing raw coal gas to pass into the heating chambers. This not only produces black smoke from the battery chimney but also interferes with temperature control which in turn can result in uneven carbonisation and consequent heavy emissions of smoke and dust when ovens are discharged. Several weeks of operation were needed until processing conditions settled down and complaint subsided but at some works the amount of repair work needed on the oven batteries was such that sub-standard emissions continued for much longer (HSE, 1986a, p. 24).

Practicability was an underlying principle in achieving the required definitions of compliance. All of the inspectorates researched were willing to accept anything which achieved the necessary results, so long as there were no unintended consequences which led to alternative or additional occupational health and safety or environmental problems. Cheaper but practicable alternatives to the more generally employed means of compliance therefore tended to be accepted. An IAPI, for example, inspecting a roadstone plant, described the pollution-control equipment as 'Heath Robinson like' but added that if it worked he was not worried. Similarly a FI was prepared to accept a factory owner's cheap alternative to a more sophisticated self-closing door device which would help ensure that fire doors remained closed. The FI commented that anything that worked would satisfy him.

Practicability was often central to inspectors' discussions with the regulated and could lead to negotiation and compromise. To this extent the processes of defining, achieving, and maintaining compliance were interactive. The definitions of compliance would not be such that they would be impracticable to attain. Indeed, as we have seen in this Chapter, considerable attention is paid in the legal, administrative, and working definitions of compliance to being reasonable.

CONCLUSIONS

The abstract concepts of the law in books need to be given meaning in everyday life. These are not disparate activities for, as we have seen, what happens at field level is structured by the law and its associated administrative guidance structure. The broad principles of law are thus given practical definition in the 'real world'. In the substantive areas on which this research focuses much emphasis is placed on the importance of the working definition of field-level inspectors. The intention is that the law should be flexible, adaptable, and sensitive to varying circumstances and changing needs. Field-level inspectors are thus attributed a vital role in giving substance to the definition of compliance.

Inspectors fulfil their role according to principles which already structure the law, most prominently according to the costs and risks associated with compliance. These are matters which pervade regulation and which, of necessity, are part of the regulatory inspector's world view. Resolving the tensions between costs and risks are both a broad rationale for the inspector's job and a point upon which the regulatory agency and officials can become the fall-guys of a system which fails to specify how stringently compliance should be defined. Moreover, the job is complicated by the uncertainties involved in giving meaning and substance to the principles of law. Inspectors did not approach these issues in any sophisticated, technical manner (cf Cheit, 1990), but rather as broad considerations across a range of issues and stages of the regulatory process. The cost of improvements was considered in relation to such factors as the levels of protection offered; the costs to production; the levels of risk posed; and the costs to the regulatory agency. Inspectors embraced a wide range of data in their attempts to construct the working definition of compliance, some of it hard data, some of it impressionistic, some of it relating to macro-economic issues, others to clues at the micro level of the individual site or situation. The data they relied on therefore ranged from the public accounts of nationalized industries to the quality of cars in the staff car parks.

It is possible to reach some broad generalizations about the impact of these tensions upon the compliance process. For instance, it is generally the case that, where the costs are higher, then there will be greater flexibility in the definition, assessment, and achievement of compliance. But where the risks of an activity are great there will generally be less flexibility—hence the definition of compliance will be strict; there will be more frequent and, where possible, more specific assessments of compliance, and an increased possibility of formal legal action in the event of persistent non-compliance or an accident. Typically risk takes precedence, so where the risks are high there will tend to be less flexibility about cost. But these are very broad generalizations, and achieving a balance between regulatory tensions may be delicate and interpreted differently from various standpoints and political perspectives. Cross-cutting these tensions are other complex considerations, some of which are common to all decisions while others are peculiar to particular circumstances.

Uncertainty characterized not just the availability of some of the data but their accuracy, interpretation, and relevance. Similar problems characterized the methods used to assess and monitor compliance. Indeed, examination of the ways in which regulatory agencies mobilized their resources to monitor compliance throws the concept of compliance into broad relief.

PART 3

Monitoring Compliance

Assessing whether or not a particular act or state of affairs constitutes compliance is itself an act of interpretation. And because regulatory activity is continuously subject to assessment this interpretation might be open to negotiation. Indeed, as we have seen in Chapter 4, there could be a series of definitions of compliance, for example in circumstances where a programme of work had been decided upon. Stringent definitions and deadlines might then be set for the most serious problems, but rather more relaxed temporary definitions constructed for the minor faults identified. And over a longer time-scale administrative definitions could change.

Officials could employ a variety of methods to assess whether or not compliance was being achieved. Some of these centred exclusively upon inspectors' own initiative and activity, with inspection and sampling being the obvious examples. Others, often those involving non-compliance, were brought to the agency's attention by a third party, such as a complainant or other regulatory agency, or, more unfortunately, by an accident or incident. The way in which agencies organize and mobilize their resources around these different modes of assessment is usually referred to in the literature by the concepts of proactive and reactive enforcement. Proactive enforcement is essentially law enforcement through agency initiative, so it involves officials seeking out offences. This is in contrast to reactive enforcement, where the agency response is prompted by an outside person or event, typically through lodging a complaint or reporting an accident (see Reiss, 1971). Alternatively, or in addition, the regulated may assess matters themselves, for instance through their own internal inspections or, if appropriate, by sampling. The Robens Committee strongly advocated self-regulation. Each of these methods is suitable for differing types of assessment and activity and each has its limitations. They all involve a complex of interpretative decisions. They also have significance for the future treatment of cases, since the way in which inspectors discover an offence may influence the extent to which they can exercise discretion in their future handling of a case.

5 Inspectors Take the Initiative: Proactive Methods

As the word 'inspector' suggests, routine inspections and check visits are the 'traditional' methods of operation for many regulatory officials and ones which are regarded as fundamental by field staff. To many enforcement officials routine inspections were the stuff of their work and a much-valued mode of operation. The amount of time spent on inspections varied between inspectorates. In all of the inspectorates examined in this research inspections comprised a major method of assessment. Of the total number of visits I undertook with inspectors, routine inspection comprised 65 per cent of FI visits; 63 per cent of IAPI visits; and 79 per cent of REI visits. This is a larger proportion than might be expected from annual work plans.[1] This seems to be explained by the fact that many of the special projects and initiatives which tended to be itemised separately in 'Plans of Work' were combined with routine inspections by field-level staff.

Spot Checks

Inspections involved either spot checks or routine inspections under formal or informal monitoring programmes. Spot checks were particularly useful for IAPIs who could readily see from a distance whether or not some of the works subject to their control were in compliance. In the case of some emissions, these inspectors could make a visual check while travelling in the vicinity of processes subject to control (see also Cranston 1979, p.79). Spot checks such as these were common during fieldwork. Inspectors would always keep an eye on regulated works while travelling in their vicinity and would sometimes deviate from the direct route to their destination if it meant that they could keep a visual check on other premises they were responsible for. Alternatively spot checks could be undertaken while visiting premises where IAPIs could climb to a vantage point and survey the neighbouring district. These

[1] See, for example, the FI's allocative guide, 1985–6 (HSE, 1985, p. 34).

visual checks were unlikely to result in visits or inspections unless something untoward was spotted. This was the case after an inspector had spotted an unusual flare at an oil refinery while parking his car at lunchtime. He commented that he was not pleased and would keep an eye on the situation over the next hour. When things did not improve and the flare from the refinery remained highly visible, the inspector visited the site to discover what was causing the problem.

If a problem is identified at a nearby works then a visit is automatic. This happened when I accompanied an IAPI to a metal recovery plant. While inspecting the plant he noticed an emission nearby. He traced the source of the black plume to an adhesives manufacturer and visited the site immediately. It transpired that the company was having problems with some new machinery. The inspector made it clear that the company should have informed him of this. He had been put into an awkward position because other companies in the area wanted to know why it was that this company was able to emit such a filthy plume when they were not allowed to. If he had known of the problem then he could have given an explanation.

This method of monitoring the regulated was also of some use to the REI and FI. REIs would always be alert to health and safety matters while travelling on the railways. Although it was obviously impossible for them to stop a train and deal with the problem 'on-the-spot', they would nevertheless take up serious problems immediately they reached their destinations or upon return to their offices. If problems were observed while waiting at stations for trains then REIs would usually deal with the them immediately. One REI I accompanied, for example, observed a gang of workmen jump from the line they were working on to the adjacent line once the lookout man had indicated that a train was coming through the station. Within seconds the lookout man in the other direction signalled that a train was travelling towards them on the line they had jumped on to, so the work gang scrambled up onto the platform. The inspector approached them and explained who he was and that he was not impressed by what he had just seen. He explained what procedures he would prefer to see them follow and why.

The FI's opportunities for spot checks of the visual type were much more restricted, the major exception being that of construction sites. FIs from any industry group could be inclined to stop if they noticed unsafe construction work, although this was most likely if they had themselves previously worked on a construction industry group. A senior inspector I was accompanying from a chemicals group spotted unsafe construction work while visiting a chemical works. The inspector interrupted travel to follow the matter through. First the workers were spoken to, but nobody would admit to being in charge of the work and it took some time to discover who was employing them. The inspector eventually established that a nearby garage-owner most probably was their employer and work was ordered to stop until they had erected proper scaffolding. Then the inspector went to see their employer to explain that the job had been stopped because the scaffolding was legally unacceptable. It was explained what would be needed before work could be resumed. This was accepted without argument. Later the inspector drove past the site again to ensure that work had not started illegally—it had not—and a memorandum was also sent to the construction group informing it of the matter. Unplanned visits of this type were especially prevalent among inspectors working for construction industry groups. This was for a number of reasons, including the short duration of many construction jobs and the serious difficulties in keeping an eye on the numerous work sites of this type in each area.

Inspectors from all three agencies would exaggerate the extent to which they could rely on spot checks in order to keep business 'on its toes'. They would ensure that managers knew that either they or their colleagues were regularly in the area and that they were taking note of the site. In order to lend credibility to these claims they would cite particular instances when they had been in the vicinity and were not especially pleased with all they had seen. It was also interesting that senior inspectors, including those at headquarters level, would refer to both their own observations and those reported to them by their staff when negotiating with senior representatives of a company or industry. This was usually in order to reinforce their arguments that certain practices were not being carried out safely.

Inspection Programmes

Spot checks were by their very definition not a regular method of monitoring compliance through inspection. Typically routine inspections were selective and planned in advance. The extent of their planning varied between inspectorates. All categorized premises according to their potential risk and deduced from this how frequently they should be inspected. In the case of the FI these decisions were formalized into an inspection programme. This took account of a variety of criteria in deciding how frequently and urgently premises should be inspected.

These included the site's present performance; the risk to employees and the public, including the number of people at risk of serious injury; and the inspector's assessment of the management's ability to regulate health and safety. The inspection ratings were therefore constructed from assessments of two types, according to apparently objective criteria such as the types of materials handled and processes used; the number of people employed on site and the proximity of housing; and to more subjective assessments, including the inspector's judgement about present performance and confidence in management. Inspection tended to be infrequent where a site was employing few people; was engaged in activities holding a negligible risk to employees and no risk to the public; and where confidence in management was high. But where the risks to employees and public were substantial and the inspector was not confident that management could or would take adequate steps to protect health and safety, then inspections would be more regular and frequent. Such a system ensured that those premises which were engaged in risky activities but which were held in high opinion by inspectors were nevertheless inspected regularly by virtue of the high rating their activities accorded them. Conversely, those who were not working with especially dangerous materials or machinery but who did not hold the confidence of inspectors were also given a higher rating to ensure more frequent inspection. Some of the premises I visited with FIs were scheduled for further visits within weeks, while others were unlikely to be revisited for as long as ten years.

The FI's inspection programme was held on computer which printed out a list of those premises due for inspection. Every attempt was made to update the rating system by incorporating any new information which could be collected by inspectors during visits or gleaned from accident reports or information supplied by the business concerned. When inspection routines were imposed in such a formal manner there was a danger that inspectors might object and regard the system as a challenge to their professional autonomy. In part this was mitigated by the fact that the rating system in FI took account of inspectors' reports. Moreover, it was often the case that inspectors would write these reports in such a way that their subsequent impact on the rating system accorded to the time when they felt the premises should next be inspected. Another problem which could be associated with these programmes was that inspections could be predicted by the regulated (Hawkins, 1984, p. 93). Again this was something which was mitigated to some extent in the case of FI by the fact that the period between visits was often so long and by the fact that visits were not announced in advance.

REIs and IAPIs did not adhere to such a formal, computerized inspection programme. They did not have formal inspection criteria, a rating system, or an inspection cycle. Instead, individual inspectors were accorded the discretion to decide how frequently to visit each site and when. Risk emerged as the most important single principle dictating the frequency with which sites were inspected. This had two dimensions, namely the potential risk inherent in the site and the current risk as indicated by past experience. One District IAPI explained that on some sites the potential for problems was so great that he felt that inspectors should exercise caution and keep a close eye on them. Some of these sites, including chemical fertilizer and steel works, were visited every six weeks to three months. If the site was also considered to be of a poor standard then visits might be more frequent. In the case of one large site in this District Inspector's jurisdiction, an attempt was made to have an inspector visit the works every two weeks. In fact, things were regarded as so risky that the District Inspector undertook regular inspections in addition to those undertaken by his staff. This was partly to ensure that more than one person had knowledge of the site should anything untoward happen. This practice was also adopted by FIs in relation to some large, potentially dangerous sites.

Other factors which were taken into account by REIs and IAPIs in their decisions about frequency of inspection mirrored those of the FI's formal inspection programme. These included the size of the site; its accident rate; and the inspector's confidence in management and workforce. In the case of REIs, for instance, large main-line stations and depots were inspected more frequently than their smaller counterparts, and particular attention was paid to lineside working, which was the most likely site of fatal accidents and serious injuries.

This research was not designed to assess whether a formal inspection programme was more efficient than one which was reliant upon individual inspectors. It should perhaps be pointed out, however, that REIs and IAPIs were responsible for far fewer sites than FIs, and as a consequence were arguably in a better position to know a greater proportion of the sites they regulated in more detail than were FIs. This said, the individual FI's knowledge was taken into consideration by their formal inspection programme.

Types of Inspection

There were a variety of types of routine inspection which again received formal definition from the FI and also mirrored the informal practices of the REI and IAPI. *Basic inspections* involved an assessment of both the 'hardware' and 'software' of a site. The former comprised the physical aspects of the site, such as its buildings and equipment, whereas software included systems of work and company procedures for ensuring health, safety, and environmental procedures. The basic inspections undertaken by FIs were more selective than general inspections. *General inspection* involved the inspector visiting all parts of a site, while basic inspection left the inspector to decide how extensive the inspection should be. The rationale was that if the inspector was happy that a company was maintaining satisfactory standards of compliance then there was no point in spending more time at the site. Accordingly, those sites which did not fully satisfy inspectors would receive the most extensive inspections. In practice, inspectors seemed to give all sites a thorough examination when it was their first inspection of a site. Thereafter, inspectors tended to follow through in detail only those matters which they had noted on previous occasions to be below standard or matters which particularly concerned them after a preliminary look around the site. For example, one FI I accompanied devoted rather more attention than originally intended to the maintenance department of a large site under inspection. The reason for this was that a number of minor faults indicated that the maintenance department might have been failing in its adherence to compliant safety procedures.

Inspectors' actions following basic inspections varied. They might only give verbal advice or they might take more formal action, such as serve an improvement notice or initiate a prosecution. In the case of the FI and REI, letters would be sent confirming matters requiring attention. When such letters were sent or a notice was served then a *check visit* might be required to ensure that the outstanding matters had been rectified. These visits were usually some weeks or months after the basic inspection, but if inspectors were especially concerned about something then they would re-visit within days or even on the same day. A FI I accompanied to a building site re-visited within hours because he was not initially satisfied with the scaffolding. IAPIs also undertook check visits although they were less inclined to write letters following inspections than the other inspectors. This was a consequence of the frequency with which they were able either to visit premises or at least keep a visual check on compliance. Indeed in the case of the IAPI the distinctions between routine visits and check visits could become blurred as some premises were visited frequently by inspectors.

The third main type of inspection was termed the *planned special visit* by FI. This was usually undertaken at the instigation of a policy branch, NIG, or working party. Often it was a fact-finding visit, with inspectors completing questionnaires about a particular type of machine or activity. Alternatively it might be part of a preventive campaign such as those targeted at the construction industry in 1983 ('Site Safe '83') and the 'Deadly Maintenance' campaign of 1985 when HSE urged industry to maintain high standards of health and safety and to pay attention to those involved in maintenance work (HSC, 1987, p. 4). These campaigns involved the publication of booklets and leaflets, letters to individual firms, media publicity, seminars, and the planned special visits. Usually inspectors would undertake some more general inspection work during this type of visit, especially if the site involved a long journey time from their office.

Inspections: Structures and Content

Once inspectors had identified a site as ready for inspection they followed fairly standard procedures for the way they structured and conducted the inspection. Not all inspections were the same—in many respects they differed greatly from one site to another and from one occasion to another—but there were some basic forms and rules that were usually followed. In the case of FI and IAPI it was not usual to announce inspections in advance, so the inspector's arrival on site was completely unexpected by the company. REIs, however, typically did announce visits in advance by means of a standardized letter stating the date of the proposed visit and sometimes giving some indication of the activities and areas they were interested in inspecting.[2]

The reason for announcing REI visits in advance was that most inspections on the railway required special safety arrangements to be made in advance, in the form of arranging lookout protection for the inspector, for example. It should be noted that FIs and IAPIs did announce some visits beforehand, notably those where they wanted to

---

[2] This is a controversial subject. See, for example, the Baryugil Report (House of Representatives Standing Committee on Aboriginal Affairs, 1984, para. 6.13 ff.); Di Mento, 1986, p. 179.

ensure that they met particular managers or specialists within a company, but these were not typically routine inspections but rather planning or prior-approval meetings. Differing views were held about the prudence or otherwise of announcing inspections in advance. Some argued that it gave the regulated the opportunity to 'put their house in order' and present inspectors with an atypical idea of the site. Others—including REIs—considered that if the knowledge of an impending visit from an inspector prompted the regulated to think about health and safety and remedy any defects, then part of their job had been completed before they started the inspection. Moreover, they argued that any problems they did pick up during the subsequent inspection would be the more serious ones, including matters which were not even understood to be non-compliant or illegal.

Once inspectors arrived on site they met a variety of people. Usually one person would be responsible for the inspector's visit, and this person I term the 'contact person'. In small businesses the contact person would more often than not be the owner and in small sites which were part of a wider organization, the works manager would take responsibility for visits by regulatory officials. When dealing with larger organizations there could even be an individual who was especially responsible for pollution control or health and safety.

The length of time taken up by routine inspections varied, most notably with the size and complexity of the workplace. Some small, relatively uncomplicated workshops inspected by FIs could take no more than twenty to thirty minutes to inspect. By contrast, a large, complicated site, such as a refinery or steel works, could take weeks to cover in even the most rudimentary fashion. The duration of the visit would also be influenced by the number and variety of problems encountered.

FIs and REIs would aim to cover most areas of a site during a basic inspection, allowing the time spent in any one section to be dictated by what they found there. During the course of the inspection inspectors would talk with members of the workforce, stopping to check that they were happy with health and safety matters in general or with a specific machine or process. Most particularly inspectors would stop if they discovered a worker not complying with good health and safety practice.[3] Very often inspectors would spot workers not using safety equipment, the most common complaints being a failure to use machine guards, ear protection, safety helmets, and eye protection. Inspectors were usu-

---

[3] See Ch. 7 for a discussion of worker non-compliance.

ally quite severe when they encountered worker non-compliance of this type and would go to some lengths to explain why the worker should comply—and sometimes the penalties which could be incurred for continued non-compliance. Most of the problems identified were referred to management for remedy. Occasionally, problems would be investigated further after a visit—an inspector might want to check details with a specialist or refer a section 6[4] problem to another section of the inspectorate. In the case of the FI unusual problems might be referred to a NIG, to an area where the manufacturer of a suspect machine, for example, was located, or to the Field Consultancy Group if further detailed inspection was required. REIs referred all such problems to their headquarters organization, and if detailed specialist knowledge of a problem was located within HSE then they would consult the relevant authority.

IAPI inspections were more limited than those of FIs and REIs. This was because their remit was restricted to particular processes on a site, and it was these and any arrestment equipment which concerned them. This did not mean that their visits took less time than those of other inspectorates, since much of what they were dealing with was complicated. Also, as with the other inspectorates, much time was spent discussing regulatory matters with management.

Inspections should not be seen as isolated visits; more often than not they represented part of a wider programme of interaction between inspectorates and companies. Typically, but not invariably, inspectors were regulating long-term, continuing activities, and there were established relationships between the regulatory agency and a company. Within this context, programmes of work were often negotiated (see Chapter 8). The process to full compliance was often gradual, and individual visits by an inspector were not necessarily designed to achieve full compliance (Richardson, 1983, p. 152). Nevertheless, what happened during the course of each inspection was significant and contributed in a variety of ways to the overall impression inspectors held of a firm (see Chapter 7).

Routine Inspection as a Method of Assessing Compliance

There were a number of ways in which routine inspection was useful as a means of assessing compliance. Its most direct and obvious use was

---

[4] S. 6 of the HSW Act 1974 refers to the general duties of manufacturers.

as a means of detecting non-compliance, but in this respect its uses were very much related to the visibility of compliance. While it might be quite clear that a guard was missing from a machine it might be more difficult to detect non-compliance when visiting a chemical works where many of the major processes are not readily visible. Generally matters of safety could be more readily assessed than those of health. The tangibility of the matter subject to control was important here. It might be possible for inspectors to pick up signals of ill-health where these were evident. For example, it was likely that excessive levels of noise would be noticed by inspectors during the course of a routine inspection. Alternatively, inspectors could learn during the course of conversations with employees that they were suffering common ill-health problems and this might alert them to possible non-compliance. Certainly inspectors were much more likely than the public to detect the less visible offences and more likely than employees to detect the least popularly understood instances of non-compliance.

The number and type of offences detected during the course of routine inspections depended in part upon the expertise and experience of inspectors (see Cranston, 1979, p. 76). This encompassed technical expertise and inspectorial experience.[5] In the case of IAPIs, REIs, and some FIs technical experience would have been gained prior to their joining their inspectorates. But in most cases specialist knowledge of health and safety or air-pollution matters would have been gained after becoming inspectors. This was also the case, of course, regarding inspectorial experience, although it should be noted that previous industrial experience could alert inspectors to some of the 'tricks of the trade' which the regulated might adopt. During the course of their careers inspectors became wise to gatekeepers who tried to stall the inspectors' entry to premises and employers who tried to steer them away from particular areas of their premises. They also acquired preconceptions and an 'instinct' which they used to aid their enforcement of the law. One REI inspecting a station which was not regarded as particularly risky commented upon entering the office, 'I don't know why but I feel uneasy in here'. A variety of seemingly minor problems were found, but the inspector was quick to point out their more serious implications. For example, two fire extinguishers were empty, so he

---

[5] The Report of the House of Representatives Standing Committee on Aborigine Affairs, 1984, para. 6.7 exemplifies the dangers of employing under-qualified and unsuitable inspectors. See also Di Mento, 1979, p. 100. No such problems appeared to be encountered by the inspectors included in this research.

explained the vital time that would be wasted while people tried to use them. In addition to all of this inspectors built up knowledge about particular sites, where they knew the premises and those who worked there.

Routine inspection is not a universally valued method of assessing compliance. The Robens Committee, for example, wrote:

Our strong impression is that routine visits tend to be brief, superficial, and usually unproductive. In particular, we think that periodical routine visits by highly qualified inspectors to very small firms employing no more than a handful of people, often engaged in processes where hazards are minimal, is a misuse of skilled manpower. [1972, para. 218].

The Committee went on to suggest that the 'occasional spot check' would be as effective as routine visits. An argument which is commonly used in support of such points of view is that many routine visits result in the discovery of only minor 'housekeeping' offences. It is argued that this is a waste of resources and that, rather than routinely inspect all premises, attention should be directed to larger businesses and those which pose most risk. I have argued elsewhere that arguments such as these underestimate both the significance of some minor offences and the multiplicity of roles undertaken during these routine inspections (Hutter, 1986). Briefly, I have put the case that some minor offences, such as unclean mess or toilet facilities and poor decoration, can create an unpleasant and possibly unhygienic working environment. Other apparently minor offences may lead to potentially dangerous situations if not checked. One FI, inspecting a large steel works, came upon a small portable cabin which had been wired up with an electrical supply so a kettle could be boiled and a light installed. The FI referred to it as a 'Santa's grotto' (it was December), trying to inject some humour in pointing out that the whole cabin was in danger of electrification. The firm's safety officer had not even seen the cabin before. A REI inspecting on-the-line repairs on a major rail route to London was concerned that a welder was not getting enough lookout protection. The inspector estimated that the welder was only getting eighteen seconds' warning when he should have twenty-five seconds. The lost seven seconds were, in his view, important, as not only had the welder to get both himself and his equipment off the tracks but the line was used by high-speed trains. The REI approached the person in charge of a nearby work gang to ask for more cover for the welder. Much to the inspector's concern he discovered that this person did not even know that he should have provided lookout protection for the welder, who was not a member of his gang.[6]

Indirectly there were a variety of ways in which routine inspections could help inspectors to assess levels of compliance. As the Chief Inspector of Factories wrote in his 1985 Report:

Certainly the inspector is . . . looking to see that there is compliance with the law . . . he will wish to satisfy himself that overall standards of health, safety and welfare are acceptable, that adequate resources in terms of money are made available to ensure that those standards are maintained and that the management of health and safety within the firm or organization is under control [HSE, 1986, p. 35].

In other words, routine visits enabled inspectors to make detailed assessments of a business. During their inspection of premises, inspectors assessed both their physical condition and the character and abilities of the personnel who managed and worked within them. They gained an impression of the morale of the workforce and picked up clues as to the financial position of a business. At the end of a visit to a station an REI's summing up of what he had found illustrates how such assessments were made. The inspector told the manager that he did not intend going through all of the problems he had found, since they should be clear enough by now. He liked to see people take a pride in their working environment. Generally he took tidiness as indicating efficiency, which in turn indicated safety. He felt that the station could be improved, and was surprised that the staff were so easy-going and scruffy. After the visit the inspector told me that he had not expected to find things so bad at this station. The station had not been inspected for six years and it had gone downhill. As a consequence he would schedule another visit soon.

All of this information was significant because it provided the information essential for the construction of the working definition of compliance. The information received and collected during the course of routine visits could also be the dynamic for a change of working definition. For example, inspectors might hear about changes in a company's financial position which led them to amend their demands.

All of this serves to highlight the fact that routine visits did have their uses as a method of monitoring compliance in all works. This included

---

[6] Carson, 1982, and the *Report of the Committee of Inquiry into an Outbreak of Food Poisoning at Stanley Royd Hospital*, 1986, both highlight the importance which may be attached to some apparently minor offences. See Hutter, 1986, p. 122.

those where non-compliance was not immediately apparent or visible. One IAPI told me that he considered it very important that he inspected the sites he was responsible for. Not only did inspections let him see what was possible with the existing plant and help him determine what modifications and improvements he could reasonably ask for, but he also found it important to have a mental image of the site when considering site plans and proposals.

FIs working in chemical groups explained that it could be very difficult looking around a chemical plant because there was not really a lot for them to see. But they could see how well maintained a site was and they could assess the character and abilities of the staff employed on site. This was not to say, however, that inspectors did not find problems through a physical inspection of the site. One FI, inspecting a small chemical works, discovered a variety of problems ranging from fork-lift-truck damage to drums of chemicals to the more serious discovery of a spillage of chemicals, some of which were very dangerous, in the dry-storage area.

It should be emphasized that inspectors valued routine inspection as a means of assessing compliance because it meant that they could see what was really going on. They were also quick to understand the symbolic value of a visit from an inspector. The visible presence of inspectors was thought to hold deterrent value to the extent that it served to remind the regulated of both the law and the agency. Moreover these visits served to show that inspectors were prepared to 'get their boots dirty' and enforce the law. But inspection could be used as a method of assessing compliance without necessarily relating directly to an inspector's enforcement functions. Inspectors often collected general data for use by other sections of the agency during the course of these visits. As we saw earlier, much of these data were used for policy-making, and while it might well be legitimate for inspectors to visit a site solely for the purpose of collecting data, they tended to combine these visits with some form of inspection.

In cases where compliance—and non-compliance—were not readily visible or tangible, other methods could be used to monitor compliance. Sampling was obviously one such method—should the matters subject to control be amenable to this.

SAMPLING

Whether or not sampling could be used as a routine method of monitoring compliance very much depended upon the activities regulated. Of the inspectorates included in this research sampling was a major method of assessment for just the IAPI. The other inspectorates used sampling whenever they could, but generally the activities they regulated were not amenable to extensive sampling.

Sampling was undertaken in accordance with a schedule or on a less systematic basis at the request of inspectors. Alternatively it could be undertaken by the regulated themselves. The HSE publication on 'Sampling and Analysis of Emissions to the Air from Scheduled Works' (ETM 1), for example, stated that '[t]he sampling and testing of emissions is an important part of the functions and responsibilities of HM Alkali and Clean Air Inspectorate, and is an obligation also on the operators of scheduled processes' (HSE, 1981b, para. 1).

Where sampling was by the agency and according to a schedule it was accompanied by the problems of predictability, which were also attendant upon routine inspection (see Hawkins, 1984, p. 92). But, given the scarcity of resources at the time of my study, this did not appear to constitute a major problem. Sampling, when by the agency, could be undertaken by inspectors or by a sampling team. Generally inspectors engaged in only the most rudimentary sampling. The more complicated and sophisticated work was undertaken by the sampling teams. Where sampling was by the regulated it was either undertaken according to a schedule agreed by the inspectorate or it was continuous. Certainly the inspectorate had a policy of encouraging the continuous monitoring of emissions (HSE, 1981a, para. 5). Indeed, the Chief Inspector's *1986 Annual Report* noted that '[t]he increase in availability and reliability of continuous monitoring instruments for both particulate and gaseous emissions is gradually rendering obsolete the simple test kit which Inspectors have traditionally carried' (HSE, 1987, p. 4).

While the greater introduction of continuous monitoring decreases the need for agency sampling it should not be forgotten that the inspectorate's ability to use this method of assessing compliance is in part determined by the availability of sampling teams. At the time of my research a fall in the availability of these teams was a persisting problem for IAPIs.[7] A more fundamental problem which could be exacer-

---

[7] In 1981 IAPIs and the sampling teams took 4,095 samples, but by 1985 this figure

bated by any decrease in the technical support was the taking of legal action, since all inspectors were advised to use specialist sampling teams when legal action was under consideration, largely because they were able to undertake more detailed and sophisticated testing.

The main purpose of sampling was as a means of assessing compliance, a point emphasized by numerous HSE publications (e.g. HSE, 1981b, para. 2; HSE, 1981c, para. 4; HSE, 1981d, para. 7). As a monitoring device, sampling could help both to sharpen the awareness of industry and to provide important 'back-up' to inspectors. Sampling was regarded and portrayed as constituting strong evidence of non-compliance, and in this respect it was invaluable if prosecution was being considered. More likely this possibility would be alluded to, so 'taking samples' and sending in a sampling team could be a threat, the drama of which could be exploited by inspectors (see Hawkins, 1984).

In some circumstances sampling was the only way of detecting whether or not there was compliance. This was the case, for example, when inspectors were dealing with a variety of substances or materials which were not visible to the human eye, and most particularly those which might not reveal themselves through smell or through immediate ill-effects upon health. There are some very harmful chemicals to which we may become sensitized, of which di-isocyanates[8] are a good example. Other substances which are dangerous if incorrectly handled or found in too high a concentration may not be visible to or detectable by even an experienced worker. A number of carcinogens fall into this category, with crocidolite (blue asbestos) being a much-publicized example. In such cases specialized sampling would be required to ascertain whether control limits are being met.

None of the above should lead one to believe that sampling is a clear-cut method of assessment. Once a concentration level has been accepted, decisions have to be made about which sampling method is appropriate. Different methods may give different results and, while the

---

had fallen to 2,302 samples. This was a matter that greatly concerned these inspectors. It was referred to in the inspectorate's *Annual Reports* and repeatedly in conversations with me. See also Richardson, 1984, p. 119.

[8] Di-isocyanate works use two highly toxic materials—TDI (Toluene di-isocyanate) and MDI (Di-iso-cyanate-diphenyl-methane). These works were one of the classes of works registered by IAPI and included, for example, foam-production plants. FI also kept a close eye wherever these chemicals were used, as workers could become sensitized to them at very low levels of concentration. See Guidance Note MS8 (HSE, 1983a) for further details of the clinical effects of isocyanates.

legal or administrative standard of compliance may remain the same, limitations inherent in the sampling method may effect a change in the working definition. The various methods of sampling for the presence of asbestos are illustrative: according to one method all fibres collected in a given sampling frame are counted, whereas an alternative method would be to count just those fibres specifically identified as asbestos. If the first method was adopted then it could be argued that a more stringent standard had in fact been imposed than had the latter method been accepted. It is partly because of these problems that the administrative definition of compliance usually specifies 'acceptable methods' of testing (e.g. HSE, 1984, paras. 20 ff.; HSE, 1981c, para. 1).

Determining which sampling method is acceptable involves a complex of decisions at a policy-making level. Determining how to implement the approved methods on site may also involve a complicated decision-making process. Some inspectors felt that there was no one technique that served all sites, but rather there were a variety of techniques at their disposal and they should select the one most appropriate for each site. Certainly many HSE guidance notes on approved methods of sampling warned that the methods would need to be adapted to suit particular sites. HSE's Guidance Note E28, for example, warns that '[w]orking conditions and practices vary greatly and it is more important to develop air sampling procedures to suit the particular circumstances than to follow exactly the details given in this Guidance Note' (HSE, 1981c, para. 4). Similarly MDHS 5, the HSE's note on 'On-site Validation of Sampling Methods' emphasizes:

The validity of any sampling method should be checked on-site if it is to be used in any environment where the effect of the atmosphere is a factor in determining the accuracy of the method. For example, the presence of high humidity or of unexpected atmospheric contaminants may reduce sampling efficiency or cause unexpected chemical reactions to occur [HSE, 1981e, para. 1].

As we can see, once the sampling method had been agreed there were still many potential sources of uncertainty. Quite large margins of error might have been inherent in the tests selected for sampling. This was particularly the case when inspectors decided that frequent testing with relatively unsophisticated equipment was preferable to infrequent sampling with high-precision and perhaps bulky and complicated testing apparatus. So routine monitoring might have relied upon relatively crude 'rule-of-thumb' indicators of compliance (see, for example, HSE, 1981b). This might, in part, have been the result of the cost of sampling, which could be very high, because sampling teams were not available or because precise results were simply not needed. Even when more sophisticated sampling methods were employed results might have been influenced by a range of factors.

Where the sample should be taken from is an example of one of these potential sources of uncertainty. IAPIs had to decide where to place monitors so as to collect a representative sample. In particular they wanted to determine whether or not it was possible to differentiate the source of contamination (for example, was it high- or low-level). The 1976 *Annual Report* of HM Alkali and Clean Air Inspectorate (as IAPI was then known) explained how complicated sampling could be. Referring in particular to BS:3405, 'Simplified Methods for Measurement of Grit and Dust Emission', the *Report* discusses the difficulties encountered by its sampling teams:

It may sound simple to say that the team samples grit and dust by means of the Airflow-BCURA sampling apparatus according to BS:3405 (1971). In practice, it is a tough, complicated job, having to be conducted in all kinds of weather conditions, in exposed positions and in many varying circumstances. As a preliminary, the process has to be examined and a suitable sampling position, or positions, chosen. Rarely can an ideal position be found, taking account of chimney diameters, duct entry and length, bends in ducts and flues, proximity to fans, valves and other pieces of equipment, etc. Having chosen the position, access has to be provided for safe operation and holes have to be drilled at right-angles to each other, possibly through a foot or two of reinforced concrete or brickwork, or perhaps through lined steel chimneys, sometimes lagged on the outside.

A convenient source of electricity has to be provided. These preliminaries can cost a works several thousands of pounds, especially if the sampling point is 100 ft or more up a chimney. Great thought has to be given in advance to the sampling process to take account of small or large diameter ducts, wet emissions (the use of a pitot heater renders the method non-standard), hot emissions, tarry or sticky emissions, swirling gases (not easily sampleable), negative pressures, horizontal ducts (deposition and stratification), and many other obstacles to satisfactory sampling [1978, p. 5].

In their prior-approval negotiations with industry these inspectors tried not only to establish continuous monitoring of emissions but also to encourage the installation of sampling points.

Once the sampling point has been determined decisions have to be made about how long to sample for, when to sample, and how frequently to sample. What constitutes a representative sample? Is it fair to convert a three-minute sample to a twenty-four-hour mean? Should the sample be taken over the course of ten minutes or twenty minutes or an hour? Decisions such as these will take into account how dangerous a substance is likely to be and, in particular, what the length of exposure is before harm is caused. HSE note ETM 1 comments that '[t]he frequency and time of testing in relation to a particular process is normally to be decided by the inspector after discussion with the works management but guidance may in some cases be given in the Notes on Best-Practicable Means' (HSE, 1981b, para. 4). The Approved Code of Practice and Guidance Note 'Work with Asbestos Insulation and Asbestos Coating' (HSC, 1985a, Appendix), for instance, recommends a four-hour sampling time. As noted above, the policy of IAPI was to establish continuous monitoring where possible.

Who undertakes the sampling and where the results are analysed may introduce further uncertainty to the process. Guidance Note E28 (HSE, 1981c, para. 5) emphasizes that sampling should be planned and executed by those who have 'adequate information, instruction and training for the task'. Indeed IAPIs were keen that the same sampling teams visit sites in their districts so as to ensure some continuity in the test results. On the subject of the need to take account of laboratory errors Guidance Note EH10 warns: '[b]ecause of the large differences in results obtained within and between laboratories with all fibre-counting methods, a good quality control procedure is essential' (HSE, 1984, p. 6). This document further states that 'in common with monitoring for other particles, errors will be introduced in sampling'.

Once the results of sampling are available inspectors have to interpret the findings and determine their implications. Again this is not always a straightforward matter. HSE Guidance Note EH10 on Asbestos provides us with a clear example of the difficulties which may be involved. The Note warns that it is not possible, using certain sampling methods, to 'distinguish between asbestos and other organic or inorganic fibres (e.g. carpet and paper fibres, gypsum)' (HSE, 1984, para. 41). The Note goes on to point out that in some situations the interpretation of results may be such that more complex and expensive analytical methods are necessary (HSE, 1984, para. 42).

It is important to emphasize that high levels of precision and accuracy were not always required by inspectors. The large bulk of tests undertaken by inspectors themselves were crude and offered them only a rough indicator of compliance. But this was often sufficient for routine monitoring, as the HSE publication ETM 1 states '[f]or routine control purposes . . . tests of high precision and accuracy are not essential' (HSE, 1981b, para. 3). Indeed, routine testing of a more sophisticated nature could be prohibitively expensive. The cost of sampling could be quite considerable. The cost of sampling teams apart, sampling equipment and the processing of samples could also pose a significant drain on agency resources. For this reason inspectors had to weigh up the costs and benefits of the sampling they undertook. An example of how high the costs of sampling could be was revealed by an inspector who was under local-authority pressure to monitor dioxin levels. This would involve regular sampling and the cost of each sample was estimated at £1,000. The inspector involved was of the opinion that the evidence of dioxin contamination was insufficient to warrant such expensive sampling.

Whatever the level of precision required, sampling was not the clear-cut method of assessing compliance it might be perceived to be. Nevertheless, it was probably the most accurate method available to inspectors, especially in the assessment of compliance with emission limits. Moreover, as Hawkins (1984, p. 89) observes, the taking of samples fostered the impression of scientific objectivity. Certainly inspectors would portray sampling as constituting a much stronger indicator of compliance in their interactions with the regulated than they would consider them to be within the agency or when considering their status as legal evidence. This use of 'scientific' equipment in the enforcement process is not confined to regulatory agencies. Manning, in his study of the police, writes: '[o]ne of the strategies employed by the police to appear professionally and bureaucratically efficient is the use of technology. . . . Technology ties the police into the most powerful symbols and belief in the mechanical, certain, unproblematic effects of employing technology to solve human problems' (1977, p. 130).

This is not to suggest that inspectors adhere unquestioningly to a faith in sampling. There were occasions when inspectors would undertake manual sampling in addition to, for example, continuous monitoring. This was done for a number of reasons. One IAPI explained that they did not place absolute faith in machines; moreover they wanted to keep the operators on their toes, so taking the occasional manual sample was both a real and a symbolic check on the company's sampling. Another reason offered by another IAPI was that agency sampling was yet another means of showing the workforce that inspectors were out and about. It was explained that taking a sample and waiting for the results was time-consuming. All of this serves to underline Hawkins' observations that sampling can be a tedious, time-

consuming activity which can at the same time be imbued with drama
(1984, p. 86).

Sampling was not always accepted as unambiguous proof of the state
of compliance. Inspectors were very aware of the limitations inherent
in their work. Manual sampling[9] and more sophisticated sampling were
taken as indicators of whether or not further investigation of a site was
warranted. Inspectors knew that they could not rely too heavily on
monitors and samples. They were also aware that monitoring did not
prevent pollution, but rather assessed it. Accordingly this method of
assessment could not be considered in isolation from the wider controls
employed to regulate health and safety and the environment.

CONCLUSIONS

Proactive methods of monitoring compliance were important for all of
the research inspectorates, but the precise methods used varied according to the visibility and tangibility of the activity subject to regulation.
A range of information was accumulated during proactive monitoring
of regulated sites. This ranged from information about technical and
financial aspects of a business to inspectors' impressions about the levels
of confidence they held in management. Proactive visits by inspectors
and sampling teams were as much symbolic as substantive, representing the visible presence of state officials actively surveying regulated
sites and increasing their knowledge of the population subject to control.

Proactive work was valued by field-level staff, and proactive methods
of monitoring compliance were regarded positively because of their preventive role. By comparison, reactive work represented the negative
side of the job, to the extent that it entailed dealing with cases where
something had gone wrong or failed. But regulatory agencies had to be
responsive to complaints and accidents; not only did they provide valuable information for the agency but, as we have seen, accident and
complaint rates informed routine monitoring programmes. Moreover,
it was often through the knowledge gained in undertaking proactive
work that regulatory officials learnt to spot the 'unusual' and potentially
interesting accidents which might be worth investigation (Hutter, 1986).

[9] See also Richardson *et al.*, 1983, although it should be noted that the inspectorates
included in this research did not seem to view sampling with such a degree of scepticism
as did Richardson's trade-effluent inspectors.

6 Responding to Complaints and Accidents: Reactive Enforcement Methods

In contrast to the relative predictability and routine of proactive methods of enforcement, reactive work is comparatively unpredictable and unstructured. There were two ways in which inspectorates were prompted to organize reactively: first, in response to complaints and secondly, in response to accidents and incidents.

COMPLAINTS

In my fieldwork 13 per cent of IAPI visits and 10 per cent of FI visits were prompted by complaints, but complaints did not figure prominently in mobilizing the resources of REIs. The levels of complaint handled by each inspectorate were not always easy to determine from the *Annual Reports*.[1] IAPI reports gave the most details about complaints, with annual figures for the number of registered and unregistered processes subject to complaint and a breakdown of which type of scheduled works were complained about each year. During the period 1983–6 the number of registered processes under complaint were:

1983	327
1984	365
1985	347
1986	399

FI *Annual Reports* did not routinely report their handling of complaints, although in 1985 it was stated that the inspectorate had handled approximately 10,000 complaints. The RI *Annual Reports* for 1983 and 1984 noted that 176 and 210 complaints by railway staff were dealt with. The 1985 and 1986 reports do not specify the number of complaints. The greater detail of IAPI reports on the subject of the complaints it receives is perhaps explained by the greater public profile and

---

[1] Some reports did not mention complaints, and where complaints were referred to the source of the complaint was not always clear. For example, it is not always possible to determine whether the complaint came from employees or the public.

accountability of this inspectorate. Generally speaking the incidents that they received complaints about affected the public to a far greater extent than did those received by the FI and RI.

Complaints were either written, for example letters or even petitions, or verbal, taking the form of telephone calls or direct complaints to inspectors. All inspectors followed up all complaints, usually within a short period of time. FIs and members of the RI expected workforce complainants to have pursued and exhausted the established channels of complaint before bringing a complaint to them. Hence inspectors expected only to become involved where these channels had broken down or proven unsuccessful. Indeed, part of their investigation of the complaint may well have included trying to determine why communication within the firm had deteriorated to the point whereby they had become involved.

IAPIs also tried to encourage complainants to call the company responsible for the alleged problem direct. Not only might this mean that inspectors were not involved, but it could have direct benefits to complainant and company alike, not least because a greater understanding could be fostered. In some cases more tangible benefits might be gained. An IAPI took me to a cement works which he told me went to great lengths to follow up complaints, for example visiting complainants with an explanation of any problem that had arisen. Subsequently when the company put forward plans to extend the plant there had been no objections. This especially surprised the inspector as the plans entailed redundancies. In cases where a site was the cause of a great deal of public concern IAPIs encouraged the formation of liaison committees. These comprised company representatives, the inspectorate, and local community representatives. They met regularly and discussed any particular problems with emissions at the site and company plans for the future. Inspectors valued these meetings, as one District Inspector's Report illustrates: '[i]n our experience an informed public is highly desirable as most people are more worried by lack of knowledge than by facts' (HMIP, 1983, p. 9).

There were two main sources of complaint in relation to health and safety and environmental matters, the workforce, and the general public. Not surprisingly it was the workforce which tended to alert inspectors to health and safety problems and the general public who were most likely to complain about environmental pollution. Both groups were potential victims, and hence both may be regarded as having a vested interest in reporting problems to the appropriate regulatory agency. Likewise, they might have other reasons for complaining, the possibility of which was usually considered by inspectors. The source of complaint was a matter taken into account by inspectors when responding to complaints: some individuals became well known as regular complainants, and they could be regarded either as the 'type' to complain about 'anything' or they may be attributed as having 'quasi-informant' status, so if they complained inspectors would receive it as a signal that something serious might be wrong. In short, a whole series of judgements were made about the complainant which could influence inspectors' responses.

Complaints could be categorized in a number of ways. First there were those which were regarded as genuine complaints, that is, cases where inspectors accepted that the complainant had a grievance which needed remedying. In some of these cases the source of the problem was readily apparent to inspectors. This was so when an IAPI visited a couple complaining about washing which became dirty when they had hung it outside to dry. The most obvious source of the problem was a nearby quarry, which readily admitted to being the cause when approached by the investigating inspector. The manager explained that inches of ice had frozen on the filters and whilst thawing this ice they had had great problems with dust emissions. The manager immediately offered to visit the complainant and apologize, something he was encouraged to do by the inspector. This particular example highlights another feature of complaints, namely that despite the problems caused only one person complained to the inspectorate. The explanation offered for this by the complainant was apparently accepted by the inspector, namely that others in the village were hesitant to complain about the quarry as they had relatives working there. In light of a recession and recent redundancies these people would not do anything which they felt might jeopardize the viability of the plant. This point was taken up by the FI in its 1986–7 *Annual Report*—'[a]reas report that fewer complaints are being received from employees and their representatives, possibly as a result of the acceptance of continued employment at the expense of poorer standards' (HSC, 1987, p. 21).

In some instances of complaint about a genuine problem the source might not have been readily apparent, particularly when complainants alleged that air pollution was the problem but inspectors could not detect any emissions from nearby plants which might cause the symptoms complained of. In such examples lengthy investigation, sometimes involving other agencies, could be involved and feelings could run high.

One of my early pilot visits with an agricultural inspector reveals how fraught such a situation can become. A lady complaining about illnesses allegedly caused by pesticides used by a neighbouring farmer became quite irate when the inspector investigating her complaint explained that he could not prohibit the use of these pesticides by the farmer solely on the strength of her evidence. He would need to investigate further. The complainant became verbally abusive and eventually tried physically to assault the inspector.[2] Clearly these situations were frustrating for all concerned, especially if the source of the problem could not readily be detected.

Inspectors seemed only too aware that a local factory could be 'blamed' for any problems in a neighbouring area, and in some cases they clearly did not accept that complaints were necessarily genuine or reasonable. In other, perhaps more typical, examples inspectors would perceive the complaint to be prompted by some additional motivation, such as intolerance or political factors. In such examples, they would regard the situation as being generally tolerated, but now the subject of complaint because of other, possibly unrelated, circumstances. IAPIs, for instance, would receive complaints from newcomers to an area who, upon moving, had not expected problems from nearby industry. One such couple regularly complained to IAPIs about steel works they had moved to within a mile of. They complained that, because of emissions from the works, the outside of their house needed frequent repainting, they could not keep the inside of the house clean, and they could not even sit in their garden without being affected. They had complained to the works but alleged that the management was rude to them. It transpired that they were the only complainants in the locality. They were surprised by this, but thought that maybe their neighbours were more accepting because they had been brought up in the area. The inspector accepted this, commenting that people do complain very much according to their expectations. He promised to do all he could to improve the situation, but told me later that he was at a loss to know what to do as the 'best practicable means' requirements were being met. So, in effect, the works were already meeting the legal definition of compliance.

Inspectors from all the agencies studied regarded some complainants as politically motivated. An industrial air-pollution complaint which fell into this category involved a factory which was causing an offensive

[2] See Frank, 1984, for a discussion of assaults against regulatory officials.

smell problem. The inspector concerned explained that there was a 'political' background to the complaint, namely that the local council was developing the adjacent area as a tourist area and clearly it, the developers, and prospective occupants would prefer the factory to go rather than to clean up. The inspectorate had already earmarked the factory as needing attention and was working closely with the company to remedy the problems, whilst remaining sensitive to—but not bullied by—the political situation.

FIs and inspectors of the RI regarded some complaints they received as being connected with industrial relations problems. A FI who received a complaint from a trade union about the dangers of one worker entering a building alone on a large industrial site believed that cuts in the workforce had something to do with the case. After investigating the complaint the inspector found that it was justified to the extent that the building needed guarding deficiencies remedied. The inspector avoided all comment about whether or not it was safe for one person to enter the building alone, which was regarded as an industrial relations problem.

Complaints were taken seriously by all inspectorates. The IAPI considered it was important to follow up all complaints as soon as possible, and the FI went to the lengths of agreeing not to reveal the name of the complainant or even that a complaint had been made at all, if they were so requested.[3] The reasons for this centred upon the importance of complaints. Clearly, they could provide inspectors with valuable information, especially if agency resources were 'thin on the ground'. Indeed, in some circumstances, inspectors would 'cultivate' informants. IAPIs, for example, often covered large geographical areas, and they used the local environmental health department as a local 'monitoring service'. Not only would they ask environmental health officers to let them know of any incidents, but they would occasionally ask them to check up on specific complaints if they were unable to visit the area themselves within twenty-four hours. Complainants were used as additional eyes and ears by inspectors—and one might add noses, for complaints were useful as a means of identifying obvious problems. One IAPI made a point of lunching in a public house near to a site registered under the Alkali Act. Over lunch he cultivated local 'informants'

---

[3] Inspectors explained that it could be very difficult to conceal the investigation of complaints. One FI I accompanied used my presence to conceal investigation of a worker complaint. Management showed me part of the site while the inspector went into a more dangerous area, where the complainant worked.

and found out what had been going on at the site. Informants such as these brought popularly-understood problems to the attention of inspectors. More specialized information was sought from managers, with respect to both their own and neighbouring works. Inspectors were to varying degrees reliant upon those they regulated for information. Indeed their reasons for cultivating informants within companies were multifarious. As one inspector explained, he might also be building a relationship with someone who would one day be in a high managerial position.

FIs offered more legalistic reasons for investigating all complaints, namely to protect against the problems which could be incurred by not investigating. If, for example, a complaint was not taken seriously by the inspectorate and subsequent events revealed the existence of a major problem, the inspectorate might quite rightly be criticized. A District IAPI, while cautioning about placing too much emphasis on complaints, spelt out some other reasons for investigating complaints:

complaints are important for two reasons. One is that they demonstrate a continued concern for air pollution and the second is that in the long run they are . . . a measure of our achievement in controlling air pollution. In the ultimate the test of our performance should be that the general public is satisfied even though this does not mean perfection [HMIP, 1983, p. 8].

This quotation emphasizes one of the major characteristics of reactive enforcement, namely the attention which may be drawn to the inspectorate and its handling of events. Inspectors may welcome the additional pressure exerted upon a business by 'outside' complainants. Indeed they may try to mobilize these people to put direct pressure on a business by urging them to complain to the works. This may give the agency an opportunity to demonstrate that it does respond quickly to problems and perhaps to explain why the agency cannot effect quicker improvements in some circumstances.

But the public attention, in combination with the other pressing reasons for investigating complaints, contributes to the major problem associated with this method of assessing compliance, namely that it causes inspectors to change their priorities and possibly give greater attention to works than they may warrant. A meeting of Principal FIs I attended voiced concern about this, in particular that basic inspections could be suffering as a result of a perceived increase in complaints. But as Manning (1988) pointed out in his discussions of police responses to citizen calls, the response is important for symbolic and instrumental reasons, since agency responses to public complaint can give the agency an opportunity to broaden its support base.

Complaints were not necessarily prompted by the most serious offences. This seemed to depend upon the type of activity subject to control. As already discussed in relation to sampling, there are some dangerous situations which may not be identifiable by human senses, and in these circumstances complaints do not arise. Similarly, their usefulness as a means of assessing compliance with health-related matters is restricted, although it should be recognized that a series of complaints about similar ill-health symptoms from one workplace could alert inspectors to possible non-compliance.

Complaints and Compliance

Although complaints may not represent a large part of inspectors' work they demand substantial resources and may have profound implications for the definition of compliance. Complaints are always taken seriously but treated cautiously. This is for two main reasons. First, inspectors (and the agency) are acutely aware that their decisions in such cases are subject to external scrutiny. Secondly, inspectors are keen to assess the status of complaints, that is whether or not the complaint is genuine and whether or not the complainant has ulterior motives. The first of these leads inspectors to investigate complaints both thoroughly and according to 'the book', in other words their discretion is reduced. But it is the second factor which has the most direct implications for compliance, for it is only if inspectors judge the complaint to have substance that they will act. If the complaint is judged to be genuine then inspectors will be seen to be doing all they can strictly to enforce the law. This implies less leeway in interpretation of the definition of compliance (see Chapter 4) and less flexibility in securing full compliance with the law. However, if the complaint is not judged to be grounded then inspectors will be sensitive in its investigation but will not be bullied into acting where they ascertain there to be no case.

The extent to which complaints influence compliance is in part determined by the source of the complaint, in particular its public profile. It is also affected by the presence or absence of alternative routes of remedy. Hence the reluctance of inspectors to become involved in disputes between workers and management. Beyond this it is significant that all inspectorates sometimes attempted to mediate in the event of a complaint, encouraging those who had a complaint to take it directly to the source of the problem. In turn, those who failed to comply were urged to offer an apology and explanation direct to the victim(s), this being especially characteristic of IAPI. It should be noted, however, that such mediation did not necessarily preclude the possibility of legal action. Indeed, at the margins the public knowledge of and complaint about non-compliance could increase the likelihood of legal action. But such a decision would typically take account of a variety of factors, of which the complaint would be but one.

It is notable that the work of the research inspectorates attracted surprisingly little public attention. Part of the explanation for this must be that the daily resolution of compliance issues is in many respects private, with these decisions typically taking place 'behind closed doors'.[4] Moreover, it must also be the case that the majority of these decisions are regarded as uncontroversial. Nevertheless, at some level there seems to be an element of institutionalized cultural disinterest with regulatory objectives. While the majority would presumably say that promoting health and safety at work, and more especially the environment, is a good cause, it is still the case that these issues, and the work of the regulatory inspectorates involved, attract little media and political comment. This is especially so with health and safety at work, where even the annual fatality-at-work statistics do not attract headline newscover or political lobbying. Indeed, there was no noticeable outcry when, during the 1980s and early 1990s, government deregulation—including health and safety standards—was a central part of the political agenda.

Pressure groups and NGOs did not figure very much in the everyday work of these inspectorates (cf. Grabosky, 1994). When there was political and media attention directed to health and safety or environmental matters (and this was by no means typical) it tended to coalesce around specific health and safety or environmental matters. These might include concern about a particular disaster,[5] a particular substance (asbestos), industry (waste disposal, nuclear), site,[6] or category of persons (children). Regulatory agencies recognize that, with respect to

[4] There have been some moves to increase freedom of information. The Environmental Protection Act 1990 and the associated Environmental Protection (Applications, Appeals and Registers) Regulations 1991 provide for some public participation in pollution-control and access to information which was previously classed as confidential. See generally Austin, 1989.

[5] For example, the fire at King's Cross Underground Station in London in 1987 which resulted in multiple fatalities and massive publicity (Fennell, 1988); or the sinking of the ferry, *The Herald of Free Enterprise*, at Zeebrugge in 1987 (Sheen, 1987); or the explosion on the Piper Alpha Oil Rig, in the North Sea in 1988 (Cullen, 1990).

[6] For example, the phurnacite site in Wales (see Ch. 8).

these particular issues, they are in the public eye to a much greater extent than is normal. Not only are they politically accountable but they are, as we have seen, anxious to maintain their credibility. They must tread cautiously in such cases, being seen to investigate and regulate thoroughly, but not being regarded as unjust or inconsistent. High-profile sites are likely to attract more frequent inspections, and similarly the agencies will be more inclined to invoke the law in the case of high-profile violations. To some extent regulatory agencies are under media and political pressure to act in prominent cases. It is precisely on these occasions that the accountability of regulatory agencies and their status as agencies of the state are highlighted (Hutter, 1992). More significantly, regulatory officials appear as the symbolic representatives of government. So in these cases methods of assessing and achieving compliance become public and subject to greater scrutiny. They also fulfil the latent function of anticipating, responding to, and perhaps appeasing public and political concern. But such cases are exceptional, and the majority of cases handled by regulatory inspectors arouse little, if any, political comment.

In routine, everyday matters field-level officers do take account of public and political concerns. IAPIs took account of the proximity of housing when regulating polluters and FIs and REIs were sensitive to public involvement in health and safety issues. All of the agencies examined were sensitive to complaints, especially petitions and letters from MPs. So field-level inspectors were exposed to public and political issues, but these were not overriding influences on their work. While the involvement of the public and the visibility of offences may increase their political profile and the possibility of legal action this is not invariably so.[7]

---

[7] The political parameters of regulation are perceived rather differently by the policy-makers within regulatory organizations. The policy-makers relate to national, rather than local, politics and in many respects this is where the political parameters are most keenly felt. Those at the top of the hierarchy are directly accountable to government and ministers and are responsible for responding to Parliamentary questions. The political context of regulation is highly important. During this research, as Manning and I have already explained elsewhere, there was a 'perceived pressure for inaction' (1990, p. 105). There was pressure from ministers, the media, and industrialists to 'reduce the burdens' on industry (Minister without Portfolio, 1986). Contemporaneously there were budget freezes and efficiency studies (Butler, 1993; Lewis and Birkinshaw, 1993; Stewart and Walsh, 1992). The political parameters of regulation were crystal clear.

ACCIDENTS AND INCIDENTS

The prevention of accidents is in many respects the *raison d'être* of health and safety regulation, so it was hardly surprising that accident investigation was an important method of assessing compliance. Usually, but not invariably, accidents were the clearest and most unfortunate indicators of non-compliance received by inspectors. It is perhaps for this reason that many inspectors were so keen to prosecute following an accident or incident, when they were in possession of apparently incontrovertible evidence that the law had been broken. It is also one reason why the FI included accidents as one of the criteria in its inspection rating system, and other inspectors considered it as part of their decision about how frequently a given workplace should be visited. This said, it was perhaps surprising how small a proportion of inspectors' time was devoted to accident investigation. In my research, visits devoted solely to accident investigation represented 6 per cent of fieldwork visits with FI and 14 per cent of visits with RI. In the case of the RI it should be understood that accident investigation was also an important role of the Inspecting Officers of Railways, especially when a major accident, possibly involving the public, needed investigation. The small proportion of time devoted to accident and incident investigation was not explained simply by the fact that there were few accidents, since this was not the case.

Since 1986 accidents have been reported to HSE under the Reporting of Injuries, Diseases and Dangerous Occurrences Regulations (RIDDOR) 1985. Prior to this, accidents were reported under the provisions of the Notification of Accidents and Dangerous Occurrences Regulations 1980 (NADOR).[8] RIDDOR requires notification of all fatal accidents, major injuries, accidents causing more than three days' absence from work, some specified diseases, and dangerous occurrences arising from the workplace. Accidents on statutory railways are reported to the RI under the Railways (Notice of Accidents) Order 1986. In addition, accidents to contractors' employees working on the railways are reportable under the Notification of Accidents Order 1986. All accidents to passengers and other persons must be reported to the

---

[8] Under an agreement with the DHSS HSE used to receive reports of anyone claiming sickness benefit who might have been the victim also of an industrial accident. However, the Statutory Sickness Pay Scheme introduced in 1983 reduced the reliability of this source of information.

inspectorate, with the exception that those to railway or contractors' employees need only be reported when the injuries cause an absence from work for more than three days. Under-reporting is, not surprisingly, a major problem for HSE (see also James, 1993). In the 1987–8 *Annual Report* the Chairman of HSC drew attention to the problem: '[t]he Commission is still concerned that the statistical base on which we rely, in deciding policies and priorities, may be compromised by under-reporting of injuries. Although under-reporting can only be estimated, we believe it to be substantial, particularly among the expanding number of new, small business' (HSC, 1988, p. 3).

Table 8 gives some indication of the number of injuries to employees which are reported to these agencies. Clearly inspectors could not investigate all of the accidents reported to them, so how did they make decisions about which of the many accidents that came to their attention to investigate?

TABLE 8. Injuries to Employees Reported to the Factory and Railway Inspectorates April 1987–March 1988

Enforcing Authority	Fatal	Major*	Over 3-day	Total
Factory Inspectorate	257	15,402	126,393	142,052
Railway Inspectorate	17	225	2,448	2,690

* As defined by RIDDOR 1985
Source: HSE (quoted in Hutter and Lloyd-Bostock, 1990).

Accident Reporting

Railway accidents have always been reported directly to the RI. Inspecting Officers were informed by telephone in the event of a particularly serious accident, such as one involving a passenger train where serious or fatal injuries had occurred. Depending upon the severity of the accident the Chief Inspecting Officer of Railways would either visit the scene of the accident himself or he would send a member of his staff. Less serious categories of accidents were reported to the inspectorate on a monthly basis. Accident reports were initially processed at headquarters level by an Assistant Inspecting Officer of Railways who would look over all accident reports sent to the inspectorate and decide which accidents to investigate and which type of inquiry was required. Most members of the inspectorate undertook accident investigations of one kind or another. Inspecting officers tended to investigate the most serious train accidents, while REIs investigated the less serious train accidents and those involving railway personnel.

FI followed much the same procedures as the RI, although in the case of FI these were much more formal. Fatalities to employees were immediately reportable by telephone, whereas other injuries were notified in writing under the regulations. FIs were much more inclined than RI to carry out an immediate initial investigation. If it appeared that legal action was likely, then inspectors were expected to carry out a thorough investigation, including interviewing witnesses and photographing the scene of the accident. Accident reports were processed at local area offices where Principal Inspectors would scan accident reports and decide how to proceed.

The Decision to Investigate

In many respects the way in which an accident was investigated depended upon its severity, the likely outcome of the investigation, and its utility for enforcement policy. FIs undertook their accident investigations under the HSW Act, the only difference between the various types of investigation being the speed with which they were carried out. The RI, however, had a variety of types of accident investigation at its disposal. Not only did it undertake the same 1974 investigations as the FI, it also undertook a range of investigations under the 1871 Regulation of Railways Act. Three main types of inquiry were undertaken under the 1871 legislation. Most were low-key investigations undertaken by REIs. But in the case of particularly serious accidents it had become the practice for the inspectorate to hold a public hearing of evidence, this being the Public Inquiry for which the inspectorate is best known (see Hutter, 1992). Finally, the 1871 legislation allows for the Secretary of State for Transport to set up a formal court of inquiry, but this type of investigation is rarely held and is reserved for the most extreme accidents.

There was a strong preference within the RI to hold inquiries under the 1871 legislation. This was partly a result of public expectation, but principally because of the opportunities the 1871 legislation afforded for publishing the findings of the investigations and disseminating information about accidents and their causes. The HSW Act, by comparison, imposes constraints upon publication. HSE can, in certain cases, direct disclosure to the public of reports. Section 14 of the HSW Act 1974 gives HSC powers to direct that incident inquiry reports be made public. Nevertheless, these are the exceptions rather than routine practice.

All types of 1871 inquiries have a number of features in common. First, all are formally ordered by the Secretary of State for Transport.[9] Secondly, the results are publicly available.[10] Thirdly, the legislation does not specify how the investigation should be conducted. The Act just requires the inspectorate to investigate the accident, determine its causes, and submit a report to the Secretary of State for Transport stating the causes and circumstances of the accidents and 'any observations thereon'. It does not direct the format and procedures of these inquiries, except that the formal courts of inquiry be held in open court.[11]

The RI had no written policy about which type of inquiry to hold, although certain informal principles were generally followed. The monthly 'bulk' railway returns on accidents were initially scanned by the Assistant Inspecting Officer responsible for accidents. Normally this inspector would decide not to investigate accidents resulting in minor injuries unless there had been a pattern or series of similar accidents. He would use his 'intuition first and the computer second' (Lloyd-Bostock, 1992) when scanning these reports.[12] This inspector also took account of the victim's age. One of the reports he scanned in my presence, for example, involved an 81-year-old lady who had fallen over at a station. This was not designated for investigation, partly because the injuries sustained were minor and partly because he would expect people of this age to be less steady on their feet. Another example cited by the inspector was that of a trespasser on the line. He would be more concerned that a case involving a 5-year-old gaining access to the line were investigated than that of a 15-year-old. This said, the inspectorate would generally request more information from the railways about where the victim gained access to the line. No further information was

---

[9] While these inquiries are formally ordered by the Secretary of State, in practice the power to make this decision has been delegated to the Chief Inspecting Officer of Railways. His decision could be overruled either way, but this very rarely happens.

[10] The Secretary of State is required to publish the report. Public inquiry reports are usually published by HMSO and other reports are typewritten by the Department of Transport and copies are available upon request.

[11] These matters are not left entirely to the discretion of the individual inspector, as a tradition has developed concerning the form and procedures of these inquiries. See Hutter 1992.

[12] RI's computerized accident records were at quite a preliminary and rudimentary stage at the time of my fieldwork, especially when compared with the more sophisticated system operated by the FI.

collected if the accident was regarded as a suicide, since in such cases the inspectorate would normally follow the decision of the coroner's inquest.[13] The source of the report was also taken into account—some local managers were regarded as less reliable than others in the accuracy of their reports. If the inspectorate was at all suspicious of the written report it would investigate further. This inspector estimated that 15 per cent of accident reports were not followed through. The rest would be investigated further. The type of follow-up involved ranged from writing to the railways and requesting more information to the initiation of a public inquiry.

Serious accidents, as already noted, were reported directly to the inspectorate. In such cases the railways kept the inspectorate fully informed of developments and the inspectorate kept the Secretary of State fully informed. Local inspectors might be sent to the scene and asked to report back to the headquarters or, if the accident was sufficiently serious or near the inspectorate's headquarters, an inspecting officer would probably attend. Public inquiries were typically held into accidents carrying a high level of public interest or concern; where there had been serious injury or fatality, especially when passengers were involved, or when there were multiple fatalities; where there was the potential for serious injury or fatality; when passenger trains were involved in a serious accident; where there was the need for public reassurance; and where the circumstances of the accident were unusual and the cause unknown. A high level of public concern or involvement in the accident featured prominently in the decision to hold a public inquiry. Similar accidents where there was no public involvement or interest could result in either a 1974 inquiry or a routine 1871 inquiry. 1974 inquiries were most likely where the inspectorate was seriously considering a prosecution. Routine 1871 inquiries were, at the time of my research, more likely. These would be held, for example, in the case of a serious or unusual accident involving freight trains or in cases involving serious or fatal injuries to railways personnel.

In the case of *exceptionally serious* or worrying accidents a court of inquiry might be set up. This form of inquiry was usually considered only when fundamental questions of policy were raised, especially when

[13] In some cases where coroners do not return a suicide verdict inspectors will try to determine the matter for themselves. It was indicated that in some cases this was readily apparent. For example, it was usually assumed that a fatality was a suicide if the victim was a psychiatric patient. The recorded trespasser fatalities and suicides on the railways were in 1984, 121 trespasser deaths and 187 suicides; 1986, 152 trespasser deaths and 160 suicides; 1988, 170 trespasser deaths and 154 suicides (source: RI *Annual Reports*).

the role of the inspectorate was brought into question (Hutter, 1992). This form of inquiry is uncommon; indeed only four inquiries of this type have ever been held. Interestingly two of these have been in the recent past, and within a year of each other, namely the King's Cross Inquiry of 1988 and the Clapham Inquiry of 1989.[14]

The seriousness of the inquiry was reflected in the personnel who undertook it. Public inquiries were undertaken by Inspecting Officers of Railways, whereas the less public investigations were undertaken by REIs. The recent formal courts of inquiry were chaired by QCs assisted by four assessors, one of whom in each inquiry was an Inspecting Officer of Railways.[15] The figures for 1983 and 1984 give us some idea of the number of the differing types of accident investigation that were undertaken.

TABLE 9. Railway Accident Investigations 1983–1984

	1983	1984
Courts of Inquiry	0	0
Public Inquiries	8	10
Inquiries into Fatal and Serious Accidents to Railway Staff	211	179
Investigations into other Accidents	299	236

Source: Annual Reports

FIs were provided with guidelines about which accidents should be investigated. In many respects these paralleled the less formal principles followed by RI. For example, all cases involving fatalities and multiple casualties were investigated, as were those cases which gave rise to particular public concern and accidents which were also the subject of complaints. Accidents which were highly likely to be investigated included those affecting children, those which seemed common to a particular industry, and those occurring on premises where there had been a series of accidents. Inspectors were also likely to investigate accidents where there seemed to have been a serious breach of the law. In

---

[14] The King's Cross Inquiry raised fundamental questions of policy regarding acceptable fire precautions and procedures on underground train systems, questions which might have drawn criticism to RI for apparently accepting these policies and procedures. The reasons for holding a court of inquiry into the Clapham accident are more elusive. See Hutter, 1992.

[15] The role of assessors is to advise the Chair on technical matters. In the King's Cross Inquiry the Attorney General also appointed a QC as Counsel to the court to aid in the investigations.

some respects the FI paid more attention to apparent breaches of the law than the RI, something which was fully in keeping with the insistent, as opposed to persuasive, strategy that seemed to characterize its work.

An important consideration for all of the inspectorates in the study was whether or not an investigation was likely to effect an improvement. In a depressing number of cases the causes of the accidents coming to the inspectorates' attention were readily apparent because of their frequency, and hence did not always lead to investigation—a typical example would be finger amputations in the woodworking industry (Hutter and Lloyd-Bostock, 1990, p. 415). In other cases accident investigation was prompted by unusual circumstances which might indicate the discovery of a new problem, for example with new machinery or a previously unknown hazard. In the investigation of such accidents the Research and Technological Services Division of HSE might become involved. The 1990–1 report of this section of HSE describes a number of cases falling into this category. For instance, the explosion of a chemical reactor vessel in 1990 'suggested the occurrence of a previously unsuspected chemical reaction' (HSE, 1991, p. 6). The explosion of a large tyre on an earth scraper vehicle led to laboratory research and eventually guidance on the safe conduct of hot work on the wheels of such vehicles (*ibid.*, p. 7).

The role of the civil police could also impinge on accident investigations. For some FIs getting to the scene of a fatality as soon as possible was partly influenced by the varying practices of the local police about moving bodies—these inspectors felt that seeing the body helped them to understand how the accident might have happened. Others were not concerned by this and did not consider that it helped them in their investigations. Railway inspectors seemed content with British Railways' wish to move fatalities away from the track as quickly as possible. Apparently if the civil police reached the scene first they would stop the line being cleared and set up their own investigation.

Investigations were conducted either formally or informally. The former involved the taking of evidence—oral, scientific, and photographic. The purpose of this might be to establish the cause of the accident (see Hutter, 1992); to construct a prosecution case; or to give those involved in the accident the impression that legal action was a possibility. Where inspectors considered that legal action was a likely outcome of an accident then they would be anxious to visit the scene of the accident as soon as possible. This was in order to take statements and photographs while items of machinery—and possibly a body—were still in place and witnesses' memories were 'fresh'. One FI explained that it could take a very long time to collect such evidence, extending over days or even weeks after the accident.

Informal investigations, as one might expect, were conducted only when legal action was not being considered. Often these investigations would not merit a specific accident visit, but would form part of a basic or check inspection. These accidents might also have been selected for training purposes, that is, to give new inspectors some experience of investigating accidents.

The length of time devoted to these investigations depended very much upon circumstances. Informal investigations usually involved just one visit to the site of the accident. More serious accidents could involve repeated visits to the site. Generally FIs' interactions with those involved took place at the worksite. RI investigations, however, might extend to the formal arena of a public hearing of evidence, which could well take place away from the workplace, in a hotel or civic building for instance. Routine 1871 inquiries undertaken by REIs usually took place on railway premises, in the local offices or perhaps the regional headquarters of the railways. Prior to the public hearing of evidence the inspector responsible for the investigation would thoroughly investigate the accident. He would visit the site of the accident, interview those involved, and liaise with the railways about the undertaking of scientific tests and the examination of any equipment involved in the accident. He might also consult with colleagues, other railways, and experts in any related fields of interest. Thus the cause of the accident would usually be known to the inspector before the formal hearing of evidence.

In all 1871 inquiries there was an established tradition of format and procedures.[16] This tradition tended to be followed both by inspecting officers undertaking the most public of inquiries and by REIs holding a hearing of evidence on local railway premises. The investigating officer was usually helped on the day of the inquiry by railway managers from departments related to the accident. Trade-union representatives would also be present and so, in the case of public inquiries, might be solicitors representing the injured or killed. None of these parties had the right to ask a question, and everything had to go through the chairman. If he considered that the question was irrelevant he could disallow it. The spatial arrangement of these inquiries was also well

---

[16] These procedures are discussed in detail in Hutter, 1992.

established. Typically the investigating officer would sit with the railway officials assisting him. Union representatives would sit at a separate table to their left or right, and so would less senior railway officials such as the rules and regulations manager. In the larger public inquiries the press and stenographers might also be present and so might members of the public, who would sit facing the formal arrangement of officials. Those giving evidence would sit immediately in front of the Railway Inspector.

The aura was one of formality and possibly an intimidating experience for those giving evidence.[17] Inspectors always stressed that the purpose of the inquiry was to establish the cause of the accident and to make recommendations to prevent its recurrence, not to apportion blame. There would then be statements from railway officials giving details of the accident, followed by statements from the witnesses and their questioning. The public hearing of evidence usually took up a day, but the more complicated and serious cases could take considerably longer. This was especially the case with the formal courts of inquiry. The court of inquiry into the King's Cross Underground fire, for instance, made British legal history as the longest public hearing yet held, lasting ninety-one days.

After the public hearing of evidence inspectors would assemble, analyse and assess the evidence before them, and then draft a report for submission to the Secretary of State for Transport. The report would describe the accident, present the evidence of witnesses and the results of technical examinations, and provide a conclusion, discussion, and recommendations. These reports would then be made available to anyone who wanted them. However the recommendations of these inquiries were not enforceable under the terms of the 1871 Regulation of Railways Act. They could be ignored by the railways. It was partly for this reason that the inspectorate liaised so closely with the railways during the course of the inquiry.[18]

FIs' accident reports were usually 'private' in that they were not published. But where special and occasional reports were produced for

[17] It should be noted that inspectors would go to great lengths to make witnesses feel at ease, speaking to them beforehand, and in some cases being prepared to hear evidence *in camera*. This was most likely when the witness might be asked to give evidence which would incriminate him- or herself.

[18] It should perhaps be noted that the railways often have an incentive to agree to recommendations to the extent that they, too, do not want the recurrence of a serious problem. This type of inquiry is presently under threat. For a fuller discussion of these issues see Hutter, 1992.

publication their objectives and format in many respects paralleled those of RI 1871 reports. The object of these reports, for example, was to give an account of what had happened and to make recommendations. The intention was not to apportion blame, and where it was felt that inspectors might have criticized particular individuals or organizations they were expected to include in the report that person's or organization's own account of what had happened. One difference from the RI type of report was that these FI reports could also include details of action taken following the accident, both spontaneously and at the request of the inspectorate.

Accidents as a Means of Assessing Compliance

The most obvious instances of non-compliance were accidents. This said, accidents were not always *prima facie* evidence of non-compliance. They could, for example, highlight a problem with practices or machinery previously regarded as compliant. The emphasis placed on accidents as a way of assessing compliance varied between inspectorates, as did the emphasis placed upon investigating accidents. In the case of the sample examined for this study, the RI undoubtedly placed most reliance upon accidents and their investigation. Its reasons for this included the sad fact that accidents were a familiar occurrence in the operation of a railway, and that when the public was involved these accidents were highly visible and were given a high profile. In any case, railway accidents were very evident and could be contrasted with some of the incidents which IAPI investigated, where the accidental emission might be 'invisible' and remain unknown to the public. Accident investigation has historically occupied a central position in the work of the RI. It is perhaps not surprising, therefore, that it was so committed to this method of assessing compliance and that it did so much to inform those working on the railways about accidents that had been investigated and their causes. The RI's retrospective approach was symbolized in its *Annual Reports*, the bulk of which were devoted to discussion of accidents.

All inspectors would do their best to retrieve some 'advantages' from an accident. Not surprisingly inspectors were keen to remind as many people as they could that accidents could and did happen. So while not all accidents resulted in a visit to a workplace, most visits involved reference to accidents. Moreover, inspectors attempted to use increased worker awareness and take advantage of improved manager receptiveness to urge full compliance wherever possible. Inspectors from all of the inspectorates studied saw the enforcement opportunities afforded by accidents—both generally and specifically. A regular ploy in persuading an individual or company to comply was to refer to accidents which had occurred because of non-compliance. A FI visiting a steel works emphasized to workers how dangerous conveyor belts could be. The inspector explained that the motors were very powerful and that the chances of coming out alive if you became tangled up in a belt were remote. The opportunity was taken to explain that accidents on conveyor belts were common. The manager accompanying the inspector supported this by pointing out one of his oldest workers in the control area who had lost an arm in a conveyor belt accident fifteen years ago. Not only did inspectors relate accidents to particular machines and particular injuries, they also referred to national statistics to impress upon the regulated the dangers which they might encounter in their working environment.

In some respects reference to specific accidents gave inspectors the greatest enforcement advantage. They were able to urge the speedy improvement of other outstanding matters. This was especially the case where inspectors had previously warned that they were concerned about aspects of a site and these warnings were not heeded by the company. IAPIs had warned a battery manufacturer that they were concerned that they had only one means of arrestment and no secondary back-up. The firm claimed that no back-up was necessary. But while the inspectorate's sampling team was on site there was an incident in which the filter system failed and, with no back-up system, the atmosphere was polluted. The sampling team took samples and these had given the inspectorate the proof it wanted to go back to the company and argue for a secondary back-up. As the inspector I accompanied pointed out, the inspectorate was no longer talking about a hypothetical situation, since it had evidence that the best practicable means requirements were not being met.

Some inspectors would take the opportunity of the evidence provided by an accident to highlight more general problems. A REI's accident report noted that the investigation of the accident had revealed a variety of malpractices. The inspector commented that 'had the accident not occurred' the malpractices 'would probably have been condoned or overlooked by managerial and supervisory staff'.

The evidence of an accident might also prompt inspectors to prosecute a company for its non-compliance. The majority of RI prosecutions followed accidents, and approximately half of all FI's prosecutions resulted from responding to accidents and dangerous occurrences (Hutter and Lloyd-Bostock, 1990, p. 418; Lloyd-Bostock, 1988). The reasons for this vary. In some cases the clear evidence of non-compliance provided by an accident was felt to increase the certainty of a successful prosecution and hence justify the resources and effort that might be put into assembling a case. This might fulfil perceived needs for either general or specific deterrence. One inspector expressed the view that it was 'vital' to investigate accidents and take the opportunity of 'making the point' as forcefully as possible.

But there was a reluctance to prosecute someone who had suffered severe injuries in an accident. This was often explained in terms of anticipated jury sympathy with the accused, the suspicion being that juries might not be sympathetic to the prosecution of someone who, while possibly causing the accident, had also been a victim of that accident. However, this would be a relevant factor only in a Crown Court prosecution and, as these were rare, it may be that inspectors also felt ambivalent about prosecuting such cases. Indeed, some inspectors were quite open about their ambivalence about prosecuting after an accident. They felt that they should consider the severity of the offence and not the injury, but most found it impossible to differentiate the two. A Principal FI always told inspectors to ask themselves whether or not they would have prosecuted had they come across circumstances that led to the accident but without the accident itself occurring. I asked several inspectors how they would answer this question: some said that they would still have prosecuted, but others said that in all honesty they would probably have given those concerned a 'good telling-off'.

Inspectors were therefore highly ambivalent about accidents. While accidents provided good enforcement opportunities most inspectors were of the opinion that their main job was preventative and that prosecution after an accident was acting too late, since the accident should never have happened. This did not mean, however, that inspectors blamed themselves in the event of an accident. Health and safety matters were ultimately seen as the responsibility of the regulated.

Accidents, especially nasty ones, had an impact on all inspectors, particularly if they were responsible for investigation.[19] At the most basic level they could be upset by seeing injuries or bodies, especially those tangled in machines. Several inspectors commented that it was psychologically easier to look at a photograph of a fatality than visit a vic-

---

[19] See generally Hutter and Lloyd-Bostock, 1990.

tim who had been permanently crippled or the victim of a chemicals accident where scalding or serious burns might have resulted and where the chances of survival were low and the injuries extremely painful. Hence serious injuries might have disturbed inspectors more than accidents involving fatalities. One of the strategies inspectors employed to cope with the horror of accidents was to talk about them. Not only did this appear cathartic, but it also seemed to enhance the solidarity among colleagues. Indeed some REIs, who were recruited largely from the railway industry, sought common ground with those they regulated through their discussions about their involvement in major railway disasters (Hutter and Lloyd-Bostock, 1990, p. 418).

The impact of accidents upon the enforcement practices of individual inspectors was discernible in their routine inspections. Investigation of especially unpleasant accidents could lead to inspectors paying particular attention to what had caused these when inspecting other sites. In effect, therefore, accidents were significant in forming what some people would refer to as inspectors' 'hobby horses'. In some cases inspectors would be especially alert to the activities of particular firms as a result of investigating either a horrific accident on one of their sites or a series of accidents on their premises. A complicating factor here may have been an inspector's perception that certain companies did not treat the victims of their accidents very well.

The publication of accident reports was often followed up by inspectors visiting similar sites and inspecting them in light of the report, which they hoped to publicize during their visits. This was routine for REIs who regularly publicized the results of 1871 inquiries within the industry. FIs also engaged in a series of visits following the publication of a special accident report. I accompanied several inspectors involved in follow-up visits after the publication of the *Report on a Petroleum Spillage at Micheldever Oil Terminal, Hampshire, 2 February 1983* (HSE, 1984(a)). The report followed FI's investigation of an incident in which approximately ninety tonnes of petroleum spirit was spilled while being off-loaded from rail tank wagons. The investigation revealed a variety of problems and made recommendations for improvements in the design and construction of rail sidings and off-loading equipment and the methods of operation. The purpose of the report was to alert the industries to the potential dangers and initiate improvements. Following publication of the report FI and RI undertook a programme of petroleum siding inspections.

By definition accidents are only useful as a means of assessment when, and because, something has already gone wrong. Their use as a means of assessing compliance is therefore retrospective, although they may have predictive value to the extent that 'past record' is usually taken to be one indicator of future performance. Another sense in which accidents may be regarded as prospective is when a series of minor accidents, or perhaps even one accident, alerts inspectors to a larger problem which, if unchecked, has the potential to pose serious danger to health, safety, or the environment. This could be, for instance, problems with a particular type of machine or substance, or perhaps with a system of work. Inspectors found accidents especially important as a means of assessing compliance in large chemical works where an accident might have been the only indication that procedures were not being properly adhered to. One FI felt that accidents on large, apparently well-run sites, were worth investigating to the extent that they might indicate problem areas. Indeed, part of most inspectors' basic inspections included looking at the firm's own accident book. The importance of accidents as a monitor of compliance is indicated by reactions to the non-reporting of accidents, where their discovery of this[20] might well result in a visit to the site which would not have taken place if the accident had been officially reported.

Accidents are, of course, only a means of assessing compliance in relation to safety, not health. Whereas the effects of non-compliance with safety-related matters are often immediate and tangible, non-compliance with respect to health issues typically has long-term effects. For example, the adverse effects of a breakdown in matters relating to health may take years to manifest themselves; hence sampling may be the most appropriate method of assessment in such circumstances.

Accidents are costly to investigate. HSC estimated that the costs of assisting the court of inquiry into the King's Cross fire amounted to £750,000 (HSC, 1988, p. 4). The Foreword to the 1988 *Annual Report* made it very clear that '[t]he Inspector's main preoccupation in 1988 was to respond to the manifest public concern about railway safety in the aftermath of the King's Cross fire' (Department of Transport, 1989, p. v). This included an Inspecting Officer of Railways serving as an adviser to the court of inquiry; inspectors paying greater attention to the London Underground; and a senior inspector joining a review team to consider the management of safety at stations on the London Underground. The report makes it quite explicit that other work had

---

[20] Often inspectors were alerted to problems by safety representatives. See Ch. 7 for a discussion of safety representatives.

been delayed by this accident and its aftermath (*ibid.*, p. v). The use of inspectorate resources in this way has not passed without comment. Cheit (1990, p. 75), in his study of standard-setting, cautions against placing too much emphasis on accidents—'[a]ccidents precipitate strong political pressures for regulatory change, but they provide little factual basis for making meaningful improvements.' In some cases accident investigation, especially public investigations, is an institutionalized way of handling social and political concern about accidents (Hutter, 1992). Some regard this as a means of protecting organizational interests:

> Both a manifest and a latent function of regulatory agencies when an accident does occur is to assure us that we shall find out why it happened and to assure us that it will not happen again. Manifestly, they should investigate to search for a causal explanation of the accident (a seeming contradiction) or conduct research on harms that gain operating intelligence for those who may be thought responsible for the harm. Latently, such investigation protects the interests of organizations that are liable for harms and may indeed absolve a particular organization from liability. The terms of such investigations, as Perrow (1984) notes, are to protect organizational interests by holding individuals responsible for particular decisions. Latently also, such investigations and actions based upon them are intended to assure us that corrective actions will be taken [Reiss 1992, pp. 307–8].

Accidents, especially disasters, draw the work of the regulatory agency to the public notice. Its activities become subject to outside scrutiny and judgement and it may feel under pressure, especially from the media, to seek out personal culprits for what has gone wrong (Gusfield, 1981). In such a climate accidents may be interpreted as moral and blameworthy, rather than neutral and technical (Douglas, 1985). The dangers of blaming individuals for an organizational or systems failure are significant, not least because this can mitigate against the wider lessons of an accident investigation being drawn and exploited. Undoubtedly the costs and benefits of each case vary and in some instances a more considered approach to accidents is to be advocated (Hutter and Lloyd-Bostock, 1990).

PROACTIVE AND REACTIVE ENFORCEMENT: ASSESSING THE
BALANCE

Inspectorates needed to strike a balance between pro- and reactive work. Their resources were not only finite but were quite strictly limited during the research period. Each inspectorate, under the guidance of HSE, set its own priorities. The programmes it set had to take account of its full range of activities—defining, achieving, and monitoring compliance.

Proactive work was accorded central importance by all inspectorates. The HSC 1987–8 *Annual Report* stated: '[t]he effort we expend in a reactive way in investigating accidents and complaints cannot represent a substitute for a credible programme of preventive inspection' (1988, p. 30). This allocation of resources was very much in keeping with the broadly accommodative approach to enforcement adopted by all of the inspectorates in the study (HSC, 1988, p. 45). Yet there were limitations on their ability to fulfil these proactive programmes of work. The reactive work undertaken by these inspectorates was unpredictable. We have already seen how accidents—in particular major ones—could consume large amounts of time and money. 'An increasing volume of public complaints and questions about industrial harms outside the workplace' (HSC, 1990b, p. 3) were also time-consuming and could involve correspondence, meetings with complainants and also public meetings. In addition to this, preventive inspections were interrupted by inspectorate involvement with promoting new regulations (such as the COSHH Regulations 1988) and by inexperience among a growing proportion of new inspectors (this being a particular problem at the time of fieldwork for this study) (Ch. 2; HSC, 1990, p. 3).

SELF-REGULATION

The methods of monitoring compliance discussed in this Chapter are distinguished by the fact that it is the enforcement agency which undertakes the assessment. This is in direct contrast to self-regulation, which would place the main responsibility for health and safety and environmental control on a business and its employees. To varying degrees this has always been the case. Nevertheless the Robens Committee felt that the responsibilities of people in the workplace should be re-emphasized and argued that self-inspection should occupy a central position, with the activities of the regulatory agencies being supplementary (Robens Report, para. 219). Moreover, it was argued that inspectorate resources should be concentrated on 'problem areas' and 'spot checks' rather than regular, systematic assessments.

The intention of self-regulation is that business will undertake its own audits and impose its own rules and disciplines for health and safety and environmental control. There are a number of advantages to this system. For example, it is cost-effective; it is said to foster good business–government relationships; and it is sufficiently flexible to be adapted to different situations. Other advantages centre on business's superior access to information relevant to regulation and its superior resources to monitor compliance (see generally Braithwaite, 1984; Di Mento, 1986). But while all of this may be very convincing in theory, the whole system is in practice dependent upon the willingness of business to self-regulate. The views of the Robens Committee seem to be premised on an idealistic view of human and corporate behaviour. This approach assumes that an organization, and those within it, can be trusted on its own to maintain ideals of health and safety as equal to, or even above, those of profit, productivity, and more comfortable industrial relations. As Di Mento writes, '[t]he audit strategy is based on a belief that, for the most part, non-compliance is an aberration that does not result from any deliberate business attempt to circumvent environmental rules' (1986, p. 55). The more cynical argue that non-compliance may be calculated, the argument being that business has little incentive to comply, especially when the compliance costs are simply for the purposes of health and safety or the environment and have no other beneficial spin-offs. Moreover, businesses vary with respect to their capacity, ability, and willingness to collect information and to comply. The evidence of this research suggests that while self-regulation might be desirable it was not sufficient to maintain acceptable levels of compliance. Even in those cases where inspectors were in close and frequent contact with the regulated they still felt the need to check and recheck levels of compliance. This was the case even where self-regulation included the continuous monitoring of, for example, emissions (see HSE, 1981b, para. 5). Indeed, the proactive programmes organized by FI, IAPI, and RI were very much geared to monitoring industry's self-regulation. But as HSC's 1987–8 *Annual Report* states '[e]ven major companies with the resources to carry out self-inspection continue to make serious mistakes' (1988, p. 45).

There were a number of reasons for this. A central reason was that monitoring compliance—even more so than defining compliance—was a continuing activity, so inspectors wanted to check that a business's own methods of assessing compliance were adequate and not in danger of becoming complacent. Moreover, they needed to keep in touch with developments in a workplace so that they knew about possible closures or new works and knew those responsible for health and safety or environmental control.

As I have explained elsewhere (1986), it is difficult to quantify the impact of inspectors' activities, hence it is hard to assess the effects if they were to be withdrawn. In many respects, one's predictions on this subject depend upon one's views about the ability and willingness of business to comply in the absence of agency vigilance. Regardless of one's optimism or pessimism concerning willingness to comply, it remains the case that if inspectors were to cease their regular assessments of firms then business would lose a valuable source of advice and education, this being especially the case for smaller firms who generally cannot afford to employ specialist advisors. Likewise inspectors would themselves lose valuable ties and sources of information.

CONCLUSIONS

Reactive methods of monitoring compliance are public and visible. They bring both the individual inspector and the inspectorate into direct contact with the victims of non-compliance. In such situations their actions are subject to the scrutiny and judgement of colleagues and those outside the regulatory organization. Hence there are symbolic and instrumental reasons to handle such cases with particular caution, promptness, and thoroughness.

Reactive enforcement highlights the tensions inherent in regulatory control, such as how one assesses the costs and benefits of regulation, or weighs up complainants' expectations with the limits of the law. It involves a complex of interpretative judgements which may have implications for the definition of compliance. In the case of complaints judgements are made about the validity of a complaint and the motives of the complainant. If the complaint is regarded as genuine then inspectors are likely to employ a strict definition of compliance and demand full compliance as soon as can be achieved within the limits of the law. Accidents tend to present inspectors with more clear-cut evidence of non-compliance, and hence they may lead to legal action more readily than, for instance, non-compliance discovered proactively. This is not only because of possible external scrutiny of the inspectorate but also because this represents the negative side of regulatory work: it is enforcement prompted by something actually having gone wrong rather than preventing harm. The information inspectors gather in their investigation of complaints and accidents gives them vital clues about those they regulate. So it is, in effect, another form of surveillance which may be used to assess compliance and predict future performance.

There needs to be a balance between the different methods regulatory officials use to monitor compliance. The methods they employ partly depend on the type of activity they regulate and the resources they have at their disposal. Reactive enforcement is costly in inspectorate time and resources, and sometimes this may be to the detriment of their proactive work. But reactive work provides an important opportunity for regulatory officials to demonstrate the significance of their work. It also subjects them to greater scrutiny and less discretion. Undoubtedly inspectors collect vital information through their monitoring of compliance. This information is used to inform the working definition of compliance and influences the methods used to secure compliance. Vitally it brings inspectors into direct contact with the regulated. Much of the focus is upon *who* is regulated rather than what is regulated and it is to this subject that we now turn our attention.

PART 4

Interactions between Inspectors and the Regulated

Defining, achieving, and maintaining compliance is an interactive process. Inspectors interact with, respond to, and try to guide the regulated; and out of these interactions compliance is defined, achieved, maintained, and changed. The regulated are the software of a site, they are as important as, if not more important than, the hardware of buildings and machines. But who are they? Certainly they are not as homogenous a group as the term 'the regulated' might lead us to believe. Inspectors regulated a wide range of corporate entities and individuals which they had to understand for enforcement purposes. Chapter 7 examines how inspectors' interactions with groups comprising those normally defined as 'the regulated' influenced the meaning of compliance. Chapter 8 considers how these interactions influenced inspectors' enforcement decisions.

7   Whose Compliance?

The regulated population comprises industries; individual companies and businesses; and employers, managers, and employees. Some of these groupings are complex, well organized, and multi-national, whereas others are simple, small-scale, and local. Compliance may vary between different sectors of an industry, and even between different parts of one site. Moreover, compliance may change over time. At an organizational level the focus of inspectors was upon safe systems of work, and at the micro level upon categories of people, for instance, employers and employees; specialists and generalists; skilled and unskilled; and the experienced and inexperienced.

Industries

The Robens Committee recommended tripartite consultations between inspectorates, trade unions, and employers' associations, a recommendation accepted and included in the HSW Act. Indeed, the HSC includes representatives from unions, industry, and local government. As this might indicate, much of the interaction that went on between inspectorates and industry happened at a *national* level and involved senior inspectors and company directors and industry associations. Indeed, many of these meetings were regular, fixed appointments, the intention of which was to sort out programmes of work and to secure the commitment of the representatives of an industry to proposed improvements in standards and working practices.

Chief and Deputy Chief IAPIs and RIs met regularly with representatives of industry. Within the FI these meetings were of two main kinds, the first involving liaison between industry and the NIG inspectors and the second involving industry and inspectors working in the policy branches of the inspectorate. HSE policy-makers were also involved in industry-level meetings if new guidelines or regulations were under consideration (see Baldwin, 1995). HSE also organized regular industry-based meetings of inspectorate, employer, and employee representatives, known as industrial advisory committees. RIAC (the Railway Industry Advisory Committee), for instance, met regularly, was chaired by the Chief RI, and included RIs, HSE representatives, industry representatives, personnel from the main railway unions, and a TUC representative. Its remit was to overview health and safety matters in the industry, identify areas of improvement, investigate any particular problems, and work out strategies for future action. These committees were discussed in the HSE's *Annual Reports*. Likewise, the Chief IAPI sometimes referred to his inspectorate's meetings in his *Annual Report*. The 1975 report, for example, mentions an annual meeting with representatives of the cement industry which 'discussed the question of a revision of our standard of particulate emission for new cement kilns' (HSE, 1977, para. 332). Sometimes these visits involved more than one inspectorate, as the IAPI 1980 *Annual Report* reveals:

Representatives of the Alkali Inspectorate, the Industrial Pollution Inspectorate for Scotland and the FI met representatives of British Steel Corporation and British Independent Steel Producers Association (BISPA) in December for the annual informal discussion on matters of mutual concern. The items included a review of progress on pollution control, proposals to amend the list of scheduled works and the reformatting and revision of Notes on Best Practicable Means [1982a, para. 167].

Senior inspectors in IAPI explained that they felt very dependent upon industry for information. Moreover, they needed time to 'soften up' industry to improve standards. The purpose of these meetings was to provide an opportunity to discuss any particular or persisting problem, policy issues, standards, or international developments, and to monitor progress. They also gave inspectors the opportunity to raise possibilities and plant ideas. Inspectors hoped that nothing they asked for would be a surprise, because they would have prepared the path ahead and these meetings would serve as implicit deadlines by which decisions would be made and action taken. In many respects the approach taken by senior inspectors towards industry representatives mirrored the approach taken at field level by more junior inspectors. Thus compliance was regarded as a long-term activity and there was constant negotiation to raise standards and change the definition of compliance.

The way in which different industries were regarded by inspectors was closely related to the type of activity they were involved in. In some industries attention to health and safety might have been imperative to the safety and viability of the whole site, so there was a self-interest in compliance (Genn, 1993). For example, chemical and petroleum works could precipitate a disaster if they paid insufficient attention to their operations. In other industries, such as precision engineering, care was regarded as an integral part of the work. In these cases inspectors worried less about the software of the site yet were required to visit the sites, often because of the theoretical risks posed by the activities undertaken there. Inspectors needed to ensure that the highest standards were maintained as far as they were able to do so.[1] Other industries had less impressive images attached to them. For example, the building industry and scrap metal merchants both had a reputation for paying scant attention to health and safety and environmental issues. But this image was related not only to the heavy, manual nature of the work undertaken there, but also to the unskilled workforce that might have been employed and to the accident or pollution records of these industries. The construction industry, for example, is and always has been particularly hazardous. Accident rates in this industry have been high, often exceeding those in manufacturing.[2] Attitudes in sectors of construction have caused HSE concern, and numerous campaigns and enforcement initiatives have been targeted at the industry in order to try to improve standards of health and safety (HSC, 1983, 1987, 1990a). This contrasts sharply with the image of the chemical industry, described in the 1990 *Annual Report* as 'currently one of Britain's most vigorous, and . . . in the forefront of modern technology. Investment ascribed to health, safety and environmental protection is claimed to be 15% of total investment' (1990a, p. 3).

It should not be deduced from this that inspectors automatically welcomed high technology, computerized, and automated workplaces. Members of all three inspectorates expressed concern about over-reliance on machines and were worried that the ability of workers and operators to know what to do if the machinery broke down might be impaired. Another factor taken into account when inspectors were characterizing industries was the way in which work was organized. For example, some industries and jobs required high levels of individual discretion. Many jobs on the railways fell into this category, especially those involving trackside work, which posed particular risks and the

[1] This was partly to protect the position of the agency and in response to perceived public expectations that regulatory agencies keep a careful eye on high risk sites. Ironically this may have been unnecessary given the self-interest these sites had to comply (see above).

[2] For example, in 1984 there were 100 fatal injuries in the construction industry compared to 290 fatal injuries in *all* industries and services (including the construction industry). In 1988 95 of the 254 reported fatal injuries were in the construction industry (HSC, 1988, p. 5).

requirement for particular systems of work which the inspectors would be keen to monitor.

A final point which should perhaps be noted about inspectors' interactions at an industry level was their role as a source of information. Inspectors visited a wide range of sites and saw a variety of practices, placing them in a better position than many others to suggest ways of complying with the law and knowing where to find particular types of safety or pollution-control equipment. But inspectors were careful not to be too specific in their recommendations so as to avoid responsibility if the solution did not work. Rather they passed on information about who to consult and how to go about considering the different alternatives to particular problems. In some cases inspectors may have sought out sources of information for companies, or were able to provide more specific information about the whereabouts of information, expertise, and even machinery within the same company. A REI I accompanied was able to tell the manager of a locomotive shed where he could dispose of some machinery he no longer wanted, since the inspector knew of another works in the region which was looking for a similar machine.

Companies

Bardach and Kagan (1982) referred to 'good apples' and 'bad apples' when characterizing the types of companies inspectors encounter. In reality inspectors operated with much finer gradations, referring to 'poor', 'reasonable', 'fairly good', 'responsible', 'very good', and 'exemplary' companies. A variety of factors were taken into account in determining how inspectors regarded individual companies, and these accorded in part to the FI's rating system (see Chapter 6). Six main criteria arose as significant in this research. First was inspectors' perceptions of the *company's commitment* to health and safety or the environment. This had a number of facets, including consideration of the time, energy, and finances the company devoted to health and safety or the environment. For example, a particular foundry was regarded as having very good standards, in part because it had devoted a lot of money and time to researching into and manufacturing safety clothing for its workers. This was considered to be particularly commendable in an industry which was generally regarded as having low, and sometimes Dickensian, standards. Also important in determining a company's commitment was the *attitude its staff had towards compliance.*

Where staff were safety-conscious and co-operative then a company was described positively, but where inspectors detected obstinacy to their suggestions and sloppiness among managers and employees the characterization was negative. A REI explained that he assessed how safety-conscious staff on a site were by looking at the general state of tidiness and the state of their records, for example, their scaffold registers (Hutter, 1986).

Closely related to the above was the third criterion identified, namely the company's *past record of compliance.* This included not only the extent to which it had complied with inspectors' recommendations but also the speed with which it had complied, its accident rate, and the level of complaint against it. A fourth criterion was the *quality of management* on site, including the management's record in responding to inspectors' demands and its record in imposing discipline about health and safety or environmental requirements amongst the workforce. Fifthly, inspectors considered a company's *ability to comply.* This included both its financial position and the degree of technical knowledge it possessed. A slag-crushing company described as 'very poor' by an IAPI was typical of a company falling into this category—the company was described as opportunist, and its owner perceived to be in need of a great deal of education about how to run the plant both safely and without causing environmental pollution. In comparison to this a chemical works was described as 'responsible' because its staff knew in advance what the standards and requirements were and usually adhered to them, unless they thought that there was good reason not to, when they would discuss this with inspectors. A sixth criterion centred upon a company's *treatment of its workforce.* The description by FIs of two different construction sites is illustrative. One was described as 'poor', partly because it provided no welfare facilities whatsoever for the contract staff working on its site. Another was regarded as 'exemplary' on the basis of its provision of good welfare facilities, such as a subsidized canteen, and high standards of housekeeping. Again this was regarded as especially commendable in an industry where these were unusual.

Typically inspectors would characterize a company on the basis of several of the above criteria. FIs, for instance, described a mill as 'very poor' because it failed to satisfy many of the above criteria. It persistently refused to comply with inspectors' demands, failing to do some things, making very slow progress on other items, and generally finding excuses for inaction. The company had a poor record of maintaining discipline within the mill; for example, guarding was often removed and there was no insistence by management that it be restored. Moreover, the company was generally perceived as having a 'poor attitude' and 'poor abilities'. An asbestos-stripping company, in contrast, was described by the IAPIs responsible for it as 'exemplary'. Its owner was found to be very co-operative and willing to invest a lot of time, money, and effort to get things right. Moreover, he was prepared to exceed the legal minimum standards upon the inspectorate's recommendation. And once again the company was run by someone whose profession/industry was generally regarded as being 'poor', a yardstick against which inspectors seemed to judge individual companies.

These characterizations of companies had important implications for the way in which inspectors regarded compliance and the action they would initiate in the case of non-compliance. For example, inspectors' assessments of an employer's attitude to health and safety were significant in their decision whether or not to initiate legal action and, if so, whether to opt for a notice or prosecution. If an employer was regarded by inspectors to have a generally good attitude towards health and safety and there were only one or two problems the inspector was concerned to remedy, then it was likely that a notice would be selected as the most appropriate enforcement tool. In contrast, prosecution was more likely in the case of an employer who was generally or persistently not complying with health and safety demands.

Improvement notices were often a response to sluggishness or lack of response to inspectorate demands. As the Chief IAPI explains, referring to an improvement notice served in 1985: '[t]he notice was served because the inspector was not satisfied that the works was taking sufficiently strenuous action to make the improvements considered necessary to provide adequate control of emissions' (HSE, 1986a, p. 3).

Similarly, several improvement notices were issued by a FI I accompanied in the case of a woollen mill which persistently displayed inaction or slow progress. Remedial work had not been undertaken on several machines so the inspector considered that the notices were necessary 'to clear up the remaining work . . . to conclude the affair'. Another FI referred to improvement notices as an 'insurance policy' where informal agreements had already been reached. None of this implies that notices were not regarded seriously by inspectors. One FI told me that when he issued a notice he always told the recipients of notices that they were lucky not to have been prosecuted. Similar views were expressed in a letter to the owner of a foundry who had failed to comply fully with a FI's demands: 'some serious matters . . . still remained outstanding. I am therefore obliged to take enforcement action and you will find enclosed various Improvement Notices which require you to remedy certain defects by a specified date. Failure to do so renders you liable to prosecution'.

It was not unknown for a business to be subject to both a notice and prosecution, especially a prohibition notice followed by prosecution. The crucial factor here was the severity of non-compliance and the high degree of hazard posed. If an improvement notice was not complied with within the time period specified then prosecution was also probable.

Poor treatment of the workforce was another factor which could increase the probability of legal action for non-compliance. One such example stood out from my research. It involved the investigation of a non-reportable accident which had occurred five months earlier, in which an employee at a mill had had three fingers severely lacerated while repairing machinery. Before visiting the mill the FI had not considered this a likely case for prosecution, but during the course of investigation the FI clearly started to look for evidence which could be used to construct a case for prosecution. After the visit the FI confirmed that prosecution was being considered, and that this search for evidence was prompted by the news that the victim of the accident had been treated very badly by the company while he was recuperating from the accident. He had been given the legal minimum support, something which was evidently perceived by the FI as morally unjust given the circumstances of the accident.

The *ownership and size* of a company could also be significant in determining inspectors' interactions with it. Inspectors could spend large portions of their time educating and advising the self-employed and small businesses. These were the least likely to know about the law and how to comply. Indeed, Dawson *et al.* (1988, p. 261) found that the gap between standards of health and safety in large and small firms was considerable. This accords with HSC's view. In its 1987–8 *Annual Report* it was reported that: '[m]any of the 19,000 new workplaces visited were found to be working in ignorance of legal requirements and basic standards for occupational health, safety and welfare' (HSC, 1988, p. 49). Large companies, by contrast, were likely to have their own health and safety or environmental departments and even legal departments. However, the sites of small firms were generally visited less frequently than those of large ones, not because they were at less risk of accidents—on the contrary they seem to have a higher risk of accident

(HSC, 1987, p. 20)—but because the risks of catastrophe were usually lower. Inspectors were also likely to spend much longer at the sites of larger companies because their sites took much longer to inspect than those of small companies. Whereas a small site could take less than an hour to inspect, inspectors sometimes took days, or even weeks, to inspect some large sites. As a result they often developed quite close relationships with those on these sites.[3]

Small businesses posed HSE a variety of problems in terms of inspection, partly through their sheer numbers and partly because there were problems in identifying them, especially as many did not notify HSE of their existence (HSC, 1987, p. 20). This said, FIs in particular devoted a large proportion of their time to visiting the multitude of small premises under their jurisdiction. In 1988–9, for example, 58 per cent of FI visits to fixed establishments were made to sites employing fewer than twenty-five people (HSC, 1990a, p. 4). Moreover, HSE has set up a Small Firms Working Group (HSC, 1990, p. 12) which, amongst other things, advises on publicity which the organization is trying to target on small firms (HSC, 1988, p. 14).

Dealing with small firms was especially the province of FIs. RI dealt primarily with British Railways but also interacted with some middle-sized firms, such as London Transport, and in the case of the minor railways it also regulated voluntary organizations which needed considerable education and encouragement (Department of Transport, 1984, p. vi). IAPIs mostly, but not exclusively, regulated larger companies.

Large firms present inspectors with different problems. An IAPI explained that in large companies local managers may not have the authority to act without reference to their headquarters, so getting anything done could take a very long time, especially if large expenditure was required. By comparison, when inspectors were dealing with small companies they could go straight to the managing director and say what improvements they wanted. Another possible problem for inspectors when dealing with large companies was the circulation of staff within the company. Changes in personnel were like changes in ownership. They could be beneficial, but equally they could introduce complications to the inspectorates' relationship with a particular site.

---

[3] This was partly for instrumental reasons such as engendering greater co-operation and easier access to information which companies could withhold from inspectors. See Ch. 8.

Differential enforcement according to size of organization is a persistent feature of regulatory enforcement. Researchers in the United States, Australia, and the United Kingdom (Grabosky and Braithwaite, 1986; Lynxwiler *et al.*, 1983; Snider, 1987) have all noted a tendency for formal legal enforcement action to figure less prominently in regulatory officials' dealings with larger and more powerful organizations than in their dealings with small organizations. Yeager (1991, p. 282) for example, found that in one region of the US Environmental Protection Agency large companies were twice as likely to receive no-action determinations and half as likely to receive warning letters as small firms. The reasons for this are various. Grabosky and Braithwaite (1986, p. 215 ff.) found that Australian regulatory officials believed that big business was more law-abiding than small business. Snider (1987, p. 49) similarly identified ideological reasons for this tendency, namely that 'regulators tend to believe that only "fly by night" organizations typically stoop to crime' (cf. Carson, 1982; Braithwaite, 1984). This belief may be partially related to the capacity of organizations to comply. For instance, larger companies are most likely to support compliance staff in a safety or environmental department (Grabosky and Braithwaite, 1986), and they may also enjoy regulatory economies of scale (Yeager, 1991, pp. 42 ff., 291 ff.). Larger companies also have a greater capacity to challenge compliance, including negotiation with other regulatory officials, appeals against legal action, and influence over the political process (Snider, 1987; Yeager, 1991).

Large companies could, ironically, pose problems for inspectors because they had 'too much' knowledge. Thus they were less susceptible to 'bluffing' and inspectors could also tend against legal action since they perceived it to be more difficult to construct a case against a larger, well-informed company than a smaller, ill-informed one. Indeed, to the extent that the sites of larger companies were larger and more complicated than those of smaller business, it could be more difficult and more time-consuming to construct a legal case against them (Snider, 1987, p. 49). Moreover, as Di Mento points out, '[s]ize correlates with differentiation in a firm and the greater the differentiation the greater the possibility of non-compliance' (1986, p. 156; see also Vaughan, 1982). It should also be noted that inspectors had greater opportunities to develop relationships with staff from larger companies, which typically received more frequent and lengthier visits from inspectors than smaller sites (see Chapter 9). It is to the question of how inspectors perceived and dealt with organizations that we now turn.

ORGANIZATIONS

Bardach and Kagan, writing about American Occupational Safety and Health Inspectors, note:

The legalistic ethos . . . induces inspectors to treat business corporations as monolithic legal entities, with a single will and an internally consistent attitude towards social and legal responsibility. To corporate managers . . . the corporation is a loose conglomeration of separate departments and managers, each with distinct problems, some very responsible and some less so [1982, p. 81].

The large majority of the inspectorates in my sample regarded organizations in much the same way as did the American managers described by Bardach and Kagan, but very few adopted the stance of the American inspectors. Within large companies inspectors differentiated between areas, both across sites and within sites. Particular departments caused special concern to inspectors. One railway company was regarded as having a particularly poor department, because of laxity in keeping adequate records, poor discipline, and (it was suspected) inadequately trained staff. One steel works was regarded by FIs as having 'good' and 'bad' areas, with sectional managers being cited as the key to how areas were categorized.

It may take inspectors a long time to become familiar with some very large and complex organizations, a task which may be made more difficult by reorganizations. British Railways is perhaps a good example, since its national organization was differentiated both on a regional basis and according to specialisms such as civil engineering, mechanical and electrical engineering, signals and telecommunications, and operations. Not only was this a complicated organization in itself but it was not a static organization. Each of the parts might be reorganized, leaving members of the RI with the problem of not knowing whom to contact, especially if jobs were awkwardly defined. However, some inspectors felt that reorganizations could help them if individual managers became responsible for larger areas, as inspectors would then need to contact fewer managers to effect improvements across a greater area.

Contact Persons

When they visited sites inspectors would invariably contact either an employer or a management representative. The contact person at each site varied. On some large and complicated sites inspectors contacted and were accompanied by specialized health and safety or environmental staff. Sometimes this responsibility would be held in conjunction with another organizational position. But if the business was financially well off, these regulatory matters could be the sole concern of a safety or environmental officer, who could be part of a whole health and safety or pollution department. Many sites did not employ such personnel and it was more likely that inspectors would communicate with works managers or sectional managers. In the case of small workshops and factories FIs were often accompanied by the owner of the business.

On 26 per cent of FI visits during this research inspectors were accompanied by the owner or director of a site; in 20 per cent of visits inspectors were accompanied by specialized safety personnel; and in 50 per cent of visits the contact person was a manager with responsibility for either the whole site or part of it. RI and IAPIs were more typically accompanied by managers. REIs were usually accompanied by area managers or their deputies, depending upon the aspects which were of particular interest to the inspector. REIs could therefore be joined by, for instance, station managers, engineers, or traffic controllers. In some departments specialized safety staff were available at regional level, but this was not widespread. The contact person for IAPIs was usually a works or sectional manager, or a chief chemist if the site was large enough to support one.

Inspectors expected to be in contact with senior personnel. One IAPI I accompanied waited some time at one site because no senior manager was immediately available to meet him. Other inspectors might have been content to be accompanied by someone more junior in these circumstances but none would have tolerated this for any length of time. Part of the reason for inspectors being so insistent that they communicated with senior personnel was that these people had more authority to effect changes and remedial work, and moreover they had this authority over a larger area of a site or company than did their more junior colleagues. In addition, the level at which they interacted with a company was regarded as a reflection of the status accorded to health and safety or environmental matters and to the inspectors themselves. Where inspectors met with these contact people regularly they would often build up quite a close working relationship and exchange personal information about families, illnesses, and holidays, in addition to information and news about the site. Certainly some inspectors thought it very important that they get on with their contact person, often for utilitarian reasons, namely that they would be given more information and co-operation in these circumstances. Inspectors and contact persons were involved in regular 'off-the-record' conversations where inspectors would gather information about such things as the company's future plans and personnel changes (see Chapter 8). It should not be deduced from this, however, that inspectors automatically got on with or respected their contact persons. These personnel were categorized like any others according to a variety of criteria.

Inspectors held ambivalent views about safety and environmental staff. On the one hand some inspectors would regard the absence of such specialist staff on large sites as symbolic that a company did not rate health and safety or the environment very highly. On the other hand, they might also be concerned that the existence of specialist departments and personnel carried with it the danger that health and safety, and to a more limited extent the environment, were seen as the preserve only of specialist personnel rather than the concern of everyone. This said, IAPIs in particular considered that the specialist environmental departments were acting very much as inspectors would, that is monitoring the whole site and possibly having the authority to issue internal notices and sanctions. Indeed, inspectors may have needed to rely heavily on a company's internal system as a means of securing compliance (Hawkins and Hutter, 1993). This was especially so with large and complex organizations.

Inspectors took careful note of the location of safety and environmental departments within the overall hierarchy of a company. Similarly they would take notice of the status of specialist personnel. If, for example, a large company did have a separate health and safety or environmental department but it was staffed by unqualified or junior staff then inspectors would be concerned about the status of health and safety or the environment within the company. If specialist staff were not sufficiently knowledgeable or senior to answer inspectors' questions or to effect action then inspectors would go above their heads. They would act similarly if they had no confidence in managers (see below under 'A Case of Incompetence and Recalcitrance').

Specialist staff were assessed according to three main criteria, namely their motivation to improve health and safety and the environment, the speed with which they acted to effect remedies and improvements, and the degree of honesty they were perceived to display in their interactions with inspectors. Specialist staff were valued not only in their own right but also for the impact they might have had on the workforce. A highly motivated safety officer, for example, was perceived to have a positive effect upon the workforce as his/her enthusiasm filtered down through the company.

In many respects the ways in which inspectors characterized and perceived their contact persons mirrored the way they regarded both companies and management in general. Before going on to discuss their views of management in more detail let us first consider the philosophy underlying the role of management and workforce in maintaining a healthy and safe workplace.

Managers and the Workforce

It was the intention of the Robens Committee that '[r]eform should be aimed at creating the conditions for more effective self-regulation by employers and work people jointly' (1972, para. 452), by making those involved understand that health and safety are their concern and not just the remit of external agencies. Health and safety, it was argued, should be the everyday concern of everyone involved in the workplace. Although health and safety were still seen as the primary responsibility of management 'the full co-operation and commitment of all employees' was regarded as essential to the promotion of health and safety in the workplace (1972, para. 59). Hence it was recommended that safety representatives should be appointed and joint safety committees should be set up to monitor the arrangements for health and safety. Not only should employers consult and involve employees in the promotion of health and safety in the workplace, but it was also recommended that inspectors should be as ready to discuss health and safety matters with the workforce and their representatives as they were to discuss them with management. Given this, the main role of the inspectorates should be to support industry in its own self-regulation.

The HSW Act 1974 places duties upon both employers and employees. Sections 2 and 3 of the Act focus particularly upon the responsibilities of employers to provide a healthy and safe working environment for their staffs. Sections 7 and 8, however, place duties upon employees, specifically to take responsibility for their own care and that of others, including an obligation not to interfere with anything provided for their health and safety or welfare. The Safety Representatives and Safety Committees Regulations of 1977 further provided for the provision and functions of trade-union safety representatives when they came into effect in 1978.

HSE policy governing the relationship between inspectors and management and members of the workforce was clear. Inspectors were expected to regard communications with employees as an integral part of inspection, to liaise with safety representatives where they existed, and to copy to them any letters resulting from inspections. In particular, inspectors were expected to maintain an impartial role.

In practice the sample inspectorates varied in their communications with management and workforce. IAPIs were in a different position from members of the other two inspectorates to the extent that they were not enforcing health and safety legislation and hence were not required to consult with the workforce in quite the same way as the other sample inspectors. Members of the RI informed management and safety representatives of their visits in advance, and all letters sent to management following visits included, as a matter of policy and practice, a sentence to the effect that the letter or accompanying schedule of matters needing remedy had either been copied to the appropriate safety representatives or should be brought to their attention by the manager. REIs, like other inspectors in the sample, copied to me letters written as a result of visits when I had accompanied them. In each case REI letters made provision for communication with safety representatives, and a documentary survey did not suggest that these visits were in any way unrepresentative. FIs informed management or the workforce of their impending visits only in exceptional circumstances, the norm being to visit unannounced. Inspectors differed in reporting their findings to both management and the workforce. Forty-seven letters were sent to employers and managers following visits, but only fourteen of these were copied to the workforce or its representatives.[4] Some inspectors sent individual letters to safety representatives; others asked employers to pass on a copy to the workforce or their representative.

All inspectors contacted management representatives upon their arrival at a site, and in the overwhelming majority of cases they would be accompanied by this representative during their visit. As discussed above, the contact person was always a management representative. This was perhaps not surprising, as the legislation and much of HSE policy places the primary responsibility for health and safety with management. Moreover, decisions about financial expenditure and safe sys-

---

[4] Some letters were copied directly to the workforce because no safety representatives had been appointed. This underlines the fact that letters should be copied to employees or their representatives.

tems of work or environmental policy were all within the remit of management rather than the workforce (see Hutter, 1993). No inspectors
invited safety representatives to accompany them on their routine
inspections of a site although they usually invited them to accompany
him for all or part of a visit where an accident or complaint was being
investigated.

Whether or not inspectors invited safety representatives to accompany them during their visits was a matter for discretion within the FI,
whereas it was a practice discouraged by the RI. What was not a matter for discretion for either inspectorate was the requirement to consult
the workforce representative (and communicate its findings to them).
All of the REIs I accompanied asked to see safety representatives on each
visit. They were not always successful, usually for reasons beyond their
control, such as the non-appointment of a safety representative or the
fact that the appointed person was working on a different shift. Likewise
all REIs copied their letters to safety representatives following visits. An
analysis of ninety-two visits on which I accompanied FIs reveals that
inspectors tried to contact safety representatives on seventeen occasions
and they were successful on fifteen of these. Twenty-five of the sites certainly had safety representatives but on forty-six sites either it was
known that there were no safety representatives or it was unlikely
because the factory was small or because the industry was largely non-
unionized. On the remaining twenty-one sites it was not clear whether
or not there were safety representatives, but the size of the site and the
activities undertaken there suggested that it was possible that safety representatives had been appointed. The important point is that sometimes
inspectors did not try to contact worker representatives. Neither did all
FIs communicate with safety representatives following visits. For example, the fourteen letters copied to employees and their representatives
by FIs were not sent by fourteen different inspectors, but by nine.
Individual inclinations and preferences seemed to be of paramount
importance here, as underlined by the file notes inspectors wrote following visits. Some inspectors always noted whether or not safety representatives had been appointed, and if so who they were. Not
surprisingly these were the inspectors who copied letters to employees.

While inspectors may not always formally have contacted worker
representatives they did speak to members of the workforce during the
course of their visits to sites. Employees were spoken to on forty-three
of the ninety-two FI visits analysed. An important function of a site visit
was to see what the workforce was doing. The extent to which this

translated into stopping to talk with employees varied between inspectorates and between inspectors. REIs were generally the most inclined to stop to have a general chat with employees. They would introduce themselves, explain their role, and check that employees were happy with their health and safety at work. Some FIs adopted a similar approach, but it was much more usual for FIs to talk to employees when they had evidence of non-compliance. Typically this would be failure to use the proper machine guards or to wear protective personal equipment such as ear protection, helmets, or adequate footwear. In some instances inspectors may have seen examples of non-compliance from afar—for example, from a train or car—and it was likely that they would then contact the manager responsible for the workforce. Indeed, inspectors would always first determine responsibility for a site before commenting upon instances of non-compliance they had witnessed. IAPIs regularly spoke to operators during the course of their visits to sites. They were keen to establish that those responsible for the production process understood how to work pollution-control equipment. Indeed, in some cases they informally supported bonus schemes which were related to the emission figures from particular sites.

In the case of occupational health and safety, inspectors would doubtless have welcomed incentive schemes which were specifically related to health and safety performance. But more typically bonus schemes were linked to productivity. This raised the fear that conditions would be created in which the workforce could be tempted to overlook health and safety issues in the interests of productivity and higher wages. Indeed in the recessionary period under consideration, the workforce might also be concerned about its job security. These issues all contributed to inspectors' assessment of the workforce and management and in turn their working definition of compliance and the degree to which firms were proactively monitored.

Variation in the interactions between inspectors and the workforce is interesting as it suggests that inspectors differed in the value they placed on workforce knowledge and opinions about the workplace. Ironically it was the most specialist and technically expert inspectorates (Hutter and Manning, 1990)—namely IAPI and RI—which appeared most committed to seeking the views of the workforce. Subsequent research I have undertaken into the impact of occupational health and safety legislation upon the railway industry suggests that the workforce is a valuable source of information (Hutter, forthcoming).

Management

As the above discussion indicates, inspectors' emphasis is in practice upon management. Indeed, their characterizations of sites often included reference to management, since how 'good' managers were perceived to be was considered to influence things greatly. One FI commented that site agents can be a good indicator of how compliant a construction site would be. Determining how 'good' or 'bad' managers were dependended on a variety of criteria which in many respects mirrored the criteria used for judging how a company was rated.

Perhaps not surprisingly, *acceptance of inspectors' recommendations* was one of the criteria against which inspectors judged managers. This comprised two parts, first the managers' willingness to accept inspectors' recommendations and suggestions, and, secondly, their ability to understand why certain health and safety or environmental provisions were necessary. One consideration here was whether or not managers treated inspectors' suggestions with enthusiasm or annoyance. Related to this was an assessment of *managers' ability to detect and remedy problems* on their own. Implicit in this was some consideration of a manager's expertise and more general intellectual abilities. In addition the ability of the manager to get things done within the company would be under scrutiny. Following a visit to a small chemical works one FI remarked: '[t]hat manager must be good at something—perhaps he's a good chemist, he's too timid for that job, he's got no initiative, he doesn't see problems for himself, they have to be pointed out, But he will do what I ask him and within a reasonable period of time.' Another FI, following a visit to a small steel works wrote to the General Manager: 'I was surprised to find so many simple items of guarding which were deficient considering that the area is on a safety audit and had been inspected recently by two safety officers.' Clearly the inspector was very concerned to find poor compliance when the works had so recently undergone a detailed examination of its risks and the systems it had in place for the safety of the workforce. As we can see, one consequence of this discovery was that the inspector wrote to a more senior official pointing out the safety officer's deficiencies. Another result of this was that inspectors visited such sites more frequently. By way of contrast IAPIs and a FI praised a particular coke-oven manager at a steel works for being conscientious in going beyond the minimum demands entirely unprompted by inspectors.

The *state of a site* was also one of the most basic criteria used to judge a site and the calibre of the person running it. At a simple level the standard of housekeeping was taken as indicative of the abilities of a manager to manage. One FI viewed with some dissatisfaction a tyre factory where the factory floor was dirty and untidy, which indicated to the inspector that time was not assigned for cleaning and emptying the bins, and the manager was unable to get the workforce to clean the place up.

Consistency was the final major criterion considered by inspectors. In many respects this accords with inspectors' definitions of aggregate compliance (see Chapter 4) whereby they considered the general state of compliance across a works and over time. As part of this process they took into account the performance of managers. This would include, for example, their behaviour towards inspectors, other managers, safety representatives, and the workforce; their ability to identify risks and remedy any deficiencies; and their ability and willingness to act upon inspectors' requests. This would be assessed over time—where there was sufficient contact between a site and the relevant inspectorate—to see how consistently managers responded. Erratic performance would concern inspectors, as would a consistently negative performance. Inspectors realized that everyone has their 'off days' and that their turning up could be the last straw. Only if managers were persistently rude or obstructive would inspectors take note and act upon this.

On occasions, particularly when dealing with new premises or personnel, inspectors would 'test' managers to see how much they knew or how much they were willing to reveal to inspectors. They did this in order to assess the trustworthiness of those they dealt with. They might, for example, have asked apparently innocent questions about processes with which they were fully acquainted in order to assess the accuracy of the answers they received. This technique was thus a check on the character of those in industry as inspectors waited to see if they were given accurate or misleading accounts. An IAPI I accompanied always asked sectional managers if they were having any environmental problems, thereby giving them the opportunity to tell him if anything was wrong and also giving the inspector the chance to assess the accuracy of the answer. On one site a sectional manager claimed that everything was in order, but during the course of the inspection the inspector discovered several problems. As a result of this the inspector's attitude towards the sectional manager changed markedly with the inspector adopting an altogether less friendly stance. The inspector determined that the sectional manager had known about the problems but had not done anything to remedy them because maintenance staff had been laid off. The inspector did not consider this sufficient justification for the problems identified, which he wanted remedied immediately. After the visit the inspector commented to me that in future he would be more suspicious of and severe with this manager as he had not been entirely honest with him.

In some situations inspectors and managers became allies rather than adversaries. Inspectors sometimes, for example, helped managers by writing letters demanding improvements that superiors might have been dragging their heels over. In some cases managers solicited inspectors' help. The safety officer and production manager of a factory employing some fifty people told a visiting FI that they were not altogether satisfied with the guarding proposed for some new machinery on order. The FI examined the proposals and agreed with these managers that there were problems, and agreed to support them. The inspector would return to the site and explain the problem to the directors, pointing out that other companies which had not provided more sophisticated guarding for these types of machines had been successfully prosecuted. The managers expressed their gratitude for this offer. In other contexts managers welcomed inspectors' visits because they had an impact upon the workforce. A construction site agent, for example, told me that he welcomed inspectors' visits, as they backed him up and made it clear that what he was asking for was demanded in law. There could, however, be difficulties if the inspector asked for less than the manager did. Inspectors also paid attention to the way in which managers were treated by their employers. An IAPI expressed some sympathy for a works manager who was not enthusiastically keeping a site up to scratch. The manager was poorly paid, indeed he was earning less than some of the workforce because he could not earn overtime, so the inspector appreciated that the manager might not be expected to be very conscientious.

There were circumstances when improvement notices might be requested by the regulated—not by employers but by managers in larger organizations. This usually happened when managers were repeatedly unable to persuade employers to spend money to achieve compliance and they considered that a notice would be the only means of convincing their employers to do so. Obviously not every manager would welcome an improvement notice. In some organizations the service of a notice could be a 'black mark' against a manager, and when this was the case the threat of a notice might have been sufficient to prompt the necessary action, if indeed this was within the capabilities of the local manager.

New managers were usually given time to prove themselves. Inspectors would start afresh in building up relationships with managers. This said, reputations did follow managers around and inspectors did pass on information about particular managers to other inspectors. The files held information about inspectors' confidence in management so information could pass from inspector to inspector in this way. In some cases inspectors would pass on verbal sketches of firms and managers to their successors. Where individual managers moved from site to site it was not unusual for their 'reputation' to move with them as information passed from one regional office of an inspectorate to another, albeit via a very informal network. Hence inspectors would often know, especially in the case of large companies, what to expect when they encountered a manager new to their area, because the inspector responsible for the manager's previous site would have passed on the information. While inspectors had not necessarily written 'black lists', some of them certainly had mental lists of people to keep a special eye on and warn other inspectors about.

Inspectors' opinions of managers were, of course, not static, and sometimes they changed quite quickly. A FI's opinion of a new manager of a brick factory was revised during the course of one visit. At the beginning of the visit the inspector noticed that very little had been done since the inspector's last visit to the site, including the failure to provide more secure guarding to machinery. The manager argued with the inspector about the feasibility of providing some of the guards, arguments not accepted by the inspector who later told me that at this stage the manager was regarded as rather unco-operative. However, during the rest of the visit the inspector's opinion was revised as the manager reacted more positively and sympathetically to some of the inspector's later requests and revealed a greater understanding of health and safety matters than he had originally conveyed. The inspector left the site with a rather more favourable impression of the manager than had originally been expected.

Where managers were regarded as especially poor inspectors manipulated the situation, perhaps writing directly to the managing director of a company to let him know of legal action being instituted against one of its works where inspectors had experienced problems with the local manager. In extreme cases inspectors might simply refuse to deal with managers they had no faith in. Instead they would by-pass these individuals and deal directly with those in more senior positions, making their reasons for this very clear to senior management. Where inspectors were in a long-term relationship with a company they sometimes took rather more elaborate steps to highlight the weaknesses of particular managers. Several such cases emerged during fieldwork, prominent among which was the case of a refinery where IAPIs were far from satisfied with the environmental staff employed. While this example involved specialist staff, such actions could equally well have been brought against any manager about whom the inspectorate was very concerned.

A Case of Incompetence and Recalcitrance

The inspectors responsible for refinery 'X' believed that the environmental staff were incompetent and insufficiently motivated in their work. This was demonstrated by the environmental officers' apparent failure to understand the types of monitor available to measure emissions from the stack or even the reasons monitors were needed. When I first accompanied the inspectors they were resolved to obtain the improvements they wanted and also to get rid of the environmental officers they were so dissatisfied with. They decided to register their discontent with senior managers and give the individuals concerned enough 'rope to hang themselves'. Over the course of the next eighteen months letters were regularly exchanged between inspectors and the company's environmental officers. Whenever the officers were slow to respond or the inspectors were dissatisfied with their reply then the inspectors would write to senior managers. Inspectors let the company concerned know informally that they were dissatisfied with the officers. Two months after I accompanied inspectors to this refinery it suffered an emergency shut-down, the cause being a problem dismissed by the environmental officers when inspectors first raised it with them.

Nevertheless, this incident did not have a salutary effect upon the company's environmental staff and the inspectorate's file reports continued to refer to the 'casual attitude' of refinery environmental officers. This situation went on for another five months until a major incident occurred: over 2,000 complaints about smell from the refinery were received in just four hours. The cause again was something the environmental officers had not taken steps to prevent when requested to do so by inspectors. This time the inspectors decided to exploit the incident. They arranged a meeting with the refinery manager and production manager. At this meeting they discussed the major incident and the inspectors raised the general problems they had been experiencing with the site. Following this meeting inspectors reported that the refinery was much more aware of the environmental controls and much more co-operative. Moreover, one of the environmental officers had left the company and the other had been severely reprimanded and was now in the inspectors' words 'a reformed man'.

This is an interesting example. It details how these inspectors took advantage of a major incident to bring the company into line: as one of the inspectors involved commented, 'all things are possible if you take advantage of situations'. It also reveals how these inspectors systematically collected evidence and exploited major incidents to highlight the incompetence of junior environmental officers to senior management within the company.

The Workforce and Workforce Representatives

As discussed earlier, the interaction between inspectors and the workforce and their representatives was variable. The most usual reason for inspectors to stop and talk to members of the workforce was because they saw evidence of non-compliance. Their role in such cases was usually educational, and the inspectors I witnessed sometimes went to great lengths to explain to the non-compliant the reasons for the law. A FI's visit to a brick factory is typical. The inspector concerned noticed that several of the brick packers were not using ear protection, so asked to speak to them about this. The inspector then gave them a careful explanation about the effects of high levels of noise upon their hearing. The explanation was quite detailed and it was notable that reference to the legal implications of non-compliance was made, albeit only in a secondary capacity. But in this case as in so many others, inspectors paid a good deal of attention to the role of management. In the letter subsequently sent to the brick factory management the inspector wrote :

The fact that some people were not wearing hearing protection at my visit when they should have been indicated supervisors were not carrying out their duties as specified in the company's safety policy adequately. If necessary disciplinary procedures should be adopted to ensure hearing protection is worn in appropriate areas . . . it is a management responsibility to determine which individual employees require ear protection.

This is an interesting response as the HSW Act imposes a duty on employees to comply with the Act, a fact which was made very clear to non-compliant employees at the time of the visit. The inspector did not copy this letter to the safety representative and appears to have decided to use the letter to emphasize the duties of management. This is not an isolated case. An IAPI, following an infraction (see Chapter 8) involving coke ovens at a steel works, wrote in his district report: '[i]t is perfectly possible for this charging to be smokeless provided the correct procedures are followed, but the operators will try to take short-cuts if the management is not vigilant' (IAPI, 1983, p. 21). Inspectors were typically of the view that worker non-compliance was a company's disciplinary matter and some inspectors felt that this should extend to contract staff, who should not be given a permit to work unless certain safety or environmental requirements were met.

The influence of the company upon the behaviour of the workforce was taken into account in a number of different ways. Company rules and policies were important, and the wording and interpretation of railway company rulebooks were often referred to in RI accident reports. Similarly FI accident reports might refer to company policies and rules, an example being a report which stated: 'I do not consider that the injured person could be held guilty of an offence under section 7 since there were clearly no management policies for him to co-operate with'. In some cases inspectors would 'help' managers by offering to send them a letter setting out the fines and other penalties which could be imposed upon workers for non-compliance, a letter which could be put up on a noticeboard. Inspectors were also mindful of the provision of safety equipment and clothing for the workforce. FIs in particular expected employers to provide a range of clothing for employees so that each individual could select the most comfortable for him/herself.

Inspectors were also very sensitive to workforce morale, in particular because of the effects it could have upon health and safety and environmental emissions. Situations which were often seen to lead to poor standards were those where staff were poorly paid, where there was a high turnover of staff, and where there had been staff cutbacks. In some cases it was possible for inspectors to pinpoint fairly precisely the cause of low standards. For example, they might have found that emission levels between similar sites owned by the same company were radically different or even that standards varied between different shifts. In these cases differences in management might reveal themselves as significant, and in one case inspectors discovered that the good results at one site were explained by the fact that the workforce was awarded bonus payments for good emission levels, whereas no bonus payments were available at its sister site where emission levels were unacceptable. Inspectors could also trace variation over time which might point to the cause of a problem; a typical cause of lowering standards here might be a reduction in the number of staff employed. In such cases, standards of maintenance and housekeeping were usually the first tangible effects of staff cuts.

Just as inspectors characterized industries in different ways, they characterized occupations according to broad stereotypes. Hence scrap-metal merchants, second-hand salesmen, and scaffolders were given negative images, whereas those engaged in more precision work, such as certain types of engineering, chemists, and craftsmen, were regarded as adhering to higher standards. The implication seems to be that people with steady, professional jobs were more likely to be law-abiding and compliant than those in manual work, especially those without secure long-term employment. Another category of worker which concerned inspectors was that of contractors. Contractors were being used increasingly during the fieldwork period as companies cut their own workforce and employed contractors on an *ad hoc* basis. Safety was not always one of the criteria for choosing these staff, and contract staff were not always familiar with the industrial settings within which they were sent to work, so inspectors considered them to be at greater risk of injury than regular staff. Inspectors tried to target sites which employed such labour for more frequent visits. In particular, they attempted to ensure that the companies employing *ad hoc* contract workers ensured that these staff knew about the peculiarities of working in the particular environment they were being brought into. This was especially so on the railways, where the working environment clearly had a number of very particular and unique dangers which contract staff needed to be aware of.

INTERNATIONAL DIMENSIONS

International aspects of regulation impinged little at district or area level. Field-level inspectors were of course aware of any new legislation which they were required to enforce, but their main contact with international issues tended to be their dealings with multi-national companies. Their understanding of international aspects here occurred in a variety of ways. They might have found, for example, that health and safety or environmental work requiring major expenditure needed to be referred to a headquarters organization abroad. This could delay a decision and lead to prolonged negotiations where British legal standards were not understood by the parent company.

Inspectors might also encounter foreign personnel in managerial positions. In some cases this could lead to misunderstandings. For instance, IAPIs visiting a refinery noticed a fall in co-operation upon the appointment of a new environmental manager who did not see the need to keep the inspectorate as well informed as it expected, partly, it suspected, because he was Dutch and thus might not have appreciated the relationships which normally existed between the inspectorate and industry in Britain (see Chapter 8). FIs I accompanied to a refinery, where they were discussing plans for new works, found refinery staff trying to refer to other national standards and practices in negotiations. But these interactions were not necessarily negative. IAPIs found that they had few problems negotiating with Danish-owned firms, as they were used to more stringent environmental regulation and had often developed more sophisticated arrestment equipment than was demanded under British law. American companies and personnel were also felt to comply without too much trouble because they would be asked to do more in the United States and would be subject to a more legalistic regulatory regime. Inspectors were aware that investment decisions could be influenced by varying regulatory regimes and were quick to point out examples where capital had been directed by a foreign company to a site in their area despite British standards being higher than they were used to in the country of the parent company.

The other respect in which field-level inspectors became aware of international comparisons was when companies they were responsible for purchased machinery abroad and then found that they did not comply with British standards. A FI explained that getting machines up to British standards can be a problem, especially when foreign goods are not always accompanied by the necessary technical information. In such cases FI would pursue the matter with the supplier/importer and the problem might be referred to the relevant NIG.

REASONS FOR COMPLIANCE AND NON-COMPLIANCE

The range of violations encountered by inspectors in this research was considerable and the reasons for compliance and non-compliance were various (Di Mento, 1986, p. 2 ff.). Different theoretical traditions have identified different reasons for compliance. As Olsen (1992, p. 16 ff.) explains, political theorists, lawyers, and economists, among many others, have come up with their own explanations of compliance, but as he points out, '[i]t is clear that no single theoretical tradition could offer a complete interpretation of all the consequences of all the total regulatory process and its effects at the company level' (*ibid.*, p. 17). Inspectors did not articulate in any sophisticated way their views about why some companies, managers, and workers complied and others did not. *Self-interest* was regarded as the main reason for compliance. The most striking example of this involved sites where strict compliance was necessary to the viability of the works. The clearest example of this was the compliance of petroleum and chemical works where the risks of non-compliance could be so great as to involve destruction of the entire site (Genn, 1993). But self-interest could take other, less dramatic forms. For instance some companies have a very great incentive to prevent emissions to the atmosphere because these emissions could involve the loss of profitable substances, such as valuable metals from metal recovery works or costly chemicals from chemical works.

Another variant on the self-interest theme was compliance motivated by a concern to protect corporate reputation. Essentially these companies did not want to be seen as non-compliant either because of a major incident or accident or because of any legal action initiated by the regulatory agency (Olsen, 1992). Most companies were considered to be concerned about their reputation, but some were perceived to be more worried than others. Large companies were seen as particularly concerned to protect their image and so were those whose relationships with the general public were actually or potentially strained. An IAPI explained that these companies do not want complaints, but to get on with their business uninterrupted. Business was clearly perceived as being susceptible to external pressures from a variety of sources ranging from consumer to peer-group pressure (Di Mento, 1986, p. 86).

The other main reason for compliance cited by inspectors was a genuine concern for the environment or the health and safety of the workforce, which some might refer to as a moral reason for compliance. It is more than compliance out of an obligation to comply with the law; it is a commitment to the spirit as well as the letter of the law. Where this commitment was absent enforcement of the regulations could itself be a motivation to comply, but, as we will see, this was dependent on other factors (Gunningham, 1984, 1987).

Other authors, notably Bardach and Kagan (1982, p. 60 ff.), have detailed a range of reasons for compliance in addition to those already mentioned. These include the threat of private lawsuits, increased insurance premiums, and worry about compensation payments and claims. These were not mentioned by any of the inspectors in this research, possibly because they were less pertinent in the British context than they were in the American context discussed by Bardach and Kagan. Other reasons mentioned by these authors, such as intra-organizational pressures to comply and avoiding the indirect costs of accidents, including 'down-time' and labour dissatisfaction, were discussed in inspector–company interactions, but never as a reason for compliance.

Reasons for non-compliance were elaborated upon in more detail by inspectors. Cost was, perhaps not surprisingly, referred to, especially in relation to remedial work requiring large expenditure. The IAPI *Annual Report* for 1985 detailed a major instance of non-compliance which led to an infraction, the reason for the non-compliance apparently being the cost:

Two rebuilt batteries were commissioned at National Smokeless Fuels (NSF) works at Cwm, South Wales. On neither has any form of containment and arrestment been provided for emissions from the discharging of hot coke from the ovens. The company has been notified of the infraction. Discussion between the Inspectorate and NSF is continuing with the aim of reaching agreement on a system which would be acceptable to the Inspectorate in terms of expected performance but at a *cost* which the company would be prepared to bear. The Inspectorate is prepared to consider less costly alternatives to full containment with extraction to high efficiency arrestment plant and is awaiting detailed design proposals from NSF [HSE, 1986a, pp. 24–5].

As we can see from this, inspectors were usually prepared to discuss alternative methods of compliance, but only so long as the standards were not reduced and only if they considered the cost to be a genuine reason for non-compliance. Obviously it was difficult for inspectors to assess a company's financial situation (see Chapter 4) but in some cases it was clear that the money was available but was being spent on other things, such as new machinery. In these cases inspectors would not regard cost as the reason for non-compliance, but would regard non-compliance as intentional and deliberate. Few authors, however, would simply relate compliance and non-compliance to cost. Wilson (1980, p. 359) notes that profit maximization is 'an incomplete statement of corporate goals'. Likewise, Di Mento (1986, p. 137) emphasizes that financial resources alone are an insufficient explanation of compliance—and, one might add, non-compliance.

Low worker morale was another major reason for non-compliance identified by inspectors. Low morale could result for a variety of reasons. For instance, it could be a consequence of low pay or industrial action, such as a work to rule or strike. Often, of course, these factors were related. An IAPI visiting a cement works found it to be much dirtier than usual. This was explained by the company as the consequence of a work-to-rule which meant that staff were not cleaning up and such things as repairs to broken ducting and spillage were not being attended to promptly. Morale was said to be low, as over 30 per cent of staff had been cut and more cuts were expected. Once again, however, inspectors were not always sure how much credence to accord to this reason for non-compliance. An IAPI, visiting a steel works because he had noticed that the emissions were particularly bad, was told that one of the major reasons for this was the recent miners' strike. The inspector clearly regarded this as an 'excuse' (sic) as he had visited the site many times during the strike and had never found the emissions to be so bad. He found it very difficult to assess how much the emissions could be accounted for by the explanations the manager gave and how much was caused by bad housekeeping. The legal implications of this, as perceived by this inspector, were that because he could not calculate the impact of the strike it was difficult to prove that best practicable means were not being upheld.

A frequently cited reason for non-compliance amongst the workforce was that safety clothing and equipment hindered it in its work. Most inspectors were intolerant of this reason. I came across none who would accept that safety equipment hindered work, although some did accept that safety clothing could be more comfortable. In this case these inspectors would suggest that alternative safety clothing be tried, but they would not accept the non-compliance. A reason for non-compliance which, not surprisingly, was not raised by inspectors but which does figure in the literature is ineffective enforcement. The basic argument here is that the threat of the law and formal sanctions must be credible for legal regulation to be effective and compliance to be achieved. Snider (1987, p. 51) sums the argument up by stating that regulatory enterprises 'have no incentive to make substantial and costly improvements, knowing that the most the inspector is likely to do is to issue a formal letter suggesting changes with no follow-up or likelihood of further action.'

Underlying all except the last of these explanations on compliance and non-compliance were assumptions about the type of people subject to regulation. Inspectors did not generally regard those they regulated to be blatant offenders. Ignorance and incompetence were more likely to be perceived as explanations of non-compliance than intent (see also Cranston, 1979; Hawkins, 1984; Hutter, 1988). In part, this explains why inspectors adopted an accommodative approach to achieving compliance although, as the differences in approach between the insistent and persuasive strategies suggest, there were variations between inspectorates. All three inspectorates were responsible for what Bardach and Kagan (1982) refer to as 'bad apples'. But it should be emphasized that such companies were considered by all inspectors to be a small minority of those they regulated. If one considered the characteristics shared by those falling into this category they tended to be short-term temporary sites and small, opportunistic firms. Moreover, they were regarded as culpable, blatant offenders who were morally deserving of the most serious sanctions being invoked against them. Blatant non-compliance was mentioned frequently by members of all three inspectorates as a good reason for prosecution. Indeed, blatant offending was mentioned as warranting prosecution by inspectors who were normally not in favour of legal action. In all cases this would involve a flagrant disregard of the inspectorates' basic requirements. The Chief IAPI's 1983 *Annual Report* cites several examples of this. It reports the prosecution of a secondary aluminium works being operated without best practicable means and without a certificate of registration. It also refers to fifteen prosecutions for illegal cable-burning, all of which were regarded as blatant non-compliance by inspectors; indeed, the *Annual Report* refers to the cable burners as 'itinerant' (1983 *Annual Report*). Conversely, in offences where there was an absence of blatant wrongdoing there would usually be a decision not to prosecute. Indeed, this was the advice of a solicitor commenting upon a case the RI was considering for legal action. The solicitor recommended against prosecution because of 'the absence of the sort of deliberate wrong-doing or omission that the Courts seem to find a pre-requisite for the conviction of individuals under the Health and Safety at Work Act'.

Of course there could be substantial economic advantage to be gained by not complying with the law, and this was something which inspectors took into account in their perceptions of intent. Another factor which indicated a lack of commitment to health and safety was persistent or repeated non-compliance. This was most clearly demonstrated by a failure to comply with an improvement notice, which could itself be prompted by a persistent failure to comply. Many inspectors felt that prosecution should be automatic following non-compliance with a notice. Indeed some felt that it should follow in cases where inspectors had given a number of formal requests and warnings which had not been heeded.

Notions of intent were also deduced from cases where the levels of aggregate compliance were regarded as generally low. In such cases inspectors could bide their time, waiting for the recalcitrant company to make a sufficiently serious wrong move to warrant prosecution. Several examples of this emerged from my fieldwork with FIs. One, for instance, took me to a plastics factory he had been visiting for several years. The inspector had a very poor opinion of the company and referred to it as 'a bad lot'. It was explained that there were generally poor standards of health and safety throughout the factory: guarding of machines was poor, the record keeping not up-to-date, and the ability and commitment of the company to remedy problems apparently nonexistent. This was set against the background of numerous financial cuts, including recently the abolition of the post of safety officer. The inspector wanted to 'run them in' but was waiting for them to do one really 'bad thing' so there was a clear-cut prosecution. The inspector did not hide a desire to prosecute the company. On the contrary, the inspector joked openly with an ex-safety officer he met on site: 'I never did manage to get you locked up did I?' Very often inspectors appeared to be reasonable with companies which they considered to have generally low standards of compliance. They would warn them that if they had not improved by the next visit then they would prosecute. This was said in the knowledge that it was highly unlikely that these companies would comply and that prosecution was 'on the cards' if a clear-cut case presented itself.

As these cases show, inspectors were quite prepared to play a waiting game with those they considered to have low levels of aggregate compliance. If they did not prosecute such firms themselves it should be noted that inspectors could be content to help another regulatory body assemble a prosecution. Such a case presented itself during a visit to an upholsterers with a FI. The FI was checking that the terms of an improvement notice had been met, and if they had not the inspector was prepared to prosecute for non-compliance. Much to the inspector's surprise the improvement notice had achieved compliance with the terms of the HSW Act 1974. However, while the inspector now had no need to prosecute the company the fire service did intend to prosecute and the inspector was pleased to supply a statement to assist it. Indicators of intent commonly lead to the prosecution of regulatory offenders. Grabosky and Braithwaite (1986, p. 188), for example, discovered that 18 per cent of the regulatory agencies they examined in Australia had a written enforcement policy which suggested that *mens rea* was important (see also, Cranston, 1979; Hawkins, 1984; Hutter, 1988; Richardson *et al.*, 1983).

We should, however, be cautious about simplifying inspectors' views about and reactions to non-compliance. As Kagan and Scholz (1984, p. 68) point out, regulatory officials do not choose among theories of non-compliance, but may combine them and make case-by-case judgements. Certainly the matter is a complex one, and probably the only thing we know for certain is that there is no simple explanation of compliance. Businesses vary in their ability and motivation to comply, and they also differ over time and across issues. Compliance is a process and the trajectories followed by different sites involve a complex of decisions and become subject to a wide variety of methods designed to achieve compliance.

Co-operation

A central feature of the regulatory relationships discussed in this study is co-operation. An American observer wrote in 1986 that:

The British system of pollution control is predicated on a high degree of co-operation between the regulators and the regulated. Co-operation is particularly pronounced in the case of the Alkali Inspectorate, but it also characterizes the relationship between the regional water authorities and industry and, to only a lesser extent, the interaction of local pollution-control authorities and industry [Vogel, 1986, p. 83].

There is no doubt that IAPI (previously known as the Alkali Inspectorate) stressed that co-operation was vital to its work. A similar view was held by RI and, to a lesser extent, FI, which sought co-operation but did not regard it as vital in the way the other inspectorates did.

At the concrete, everyday field-level of regulatory enforcement these relationships between inspectors and the regulated may be personalized and located in the signs and symbols of a 'good relationship'. Names are frequently used symbolically, and typically the degree of formality in the regulatory relationship was reflected in the formalities of address. So those keen to establish close working relationships would use first names more readily than those who were likely to take a more severe and distanced stance. An IAPI explained to a newly registered business that he would use first names and be known by his first name while he was satisfied with their environmental control. But if he had cause for dissatisfaction he would refer to the regulated by their formal titles and expect to be similarly addressed by them. Inspectors would often reinforce working relationships with social chit-chat about topics of communal interest extending beyond the workplace, for example children's education, hobbies, or holidays. Such talk was not part of more distant and formal relationships.

Inspectors interpreted the reception they received from the regulated according to the nature of their relationship. For instance, difficulties in parking could be interpreted as a company being awkward or as an understandable pressure on parking. Being asked to sign a visitor's book would be seen either as a sensible precaution in case of fire or as obstructionist and rude. Inspectors also reacted differently to offers of coffee and lunch according to the social distance they wished to maintain between themselves and the regulated. Where there was a close and co-operative relationship inspectors would expect to be offered coffee and possibly lunch. Few inspectors would refuse coffee, but some FIs, certainly from my observations, refused offers of anything more substantial.

Inspectors' reactions to and handling of these matters, which on the face of it may appear trivial, reflected the boundaries of the relationship and the degree to which inspectors wanted overtly to underline their authority. These were symbolic of the extent to which inspectors trusted the regulated and to which they were prepared to trust them. Some inspectors, and in some circumstances most inspectors, were keen to avoid feeling indebted, in however small a way, to the regulated. They were concerned that they might develop 'too cosy' a relationship which would compromise their discretion and appear 'too pally' both to other groups within a business and to outsiders.

Co-operative relationships established at site level were mirrored at *industry level*, where senior inspectors and industry representatives were in regular contact. These contacts were most prominent where the reg-ulated population was small and closely defined and where the turnover of senior personnel was low, for example IAPI and RI. Members of these inspectorates referred to 'good working relations', 'amicable' and 'happy' relationships with the regulated. They had both regular, formal meetings and informal *ad hoc* meetings plus regular telephone conver-sations. As at field-level the intention was to hold full and frank discus-sions and use these meetings both as a 'sounding board' and as a means of keeping industry 'on its toes'.

Explanations of why such relationships develop are related to expla-nations of variations in enforcement styles. One view is that co-opera-tive relationships are instrumental, a view exemplified by John Scholz (1983) in a paper which discusses the relationship between regulatory agencies and regulatory companies. The company, it is argued, has the choice either to comply voluntarily with regulations or to evade them. The agency can choose either a flexible or a coercive enforcement approach:

If the agency enforces with flexibility and the firm complies with the rules, then both the agency and the firm benefit from mutual co-operation. The agency benefits from the company's compliance and the company benefits from the agency's flexibility. Both sides avoid expensive enforcement and litigation pro-cedures. Society also gains the benefits of full compliance at low cost to the economy. But if the firm evades and the agency uses coercive enforcement, both suffer the punishing costs of the resultant legalistic relationship. The firm also faces a temptation to evade if the agency is using a flexible enforcement policy which is unlikely to penalize evasion. And the agency faces a temptation to use the strict enforcement mode with a complying company in order to get the benefits of enforcing even unreasonably expensive rules [cited in Axelrod, 1984, p. 156].

This is a social-exchange approach where the inspector's ability to 'win co-operation is rooted in the relationship of reciprocity or exchange that he manages to establish' (Bardach and Kagan, 1982, p. 130; see also Shapiro, 1987). But the evidence of this research is that this is an insufficient explanation of co-operative relationships and accommoda-tive enforcement strategies. There is little evidence that the inspectors and inspectorates in this study were as calculating as the social-exchange model suggests. Neither were the advantages and disadvan-tages of different regulatory strategies so amenable to calculation. Regulatory work emerges as complex and changing and regulatory decisions as the outcome of complicated interpretative judgements.

Regulatory relationships and strategies are rather more adequately explained by the exigencies of regulatory work, foremost amongst these being *organizational* factors. These ranged from inspectorate resources and their organization to policies which directly or indirectly encouraged or discouraged the development of relationships between inspectors and the regulated.

The organizational resources available to each inspectorate varied, especially the staff numbers in relation to the number and complexity of environmental problems encountered. Table 10 compares FI and IAPI resources, examining the ratio of inspectors to premises regulated.[5]

TABLE 10. Comparison of FI and IAPI Resources 1980–1987

YEAR	FI			IAPI*		
	ΔN	Premises Regulated	Ratio	ΔN	Premises Regulated	Ratio
1980	759	309 000	1:403	48	1969	1:41
1981	735	550 000	1:748	46	1915	1:42
1982	678	500 000	1:737	46	1871	1:41
1983	654	400 000	1:611	42	1950	1:46
1984	627	—	—	40	1975	1:49
1985	561	400 000	1:713	40	1978	1:49
1986	562	>400 000	1:711	39	1985	1:51
1987	562	>400 000	1:715	44#	1986	1:45

Source: HSE Annual Reports
*   England and Wales
\#   Number of HMIP Inspectors allocated to air pollution work
ΔN Number of Inspectors

As we can see, the ratio of IAPIs to premises was considerably higher than was the ratio of FIs to premises. Similarly Table 11 reveals how RI resources were greater than those of FI. In the context of this research we can see how these differential resources gave FIs less opportunity than either IAPIs or members of RI to revisit premises and establish relationships.

The ways in which resources were mobilized also influenced the ability of inspectors to establish working relationships with the regulated. The setting-up and maintenance of these relationships was more likely

---

[5] RI are not strictly comparable as they are responsible for railway premises and track.

TABLE 11. Comparison of FI and RI Resources 1980–1985

	FI			RI		
YEAR	N*	Employees Regulated	Ratio	N*	Employees Regulated	Ratio
1980	759	17.0M	1:22,398	15	232 000	1:15,467
1981	735	15.6M	1:21,224	22	229 000	1:10,409
1982	678	15.2M	1:22,419	22	221 000	1:10,045
1983	654	15 M	1:22,936	22	218 000	1: 9,909
1984	627	—	—	23	209 000	1: 9,087
1985	561	16 M	1:28,520	23	181 000	1: 7,869

Source: HSE Annual Reports
N* Number of inspectors

in proactive rather than reactive work. Clearly this is related to the resources available, as proactive strategies are most likely when there is a smaller ratio of premises to inspectors.

The establishment of co-operative relationships is not just a matter of chance or circumstances. It may be a matter of policy. For instance, there may be policies about the rotation of staff. FIs were moved regularly between industry groups and area offices. This was to broaden their experience and also to counteract any complacency which it was feared might be introduced if inspectors got to know personnel in an area well. IAPI and RI, however, encouraged their inspectors to develop relationships and were not concerned to move their staff between duties on a regular basis. Indeed, some REIs even worked as inspectors in the same geographical areas where they had previously worked as railway managers.

The *type of business* regulated may also influence the frequency of interaction between enforcement officials and those they regulate. Generally, inspectorates visited large, potentially dangerous, and complicated sites most frequently. IAPI and especially RI typically regulated businesses falling into these categories, but FI was responsible for a very wide range of industries and businesses. The circumstances under which inspectors were able or unable to develop relationships with the regulated are illustrative. FIs, as we have seen, were most likely to sustain a formal, official relationship with the regulated. The exceptions were large, technically complex sites, such as chemical works, where individual inspectors, often senior inspectors, visited regularly and built up a relationship with safety officers, senior managers, and sometimes union safety representatives. It was on visits to sites such as these that FIs were observed to 'relax' the normal rules and, for example, agree to be on first-name terms and accept meals. Conversely, all inspectors were most formal where their meetings with the regulated were transitory and infrequent. This was often related to the *nature of the activity* regulated. The possibilities of a co-operative relationship developing are in part dictated by whether or not the regulated are engaged in continuing rather than episodic activity (Hawkins, 1984; Shapiro, 1987). It is perhaps significant that inspectors were often more sanctioning in their dealings with transitory operators. For instance, many of the prosecutions initiated by IAPIs pre-1984 were against metal recovery works, especially illegal cable burners (see Table 12).[6]

TABLE 12. IAPI Prosecutions, 1978–1983

PROSECUTIONS HEARD	YEAR					
	1978	1979	1980	1981	1982	1983
Metal Recovery Works	8	5	10	15	n.a.	15
Total Number	13	7	10	17	n.a.	17

Source: Annual Reports

While these inspectors would have acted stringently against any unregistered business operating without pollution-arrestment equipment, it is noteworthy that these were typically transitory operations where inspectors had to act quickly and had no opportunity to establish long-term relationships. Similarly FIs working in construction industry groups tended to be more sanctioning than many of their colleagues. Again they were often dealing with transitory operations, whose operators were unknown to them.

Where inspectors were regulating complicated operations and where non-compliance was invisible and intangible—as was often the case for IAPIs and FIs regulating, for example, petrochemical works—then inspectors might have been dependent upon the goodwill of the regulated. Many IAPIs considered that co-operative relations were vital to their jobs as they were reliant upon companies for information, much

---

[6] As a result of amendments to s. 78 of the Control of Pollution Act in the Health and Safety (Emissions into the Atmosphere) Regulations 1983, IAPI ceased to be responsible for itinerant cable burners (see Hutter, 1989, p. 169 ff.).

of it confidential. Vogel, discussing British pollution control in the 1980s, noted that:

On balance, the ability of British pollution-control authorities to require compliance by industry is limited. British industry is under no statutory obligation to develop new technologies to control pollution. . . . No law requires industry to keep the government informed of improvements in its technical ability to control its emissions, nor are firms under any obligation to share with government officials data on the costs of abatement. . . . Not only is the co-operation of industry thus critical to the government's ability to define what in fact constitutes the best practicable means of pollution control, but since much of the monitoring of industrial emissions is actually carried out by the companies themselves, British officials are also dependent on a high degree of voluntary compliance by industry with pollution-control requirements after they have been negotiated [1986, p. 83].

As Vogel indicates, the legal and political parameters of regulatory work again reveal themselves as significant.

Regular contact is perhaps a necessary condition for co-operative enforcement relationships, but it is not sufficient. Inspectors in frequent and regular interaction with the regulated have the opportunity to acquire detailed knowledge of a company, to discover its strengths and weaknesses and who to trust, to keep a close eye on how a company is performing. They acquire knowledge of the 'hardware' of a workplace, its machinery, processes, and site, and information about its 'software'. This includes knowledge of the people associated with a site, including its ownership, management, workforce, and the relationship between these. It also includes information about systems of work and the financial position of the business. As a result, inspectors build up a picture of a business's trustworthiness and abilities.

CONCLUSIONS

The regulatory community is at the core of the compliance process. It comprises the broad groupings involved in regulatory policy and practice and the relationships within them (Meidinger, 1987, p. 364). The regulatory inspectorates are clearly one central grouping, and this research has considered three very different regulatory inspectorates in Britain. The other central grouping is the regulated population, which encompasses a wide range of industries and organizations.

The range and sophistication of the industries regulated by each inspectorate varied, as did the risks associated with each type of site. Whereas FI regulated a very wide range of industries and processes, IAPI was responsible for a small and well-defined population of industries and processes. RI, meanwhile, devoted much of its effort to one major company. FI also dealt with a higher proportion of smaller and less complex businesses than did IAPI and RI. Large, complex sites in multi-national ownership usually demanded a different enforcement approach from smaller, simpler sites. This was for a number of reasons. As Yeager (1991) reminds us, larger and more powerful organizations are more able to set regulatory agendas and challenge inspectorate decisions. They are also more likely to have the ability to comply, both financially and technically. This means that this type of company was more likely to comply and that inspectors would not need to devote time to educating personnel about regulatory requirements. But it also meant that inspectors could not bluff and needed to be careful that their demands could be construed as legally valid. And on large, complex sites it could be difficult to discover the source of a problem, so there could be difficulties in assessing compliance and the methods of achieving compliance could be compromised. All of this serves to highlight the difficulties enforcement officials faced in attempting to regulate activities which were a routine part of economic life and where such offending as could be identified was committed by organizations as opposed to persons. The effects of this were heightened by the uncertainties surrounding offending. Rock (1995) explains that in such a system offenders 'may not so much have done or omitted to do some definitive thing in a past now closed as failed merely to perform an act so far . . . whose behaviour . . . is phenomenologically open, uncertain as to its precise intention, meaning and consequence.'

All of these issues relate to the nature of the regulated community, and it is this which emerges from this research as a crucial variable in the compliance process. The relationship between the regulators and the regulated is especially important to our understanding of regulation, with co-operation being a hallmark of many regulatory relationships. The precise nature of regulatory relations is not simply worked out at the level of everyday interactions between inspectors and those they regulate. The scope for co-operative relationships is itself a product of broader structural features of regulatory work, such as its organization and the nature of the activities and businesses subject to regulation. These in turn are the product of broader social, political, and economic tensions about the regulation of economic activities.

8 Compliance as a Process of Enforcement

In the context of regulatory enforcement it is particularly relevant to regard compliance as processual. Regulatory agencies are typically—but not inevitably—in long-term relations with the regulated, whose compliance is of ongoing concern (Bardach and Kagan, 1982). The relationship between the agency and the regulated is reflexive, with each party adapting and reacting to the moves and anticipated moves of the other (Hawkins and Hutter, 1993). Enforcement is often serial and incremental (Hawkins, 1984) and the whole process of enforcement may be usefully characterized as a 'career'.

ENFORCEMENT CAREERS

The notion of an enforcement career emerges from the interactionist tradition, in particular the sociology of deviance. Rock (1973) uses the concept in an especially illuminating way to describe and explain the debt-collection process. He regards enforcement as a status passage, where defaulters progress through a variety of definable stages in the 'process' of 'becoming'. Enforcement careers are in many important respects moral careers where critical benchmarks mark the passage from one stage to the next and where moral characterizations may change. Thus enforcement officials interpret, classify, and test the regulated and act accordingly. Indeed, they may act on the basis of very little information. The process is a complex one where, to quote Rock, '[s]ocial control is not taken to be a mere context of deviation. Instead, it defines, shapes and infuses rule-breaking' (1973, p. 2).

Early sociologists of deviance applied the concept of an enforcement career to rule-breaking which in many respects accorded with conventional images of crime and deviance. The focus was upon 'street people', young male deviants, and their interactions with the police.[1] Rock moved thinking on in his application of the concept to civil rule-breaking where individual defaulters were pursued, for sometimes very

[1] See Rock, 1995, for an excellent account of the development of these ideas and their application to new areas of research.

long periods of time, for recovery of unpaid debts. More recently, the concept has been used in the study of regulatory control (Hawkins, 1984; Richardson, 1983), where it is used in a slightly different context again, for it refers to both individual and corporate careers. Moreover, the concept of career often refers to a long-term, ongoing relationship where regulatory agencies may be dealing simultaneously with some areas of a site which are in compliance and other areas which are not. Indeed, sites may be in compliance on one visit but not on another. The career may therefore involve more than one set of related, definable stages, running sometimes in parallel and at other times cross-cutting each other as inspectors trade off temporary compliance in one area for full compliance elsewhere on a site. All of this, of course, serves to emphasize the complexity of enforcement careers and the fact that they are not unilinear.

So far in this research we have discussed a variety of aspects of compliance which may be ordered as a 'career'. Defining compliance is a continuing activity embracing a range of working definitions of compliance, for example, temporary compliance and full compliance. Initial compliance has been distinguished from compliance maintenance, the latter being another ongoing activity. Throughout the process compliance takes on different meanings depending upon circumstances. This Chapter will consider the progression of the enforcement career in terms of the enforcement moves and techniques used by regulatory officials to gain and sustain compliance.

Entering the Career

Companies and individuals enter a regulatory enforcement career immediately they set up and often before they open for business. In the case of all three inspectorates in this research there were premonitory procedures which defined the populations subject to control. The Factories Act 1961, section 127(b), for example, requires that 'any person undertaking any building operations or works of engineering construction to which this Act applies' shall notify the appropriate authorities of his or her occupation of a 'factory' (section 175) or, in the case of construction work, report the commencement of work which will be of more than six weeks duration. These notification procedures were particularly helpful in denoting the population subject to the control of FI.

IAPIs operated with slightly different and more stringent requirements. Under the terms of section 9 of the Alkali etc. Works Regulation Act 1906, all works operating a scheduled process (see Chapter 2) had to be registered. This involved application to the inspectorate for a certificate of registration which was issued only if the inspectorate was satisfied that the best practicable means requirements had been met. Businesses were required to re-apply for registration annually. The effects of these requirements were to make prior approval procedures an integral part of IAPI's job with regard both to new works and modifications to existing works.

RI also had powers of prior approval. Indeed the inspection of new railways was one of the earliest tasks of RI (see Chapter 2). The Road and Railway Traffic Act 1933 requires the railways to inform the inspectorate of any major new works, such as new stations, signalling, or level-crossings. Under the terms of the 1842 Regulation of Railway Act the inspectorate is given 'teeth' in the form of a power to postpone the opening of a railway until its requirements are complied with (see Chapter 3): it can simply refuse to give permission to open a line until satisfied that it is safe. RI does not have the statutory authority to approve new railway stock, although in practice the railways usually consult it at the earliest possible stage.[2]

Another respect in which RI's role is crucial in granting prior approval is in its advisory role to the Secretary of State for Transport. This was especially the case in relation to proposed changes to level crossings. Section 66 of the British Transport Commission Act 1957 requires the Secretary of State's approval before British Railways can change a level crossing. RI undertook the investigations upon which these decisions were taken: it examined and commented upon the modernization proposals and examined each scheme to ensure that the terms of the order issued by the Secretary of State had been met. It also undertook public hearings about proposed changes to level crossings. Following the court of inquiry into the accident at Hixon in 1968, when a heavy road transporter and a passenger train collided on an automatic half-barrier level crossing (Ministry of Transport, 1968), there has been increased consultation when changes to level crossings are

---

[2] The Hidden Report into the Clapham Junction railway accident criticized the prior-approval arrangements relating to the railways, partly because only certain schemes of work needed approval. The report stated that the legal provisions for prior approval were unworkable and placed the RI in an 'extremely difficult position'. This was partly because there was no way of forcing the railways to submit, in good time, plans to RI for a whole scheme of work. The report recommended that a scheme for the approval of new works on the railway should be designed (Hidden, 1989, paras. 12.35–12.38, p. 115).

proposed. British Railways must send the County and District local authorities concerned notice of their proposals. If it considers it necessary RI can then make recommendations to the Secretary of State.

Inspectors took premonitory procedures very seriously and, quite unusually given their general reluctance to prosecute, would switch immediately into a repressive system in cases of non-compliance with legal requirements. FI regularly prosecuted for a failure to notify the inspectorate of, for example, occupation of a factory; of the commencement of construction works; the use of radiation; or overtime.[3] However, it should be noted that FIs did not prosecute every case of non-compliance they detected. They appreciated that some people setting up their own businesses might not be fully aware of the notification procedures and some inspectors overlooked minor infringements of the laws relating to hours of work. It was normally the persistent or blatant offenders who were taken to court, with the latter group including large companies which inspectors considered should be fully aware of the relevant legislation and employers who had flouted similar laws in the past. Hence judgements were made about the moral deviance of a firm that did not comply.

One reason the FI took a certain view of what some may regard as a technical offence is that these notification procedures were the only systematic means that this inspectorate had of knowing the populations subject to its control. The annual registration requirements of the Alkali Act were similarly important to IAPI as a means of defining the population it was responsible for and providing relatively up-to-date information. The force of these registration requirements should not be underestimated. Failure to register a scheduled process is an offence, and one which could provoke a strong reaction from IAPI. But this did not necessarily mean it prosecuted. In the case of the one site I visited with an inspector, which was not registered when it should have been, an immediate closure of the works was effected until best practicable means had been negotiated with the company concerned. A chance remark made during one visit alerted the inspector to the fact that there could be premises operating nearby which had not sought the necessary registration from IAPI. The possibility of this greatly concerned the District Inspectors. This was partly because several applications by the company involved to site a mineral works in the area had been turned down. Inspectors had also written to the local management informing

---

[3] In 1984 there were 65 convictions for these offences with an average penalty of £172 and, in 1985, 39 convictions with an average penalty of £226.

it of the need to register and to comply with the best practicable means requirements, a precaution taken because its parent company had set up business elsewhere and claimed ignorance of the registration process, using this as a reason for non-compliance. An extract from fieldnotes takes up the story:

Before lunch John (a pseudonym for the inspector involved) decided to go and have a look at the proposed site of the mineral works: it was on a rough piece of land on the estuary, an area taken over by small commercial enterprises. At the entrance to the area was a sign advertising the roadstone plant and giving directions. This worried John a little but he really didn't expect to find an operating plant. Indeed, when we arrived on site the plant was there but not in use.

We took some time to find the site manager—John introduced himself and the manager replied that if he had come this morning he would have seen the plant in operation, but as it was they had stopped production for the day. John replied by telling the manager that before they started operation they should have had the process registered. The manager obviously didn't know anything about this. John continued to say that by operating the plant without having attained best practicable means and being registered the company had broken the law and he had no option but to declare an *infraction*[4] of the Act. The manager asked if the company should have known about this. John said that most certainly they should and he asked which company now owned them. The manager replied that they were working on a contract for 'a national company', this was not the company on file as the backers. John was more annoyed, he said that a large company like that certainly knew the rules—the manager asked if they would have other sites like this one that needed registering. John said that they would. So, asked the manager, could it be that they had a nationwide registration? John explained that this was not possible and that best practicable means had to be worked out for each site. He added that this type of plant was different from most roadstone plants and there would be certain restrictions on its use as particular pollution problems are associated with it. For a start they would have to raise the height of the chimney—it should be at

---

[4] Infractions were administrative devices used by IAPI to signal formally to the regulated that they had committed an offence and might be considered for prosecution. See below for a fuller discussion.

least 70 feet and it patently wasn't that high now. He asked the manager what sort of minerals they were processing—he replied the full range. John said that this wouldn't be allowed either . . . The manager then said 'Are you saying that we can't continue production, that we have to close down?' Yes said John, in fact a letter declaring an infraction of the Act would be sent and a meeting requested to discuss best practicable means. Also a copy would be sent to John's HQ where the possibility of prosecution would be discussed. The manager said that he would have to get onto his employer straight away as he didn't know anything about this at all . . .

On our way to the new site the manager repeated that he had never heard of this before, he was going to have to get on to his boss immediately. John told him that the Inspectorate had even written to the contractor to let him know of the requirements. Also he noticed the company who had provided the equipment had said that they too were fully aware of the need to register with IAPI so there really was not any acceptable excuse. He asked the manager if the company he worked for owned any similar sites. Yes they did—in fact the manager had just moved from one in Surrey—John asked where they were situated and said that it would be interesting to see if they had been registered.

We eventually looked at the site in the company of the manager: John turned to me and asked how far I thought we were from the nearest housing; I was non-committal, he then said do you reckon that it's a good half mile. I said that I did. (Later I asked John if the site was too close to the housing, he replied that it wasn't anywhere near the limit. This suggests that he was merely adding to the drama and tension when he asked me this). He muttered that it looked OK to him but he would have to check the planning permission.

John was evidently surprised by what had taken place and was angry that the local planning department had not let the Inspectorate know about the site. An infraction letter was subsequently sent to the company and meetings arranged with a director, at which the company's non-compliance was emphasized to them. A prosecution did not result but the company was unable to operate the plant for a week which was arguably a greater blow than prosecution. Best practicable means requirements were eventually complied with and a year later the inspectors involved reported that they had not had further problems with the works.

Like their counterparts in FI, IAPIs did not take such drastic action in every case of non-compliance with premonitory procedures that came to their attention. In the case cited above a significant factor in the decision to close the works was that it was owned by a large company which knew full well that it should register with IAPI. In some respects, therefore, the closure of the works was as much a reaction to what was perceived as a symbolic assault on the authority of the inspectorate as it was a consequence of non-compliance with the law (see below, under 'Pyramid of Enforcement Strategies'). Non-registration was thus regarded as particularly serious if it was perceived as flouting the law and challenging the agency's legitimacy. Yeager (1991, p. 28) similarly found that the Environmental Protection Agency region he researched used its most serious sanctions for a failure to apply for a discharge permit.

Prior Approval

The force of the Alkali Act's registration requirements not only defined those processes subject to control, but also established prior approval as an integral aspect of IAPI's work. Prior approval procedures could be lengthy and time-consuming and could involve considerable negotiation. But as a District Air Pollution Inspector noted in his 1983 *Annual Report*: '[f]rom the point of view of air pollution the newer plants are welcome as it gives an opportunity to upgrade the air pollution control equipment.' It is for this reason that inspectors were prepared to devote months of hard work and negotiation to one which was planning to invest in new equipment or to a company which had recently changed ownership. IAPIs seized these opportunities to improve pollution control. Indeed a company decision to invest could come after months or even years of pressure from the inspectorate to improve standards of pollution control. In this sense much of IAPI work could be regarded as premonitory.

Prior-approval procedures were not only for the benefit of inspectors, since it was in the interests of the regulated to take account of the requirements from the beginning of a scheme. This, as all inspectorates pointed out, was because it was usually more practical and cheaper to allow for regulatory demands at the design stage rather than be forced to add them at a later date. In the case of those coming under the remit of IAPI a failure to comply could delay registration, and hence operation of new plant.

The benefits to both parties became obvious in the case of works subject to the regulation of the FI. Although FI could legally secure co-operation at the planning stage it often arranged to go through plans and offer comment on an informal basis. This was particularly the case with major new works such as a new chemical plant. These arrangements benefited both the regulated and the inspectorate: if the regulated were to incorporate anything which was unacceptable to the inspectorate, or failed to include something required by the inspectorate, then it could be expensive to remedy at a later date. From the inspectorate's view point, a lot of time and effort could well be saved in avoiding the need to negotiate post-construction remedial work. It was for similar reasons that Inspecting Officers of Railways were asked to approve rolling stock which did not legally have to be officially approved before use.

In his 1983 *Annual Report on Railway Safety* the Chief Inspecting Officer of Railways summarizes the importance of premonitory procedures, with reference to plant and equipment:

Safety improvements introduced at the design stage can often be made at little or no increase in cost of the finished machine. Indeed, when account is taken of the cost of accidents due to compensation to staff, repairs to the machine, or lost working time of the machine itself and others who are dependent upon it, the safety improvement can result in an overall saving. In addition to discussion on safety matters at the design stage, it is important to inspect the completed machine since this often shows up other points not noticed when preliminary drawings are examined. Furthermore, both at the design stage and when inspecting a prototype, it is possible to incorporate in subsequent machines minor improvements which could not be justified if the machines had already been built (Department of Transport, 1984, p. 26).

Inspecting Officers of Railways devoted a large proportion of their time to inspecting new works and discussing new proposals. The railways submitted plans for new works to the inspectorate. Major works, such as new signalling schemes, were checked through by an Assistant Inspecting Officer who then prepared a report, including his recommendations, having regard to such matters as suitability of the proposal or the need to inspect the works before giving approval. This report—and, if appropriate, inspection results—was then forwarded to the Chief Inspector who made the final decision about how to proceed. He decided whether to approve the works and whether an inspection was necessary, either prior to approval or afterwards, to ensure that everything was running smoothly. Many works were approved from plans but there were occasions when an inspection was considered necessary.

For example, officers carried out an inspection when they were not satisfied with the plans, or when a particular railway or department of a railway had not been inspected for new works for some time. In addition, any electrification scheme was always inspected before it was energized, because of the obvious dangers associated with electrification. It was generally the case that the inspectorate inspected a wider range of new works when they were proposed by smaller railways, especially those run by volunteers, which may have welcomed the specialist opinions of Inspecting Officers.

It should be emphasized that Inspecting Officers were prepared to hold up new works and the opening of new schemes if they were not satisfied that safety standards had been met. They also kept in close contact with the railways when new plant and machinery were being developed. While they recognized that any decisions regarding these matters were for the railways to take, Inspecting Officers nevertheless made their standards and requirements very clear. Clearly the railways respected this, for they sent the inspectorate detailed plans highlighting proposed safety arrangements and they also appeared to welcome the inspectorate's inspection of any prototype plant or machinery.

Level-crossing inquiries also took up considerable time. As noted earlier, Inspecting Officers were responsible for advising the Secretary of State about any proposed changes to level crossings. This involved them in a lot of work. Not only did they have to go through the plans submitted by British Railways, but they were also involved in site meetings and public hearings. Inspecting Officers usually visited the sites of the crossings before the public hearing so that they were familiar with them.

In deciding what type of crossing to allow a number of factors were taken into account. These included the road-traffic flow, the speed limit for trains, and the cost. The last was really only a consideration for British Railways, since if it met the safety requirements then the decision about which type to use was for its commercial judgement. The requirements it should meet are laid down in *Railway Construction Operation Requirements—Level Crossings* (Department of Transport, 1981) (see Chapter 3).

The public hearings held by Inspecting Officers had three purposes. The first was to explain the main characteristics and safety measures associated with the type of crossing British Railways proposed to install at a given site. The second was to obtain and discuss the views of all of those present, while the third was to resolve any technical problems associated with such installations with representatives of the Highway Authority and British Railways. The public meetings were chaired by an Inspecting Officer and also involved representatives from British Railways, the district council, parish council (as representatives of the local community), the National Farmers Union, the local police, and the local highway authority. Each of these hearings could take up at least a day once travelling time was taken into account, which, together with the desk time devoted to each case, posed a considerable demand upon the inspectorate. This was especially the case given that British Railways was undertaking a national modernization programme for level-crossings.

The HSW Act 1974, section 6, also provides for some checks on the design of new plant through the general duties it places upon persons who design, manufacture, import, or supply articles for use at work. These duties cover such matters as ensuring 'so far as is reasonably practicable, that the article is so designed and constructed as to be safe and without risks to health when properly used' (section 6(1)(a)); arranging for the testing, research, and examination of articles to ensure their safety; and ensuring that adequate information regarding the use of articles is provided.

FI was most concerned with the provisions of section 6. FIs had compiled lists of manufacturers, suppliers, and importers of tools, plant, and machinery for use at work, and they aimed to visit a proportion of these each year to review existing machinery and discuss plans for new products. But not all of the work associated with section 6 was premonitory; much of it was postmonitory. This occurred, for example, when an inspector discovered a problem with a machine, which might have come to light through an accident. When this happened he would contact the supplier of the machine to inform him of the problems and, if there had been a breach of the law, this could result in prosecution. If, as was usually the case, the supplier was located in another part of the country then the contact would be made through the supplier's local inspector. In its *Plan of Work 1983–4* HSC identified yet another way in which HSE could influence the initial integrity of plant and equipment, namely through its participation in preparing British Standards or EC technical standards and regulations (HSC, 1983, p. 28). In this way, of course, HSE was very much involved in defining compliance.

As we can see, the law specified formal procedures for most new entrants and also required that some changes introduced by existing companies were legally processed as compliant by regulatory inspectors.

The 'starting points' for those entering an enforcement career varied. Some new entrants were large companies with other sites which were all too familiar with the regulations and regulatory agency; others were starting up a business for the first time. The degree of flexibility exhibited by inspectors varied according to such factors (see Chapters 2 and 7). Also relevant were the type of activity subject to control, the risks associated with it, the costs of regulation, the political profile of the activity, and so on. Throughout this book regulation has been seen as an interplay between a variety of diverse factors. Now we will turn our attention to considering the goals of this activity and the methods used to achieve them.

REGULATORY GOALS

All of the inspectorates in this study had a common primary objective, namely to secure the compliance of the regulated. The importance of this objective is perhaps underlined by the notion of *immediate compliance*—that is, a situation where an inspector discovered non-compliance while visiting premises or a site and the offending fault was remedied immediately. Usually this was sufficient to satisfy inspectors, and no further action resulted. This was the case even when the non-compliance had been causing an imminent risk to health and safety. Indeed, immediate compliance could be sought when inspectors would otherwise consider issuing a prohibition notice.[5] In such situations inspectors were typically seeking to achieve full compliance with fairly clear-cut requirements, for example, the destruction of a broken ladder so as to prohibit its further use or the placing of toe-boards on scaffolding.[6] Where compliance to the full standard was more complicated or costly to achieve, temporary compliance could be tolerated for a specified period of time until full compliance could be achieved. The goal here was to achieve full compliance. Once full compliance existed the goal became one of compliance maintenance. And in some cases the regulatory goal was to exceed existing standards, that is to effect higher standards than the legal definition of compliance. IAPIs, for example, would try and

---

[5] Whether immediate compliance was effected voluntarily or after the inspector had asked for an immediate remedy was all information inspectors would note when assessing the attitude of a firm or individual manager for future reference.

[6] These are boards placed at foot level on the outside of scaffolding in an attempt to prevent objects falling off the scaffold.

engage in a continuing process of raising standards, something they referred to as 'tightening the noose'.

An enforcement career is characterized by a gradual progression of increasing standards of compliance. Indeed, IAPI claimed that it often increased the standards of the administrative definition of compliance, namely BPM Notes, once a majority of companies had complied with the higher standard. Certainly at an industry level the regulatory goal-posts were continually moving. Once inspectors achieved one standard then they started agitating for more. This was mirrored at company level, something which was well understood by some managers. Indeed, one took me aside during an inspection and informed me that he never did everything the inspectors ask of him, because it gave the inspector something to dwell on during the next visit, rather than find something else for the company to start working on.

In a sense, therefore, regulatory objectives are never achieved nor are they achievable, for the standards keep increasing. Full compliance is a concept which has short-term meaning. Enforcement careers are a series of ever more stringent deadlines, whatever the starting point at entry to the career.

ENFORCEMENT STRATEGIES AND TACTICS

The enforcement strategies and tactics inspectors used to achieve compliance and move the regulated on in their 'careers' were many and various. They ranged from the informal, unrecorded exchanges which took place in the privacy of a visit to the formal and legal and public strategies which might have culminated in prosecution. The strategies and tactics varied according to circumstances. The process is captured well by Ayres and Braithwaite (1992) who introduce the concept of an enforcement pyramid.

Enforcement Pyramids

Ayres and Braithwaite describe two enforcement pyramids, one involving a hierarchy of sanctions and the other a hierarchy of regulatory strategies. These pyramids subject the regulated to increasing regulatory interventions in the face of persistent non-compliance or decreasing intervention in the face of compliance. Their purpose is to encourage regulation which is responsive to the behaviour of the regulated.

The pyramid of sanctions is targeted at the level of the firm, whereas the pyramid of enforcement strategies is targeted at industries. Although Ayres and Braithwaite give examples of these pyramids, they acknowledge that the components of each layer of the pyramid may vary. The principles of construction, however, remain the same. First, the least intrusive interventions occupy the base of the pyramid and the most intrusive the pinnacle—'[e]scalation up this pyramid gives the state greater capacity to enforce compliance but at the cost of increasingly flexible and adversarial regulation' (1992, p. 38). The second principle is that most regulatory activity takes place at the base of the pyramid—'[t]he key contention of this regulatory theory is that the existence of the gradients and peaks of the two enforcement pyramids channels most of the regulatory action to the base of the pyramid—in the realms of persuasion and self-regulation' (*ibid.*, p. 39).

Sanctions Pyramid: Research Findings

Let us now use the notion of the enforcement pyramid to consider the enforcement tactics and sanctions used by the inspectorate. The hierarchy of enforcement tools at inspectors' disposal was broadly similar for each of the research inspectorates. At the base of the pyramid were the least repressive and coercive methods.

In this research, as in Ayres and Braithwaite's model, *persuasion* appears at the base of the pyramid. This comprises a number of enforcement techniques, the least coercive of which were *education and advice*. The inspectors in this study were no exception. They all spent at least part of their working day helping the regulated understand what was required of them and why. A FI's visit to a small foundry illustrates this point. It soon became apparent to the inspector that neither the owner nor the manager of the foundry was fully aware of the dangers associated with lead and the precautions that should be taken. Education and advice thus became the hallmarks of the visit, with the inspector carefully going through the relevant information. After the visit the inspector sighed and said that it was going to take a lot of work to bring the place up to standard, but the inspector was confident that things would improve. The subsequent letter gave advice and offered further advice to the owner. The file report stated that the owner 'appears well meaning and reacts to advice but is generally ignorant of appropriate standards with respect to dust control and lead. However, the health risk is small because of the small number of employees involved.' Two points are worthy of mention here. First that the risks were estimated to be low. A sterner approach could well have been adopted if the risks had been more substantial. Secondly, the characters of the owner and manager were judged to be significant, especially because they were willing to accept and act upon advice. This second point is highlighted by another FI's visit to a mill which repeatedly failed to act on advice. The file notes 'they need to be continually spoonfed regarding basic safety requirements'. But in light of the company's recalcitrance there must be limits to the educative role: 'this close attention cannot continue at this level forever and legal proceedings may be merited if signs of commitment are not noted in the next 12 months'.

The extent to which inspectors adopted an advisory or educational role depended in part upon the size and sophistication of the businesses they were regulating. In general smaller, less complex, businesses required the most help from inspectors. Indeed, in some cases it seemed that the inspector was the main source of information about health and safety or environmental regulations. Larger businesses, especially those involved in complex or dangerous processes, often employed specialist health and safety or environmental staff whose job it was to monitor compliance within the company. Nevertheless inspectors could still be a valuable source of information to these personnel. They could offer a broad view of problems and had experience of how other companies met their demands. Even within the same company inspectors could be an important source of information. For example, REIs appeared to be important disseminators of information within British Railways, passing on details of how other sectors of the railway managed particular technical problems, informing managers of where to find specialist help within their own organization, and even passing on information about where spare machinery was available. In all cases inspectors might be called upon for advice about how to interpret complicated regulations—the COSHH Regulations[7] were causing business the greatest difficulty at the time of my fieldwork and were, if the

---

[7] The Control of Substances Hazardous to Health Regulations (COSHH) came into force on 1 Oct. 1989 after extensive consultation. HSC (1990, p. 45) referred to these regulations as 'the most important health and safety legislation since the HSW Act itself'. Their purpose was to protect health from hazardous substances at work and they applied to the large majority of workplaces in Britain. The regulations required risk assessments and measurement of worker exposure to hazards. HSC issued guidance but many employers seemed, at the time of fieldwork, at a loss to understand them.

inspectors I accompanied were representative, taking up a lot of inspectorate time.

Some inspectors used *dramatic techniques* to highlight problems and explain the need for compliance. During his inspection of a station one REI intentionally lost his balance on a rotting wooden platform which he was insisting to a rather unreceptive assistant manager was a danger. Later in the inspection he drew a wet rag across the wall of a mess room which he wanted cleaned, using the clean line he drew across the wall to support his request. In a subsequent letter he stated that anti-slip treatment had to be applied to the rotten platform and requested a 'special report back on this item' revealing no scope for negotiation on this matter.

'Dramatic' techniques were similarly used when a FI was accompanied on a check visit to a small foundry, where there was a lot of outstanding work the inspector suspected would not have been completed. This visit confirmed the inspector's suspicions. The FI was especially concerned by the extraction at the fettling positions,[8] since the air-flow rates did not meet the requirements. The inspector asked the works manager to correct this, pointing out in response to claims that it would be too costly that the purchase of new equipment was not being suggested but the maintenance of existing equipment. Two fettling positions were served by one extraction flue and the flow between the two was controlled by dampers.[9] When the inspector learnt that only one fettling position was in routine use he asked the works manager to divert the air flow from two benches to one so that at least one would comply. The works manager was left trying to achieve this, but he could not move the dampers. The manager became visibly agitated, and the more angry he became the more protracted became the FI's conversation with the employees and senior managers who were present. The visit resulted in the service of an improvement notice. Afterwards the FI remarked that the works manager was looking too smug about not having made any improvements, so it was thought the manager should have the problem brought home to him in front of everyone else. Hence the inspector insisted that the manager should try to move the dampers in the inspector's presence.

Another method used to persuade the regulated that they were non-compliant and needed to improve was to take *photographs* of problems of particular concern. Photographs were especially helpful where

---

[8] This is the area where the rough edges of metal castings are trimmed and cleaned.
[9] Dampers are metal plates in a flue which control air flow.

inspectors were at remote or transitory sites such as REIs and FIs in the Construction Industry Groups regularly encountered. A REI I accompanied photographed a dangerously overloaded line truck he had seen on a night inspection. When he presented the photograph to the area manager responsible for the workforce concerned he asked '[h]ow are you going to wriggle out of this one?' The inspector clearly had evidence he had been waiting for, and there was little the area manager could do except promise to look into the matter forthwith. The REI showed this photograph to several local managers as an example of non-compliance he would not accept, increasing the embarrassment of the area manager involved. In examples such as these the inspector was in a position not just to highlight a problem but to use the evidence of non-compliance to negotiate about other issues, in other words to maximize the advantages of the evidence.[10]

Deadlines were regularly imposed by inspectors. They were often included in the letters inspectors sent following visits. In some cases inspectors would specify the period of time within which they expected compliance and a check visit (see Chapter 5) might follow to ensure that compliance had been achieved. For example, inspectors could ask for a written reply giving details of remedial action taken by the business. They would often include a date by which they expected to have received a progress report. One REI I accompanied on an inspection of a main-line station sent a letter one week after the inspection detailing items requiring attention and requesting a progress report within six weeks. The inspector told the manager that if he had not heard from him two weeks after that he would send a 'nasty letter'. His letter was replied to well within the time limit set, but the REI noted that some matters were still outstanding and explained: 'I will be chasing them in a month or so if no further answers are forthcoming. I do not intend to make a special check visit because I will look at these things when I pass through the station on my travels.' The speed and efficiency with which inspectors' demands following inspections were met was taken into account by inspectors in their assessments of businesses.

Local inspectors sometimes held annual meetings with industry. IAPIs from one of my sample districts held such meetings with a mineral works. Each year the District Inspector and the inspector responsible for the works met managers from the site and representatives from its foreign parent company. The inspectors emphasized the value of

---

[10] The use of photographs in such cases is of course distinct from their use as evidence in a prosecution.

these meetings with respect both to seeing how much had been done about environmental control in the past year and to discussing what was proposed for the coming year. IAPIs were particularly keen on securing target dates from industry, and one commented that industry always worked to dates for itself, so he could not see why it should not work to target dates for him.

Each of the inspectorates in the study discussed *programmes of work* with firms. This was recognition that full compliance could not always be attained immediately, especially in situations where there was a lot to be done, where the remedies were complicated or time-consuming, and where costly remedies were called for. Programmes of work were arranged with all types of companies, the universal principle being that those things which represented the most risk should be remedied first, with inspectors being prepared to stand down on less risky matters and let them be corrected later in the programme. The time period covered by the programme varied. One FI considered a year to be the maximum for getting everything done: if nothing was done after six months then a notice was served. However, when questioned further this inspector said that a number of factors would be taken into account, for example, the cost involved and the technicalities of the remedy. There were seldom any hard-and-fast rules on these matters, and much depended on the circumstances of each case.

Two examples illustrate the sorts of programmes which might be agreed upon. The first was the case of a metal recovery works where the IAPI spent several years telling the company what it required it to do. Eventually the company went to the shareholders to get the money approved, and over the course of two years the inspectorate achieved a higher standard than it had originally intended. The beginning of the programme was a survey to identify sources of emission—some thirty sources were identified and the worst of these dealt with first. Over the course of the following two years a number of major works were undertaken. These included new buildings where materials previously stored and blended in the open would be housed; the installation of hygiene scrubbers; and the replacement of obsolete furnaces. Some of these were improvements the company would have made for its own benefit anyway and others also improved the working atmosphere for the workforce, but all benefited the environment and some, such as the electrostatic precipitator, were entirely for environmental control. The inspectors involved explained that the expenditure was in part the result of their constant visiting and laying the foundations for improvement.

They were convinced of the importance of working gradually towards major improvements, thinking in terms of the long term. In this example over £3 million was spent throughout the programme of improvements. In other examples less spectacular sums were spent, but they still represented a major expenditure to those involved.

The second example concerned a small electronics business set up by two people using their redundancy money. The FI responsible for the works explained that they were struggling to make a go of things, and it was felt that they would be lucky to succeed. When the inspector first visited the site the building was in a dreadful state. The business had first been persuaded to attend to the main worries, namely heating for the employees, the provision of fire escapes, and a proper storage area for flammable substances. Once these matters had been remedied the inspector urged the business to work through a programme of less urgent, but nevertheless necessary, matters. The requirements and how best to attain them were explained and the inspector also offered suggestions about other vacant sites and the availability of grants. The inspector felt that the business needed a lot of education and coaxing in order to understand the programme of work and the need for the improvements.

An IAPI discussing the requirements he placed upon a steel works explained that he and the company both had 'shopping lists', and that part of his job was to persuade the company to put the same things as he did at the top of the list. He had a list of priorities and often he did not mention the lesser matters until the programme of more important matters had been dealt with. Implicit in this explanation was that a certain amount of negotiation was entered into. In writing about the police Peter Manning notes: '[s]ocial control encounters, those where reaction to deviance is central, involve degrees of mutual dependency, thus all rule enforcement is a matter of negotiation' (1977, p. 247). The growing literature on regulatory enforcement suggests that nowhere is *negotiation* more important than in the enforcement of regulatory legislation (see Carson, 1970; Hawkins, 1984; Hutter, 1988; Richardson *et al.*, 1983). The inspectorates in this study add further support to this finding.

Inspectors and the regulated negotiated about three main factors. First, what needed to be done; secondly, how to do it; and thirdly, the time period within which this was to be achieved. The last of these was exemplified by the setting of deadlines and programmes of work discussed above.

The clearest example of negotiation arising from my fieldwork occurred during an IAPI visit to a refinery which proposed building another catalytic cracking unit.[11] Before the meeting began the inspector involved decided to adopt a strict negotiating stance and to refer to the reputation and competition of another rival company as a negotiating technique. Three refinery representatives and two IAPIs (a District Inspector and one of his staff) were involved in the meeting and business started promptly when the inspectors arrived on site. Negotiations centred upon three main points: the number of stacks there should be; the height of the stacks; and emission limits. On each of these points an agreement was negotiated. The company wanted a total of three stacks, including one already on the site and two new ones; the inspectors wanted just the existing stack. Negotiations resulted in one new stack. The refinery wanted the new stack to be 150 feet high and the inspectorate argued for 500 feet, with an agreement of 375 feet being reached. The matter of emission limits very much cross-cut the first two factors, and an overall reduction in emissions of sulphur dioxide was achieved and a sampling point agreed upon.

Throughout the negotiation a number of tactics were employed. The inspectors remained adamant that they would not accept a deterioration in the existing levels of pollution control and they argued for flexibility in case something went wrong. Inspectors frequently referred to the rival company and on occasions mentioned past difficulties with the refinery. The refinery representatives repeatedly argued that the inspectors' demands were too costly, but the inspectors tended to ignore this, arguing that the improvements they wanted were negligible compared to the total cost of the project. Moreover, inspectors were quick to point out that additional profits would be generated by the new plant.

The meeting revealed that the company representatives fully understood the inspectors' demands and had fully anticipated them in advance of the meeting. On three occasions the company representatives produced printouts, prepared in advance, of schemes suggested by the inspectors. In each of these cases they had first resisted the inspectors' suggestions. Afterwards the inspectors told me how pleased they were that their demands were already understood by the company and the printouts had been prepared in advance. They regarded this as a good example of their co-operative relationship. The inspectors were very pleased with the results of their negotiating and suspected that they

[11] A catalytic cracker is a device for cracking—that is decomposing petroleum oils by heat and pressure with a catalyst—to produce lighter hydrocarbons such as petrol.

had achieved more than the courts would have allowed, had the matter ended up there.

The scope for negotiation varied. As noted in Chapter 3, the structure of the law itself may encourage negotiation. Indeed regulatory law may be characterized by ambivalence and ambiguity (Carson, 1980; Hutter, 1988). Negotiation about compliance could also be encouraged by the nature of the activities subject to control. Regulatory offences, for example, were often amenable to correction before causing harm (see Hawkins, 1984, p. 6). Unlike more traditional crimes, such as murder and arson, regulatory offences, such as using unguarded machinery or polluting the environment, are often—but not invariably—capable of remedy.

Shaming techniques could also be employed to persuade the regulated to comply (Braithwaite, 1989). For example, inspectors would, if possible, try to exploit competitive situations. They might refer either to another company or to another works within the same company. Competition, explained a FI, could be especially intense within the same company, particularly if the industry was in recession. In the case of reference to another company, inspectors were playing upon the importance of corporate image. One IAPI discovered that a roadstone company he was having difficulty with was quite susceptible to comments that its plant fared very poorly in comparison with its main competitor. Indeed, at a site meeting with inspectors, senior management of the company was very concerned by this. This inspector felt that he was able to exploit this to achieve higher standards of compliance.

Appeals to higher authority were another common device for shaming in the face of recalcitrance. Incrementally this was a more stringent sanction to be used against particular individuals or areas of a company (see Chapter 7). For instance, if an IAPI came upon a situation which he considered to be particularly unsatisfactory then he could write a letter and request a meeting with a senior member of management. Indeed, an IAPI was much more likely to approach senior management than he was to write a letter—although this varied to some extent between inspectors. Certainly members of all inspectorates would appeal to a higher authority—if there was one—within a business.

In addition to appealing to a higher authority within a company, inspectors also referred to senior authorities within their own organizations. They could transfer responsibility for their own actions to their superiors by inferring that they were being pushed by them into a particular course of action.[12] Inspectors could, for instance, refer to HSE as the instigator of particular initiatives. Alternatively they might call Chief Inspectors or other senior inspectors in their support. Chief Inspectors could take on a special symbolic significance which could be exploited. To the extent that both the regulated and regulator were concerned with public image, *Annual Reports* could be very interesting documents as they contained references to specific industries, and sometimes companies, which could well influence their public image. Indeed, in this respect inspectorates seemed to be well aware of the importance of publicity as a form of social control (see Fisse and Braithwaite, 1983; Gerber and Short, forthcoming).

Warnings

As with the sanctions pyramid described by Ayres and Braithwaite the next broad layer of sanctions in the enforcement pyramids used by the inspectorates in this research was *warnings*. The least threatening warnings were verbal warnings.

Verbal *threats to proceed with legal action* were possibly more common than written threats. In the context of a long-standing relationship with a company these threats could be very real. This was the case when a FI visited a steel works where the coke ovens were regarded as being in a 'diabolical state'. Over lunch with the safety officer and the manager responsible for the ovens the FI made veiled threats of improvement notices, and no-one around the table seemed in doubt about the inspector's seriousness. In other cases threats of legal action were made to avert complacency. A FI making a check visit to a small bedding factory discovered that, while some previous requests had been met others had not; in particular the company were not keeping the gangways in the factory clear. The FI did not accept the owner's explanation, namely that they were too busy to keep the gangways clear. Rather, the inspector regarded this as an even more pressing reason to comply, and the manager was informed the matter should be dealt with as soon as possible. The manager was expected to telephone the inspector's office confirming that the gangways had been cleared, and he was warned that if the inspector came back and found the factory in the same state again there would be no hesitation about prosecution, since the

---

[12] Cranston (1979, p. 80) similarly describes how consumer officers may adopt a strategy of presenting themselves as 'neutral agents of legislative and departmental masters'. He explains that by doing this 'consumer officials purport to be merely discharging their rather unpleasant obligations'. Rock (1973) makes a similar observation about bailiffs.

indicating those matters requiring attention either within the letter or in a schedule sent with the letter, whereas IAPIs usually sent letters only if they discovered important matters requiring attention and they stated explicitly that the law had been contravened only if they came up against something very serious. In the latter case legal proceedings could be mentioned as a distinct possibility. Indeed, IAPIs sent out the most severe letter threatening legal action in the form of an *infraction letter* (Weait, 1989).

Infraction letters were administrative devices which signalled formally to the regulated that they had committed an offence and might be considered for prosecution. Although it was not a legal document, an infraction letter quoted the legislation contravened and might be accompanied by copies of the relevant sections. Inspectors could send such letters of their own volition, unlike the service of notices where permission from a senior authority was required. The number of infractions declared by IAPIs in a year were reported in the inspectorate's *Annual Report* and it is perhaps a sign of the seriousness with which they were regarded that they were reported in the same paragraph as prosecutions and notices. It was certainly the case that before declaring an infraction inspectors should have sufficient evidence to prosecute. And should the offending business not comply promptly then prosecution was likely, especially if the inspectorate already had a poor opinion of the business.

Letters of infraction were not sent automatically following every offence coming to the inspectorate's attention, but were reserved for the most serious and flagrant cases they encountered (see Table 13). These might forestall a prosecution by giving offenders the opportunity to remedy outstanding problems and explain why they were not complying with the standards required of them. To this extent they might also involve an element of bluff. Nevertheless, an infraction letter did not preclude prosecution.

Two infractions were witnessed during the course of fieldwork. The first was the result of a single flagrant violation, namely a failure to register a process with IAPI (see 199 above). The second infraction was the result of persistent non-compliance and a steady flow of complaints from neighbouring businesses about emissions of dust from a small factory. The premises were brought to the IAPI's attention by a FI who was dealing with dust problems within the factory. The IAPI which subsequently became involved in the case felt that it had fought an uphill battle to try to improve matters but with few positive results. So

TABLE 13. Infractions Declared by IAPI 1980–89

Year	No. of Infractions
1980	80
1981	69
1982	77
1983	41
1984	32
1985	24
1986	26
1987/88	25
1988/89	34

Source: Annual Reports

it was decided to send in a sampling team. It reported emissions double the accepted limit, so it was decided to send an infraction letter to the company. The owner's response to this was, in the inspector's words, 'rude, inaccurate and insulting'. Largely because of this perceived assault on IAPI credibility another letter was sent to the company, again explaining that prosecution would be a distinct possibility if the emissions were not improved. One year later the factory was still the subject of complaint and the District Inspectors involved wrote to the Deputy Chief IAPI suggesting that an improvement notice be served. The Deputy's response recommended prosecution in the event of further non-compliance.

Notices

The next layer in the sanctions pyramid comprises *improvement* and *prohibition notices*, the least coercive of the formal legal sanctions available to inspectors. All inspectors tended to adhere to similar general principles when deciding which type of legal action to invoke. The sort of non-compliance likely to prompt consideration of a *notice* was failure to provide basic safety or pollution equipment or a failure to comply with inspectors' requests from earlier visits.

Typically a notice was preferred to prosecution when inspectors did not consider that recurrence of the problem was likely. An improvement notice would therefore be considered most appropriate for initial compliance, for example to achieve the purchase and installation of new safety or pollution-control equipment. Compliance maintenance, for example encouraging the use of equipment already installed, may prompt more immediate action such as a prohibition notice, or more severe action, depending upon circumstances.

Although prohibition notices were seldom suitable for IAPI, given the need to prove imminent danger to health, this does not mean that these inspectors never used them. The Chief Inspector's *Report* for 1985 notes the 'rare event' of an IAPI issuing a prohibition notice when he discovered the owner of a chemical-waste incinerator attempting to dispose of waste pharmaceuticals in an unacceptable manner: '[t]he inspector decided there was a risk that the practice would result in harmful substances being emitted from the chimney in an uncontrolled way and so took this immediate step to stop the operation' (HSE, 1986a, p. 3).

Prohibition notices may also be preferred to improvement notices when inspectors were dealing with temporary rather than permanent sites. FIs, for example, opted for prohibition rather than improvement notices if possible when they encountered problems on construction sites. An improvement notice gives the offender at least twenty-one days to comply and a contractor or firm might not be on a site for this long.

When deciding whether to initiate legal action and, if so, whether to opt for a notice or prosecution, inspectors were involved in assessing an employer's attitude towards health and safety. If an employer was regarded by inspectors to have a generally good attitude towards health and safety and there were only one or two problems the inspector was concerned to remedy then it was likely that a notice would be selected as the most appropriate enforcement. In contrast, prosecution was more likely in the case of an employer who was generally or persistently not complying with health and safety demands.

Prosecution

Prosecution was the most serious form of legal action available to inspectors, and as such it denoted the ultimate sanction in the sanctions pyramid. The *purposes* of prosecution are usually broadly identified as either retributive or utilitarian, the former being an essentially moralistic, punitive approach and the latter focusing on deterrence. In the case of all three inspectorates prosecutions were, more often than not, instituted for a complex mixture of retributive and utilitarian reasons.

Cases where the dominant reason for prosecution was retributive were those involving deliberate offending. IAPIs cited such a case, namely working at night so as to avoid inspectors and because emissions were less visible then. Even in these cases, however, there was an element of general and specific deterrence in the decision to prosecute. Inspectors regarded the prosecution as a warning to the offender involved and to other potential offenders that flagrant offending would not go 'unpunished'. Indeed, flagrant offending could be perceived by inspectors as an attack on their credibility and this, too, informed the decision to prosecute, with legal action serving to underline the authority of the inspector.

Of the three inspectorates examined in this research the FI was most likely to mention retribution as the purpose of legal action. A much quoted phrase was 'a punishment of wrongdoing'. But even FIs did not always prosecute serious or negligent cases, since legal action was not always considered appropriate. This was most usual when someone had already been 'punished' either by a serious injury or by another regulatory agency deciding to prosecute. In such cases inspectors did not always consider legal action worthwhile. Where the person responsible for an accident was also its victim, inspectors could consider that there was no need for specific deterrence and that there would be no public sympathy for retributive action. More pertinently, there might not be sympathy in a court, especially in a Crown Court with a jury.

Utilitarian reasons for prosecution came into prominence when inspectors were concerned about a high incidence of a particular type of accident in an industry. The decision might then be taken to prosecute the next major accident falling into this category. The RI pursued such a strategy following a spate of accidents involving overturned cranes. New regulations requiring the reporting of some crane accidents (regardless of injury) had revealed a high incidence of potentially dangerous accidents (Department of Transport, 1982, pp. 61–2). The inspectorate quickly investigated the issue and identified overloading as a major problem. Measures to improve the situation were discussed with the industry and there appeared to be some improvement in the short term (1983, pp. 24–5). Yet it was clear that little further progress was made, for further accidents of this type were recorded in the 1984 *Annual Report* (1985, p. 25). Having pursued a strategy of persuasion, and in the face of continuing offences, an exasperated inspectorate decided that the only course open to it was legal action. Accordingly the 1984 *Report* records the first successful prosecution for an overloaded and overturned crane.

A prominent reason for prosecution in all inspectorates was to 'get things done' and to remedy problems. Even though such prosecutions could follow persistent non-compliance and it might be considered that there was an element of retribution involved in the decision to prosecute, this was not necessarily so. Prosecution did not necessarily result from aggregate non-compliance. It could also be the result of a single act of negligence or carelessness in a normally compliant company. This was possible, for example, when the reason for prosecution extended beyond the individual firm to an entire industry. In the case of exemplary prosecutions, intended often as a warning to an industry, the business subject to prosecution might not have a past record of non-compliance. Moreover, inspectors might not have intended any punishment but may simply have wanted to remedy a problem.

The stigma and loss of reputation which might be suffered by a business following a prosecution was appreciated by inspectors. They recognized the consequences of their legal action and in many cases they would try to exploit this by threatening to prosecute. Some inspectors felt that prosecution, whether or not successful, was the most significant act because it would keep the regulated 'on their toes' and keen to avoid the publicity of another court case. In some cases securing a conviction was so highly valued that 'horse trading', or 'plea bargaining' as it is more formally known, was entered into. In all of these cases the reputational damage which could be incurred by a prosecution was clearly intended as a specific deterrent. Similarly, prosecution as a reminder of obligations and responsibilities was intended as a specific deterrent, although the cause of general deterrence could also be met. The evidence of other studies suggests that these inspectors were correct in their assumption that companies are concerned to create and maintain good reputations and are hence susceptible to adverse publicity being used as a form of social control. (Fisse and Braithwaite, 1983; Gerber and Short, forthcoming; Olsen, 1992).

Prosecution was both a rare and an important event for the regulatory inspectors in this research. Moreover it had both pragmatic and symbolic significance. Pragmatically it accorded with the prime regulatory objective of gaining compliance. Symbolically prosecution underlined the authority and legitimacy of inspectors in the face of flagrant, blatant, or persistent non-compliance (Hawkins, 1989; Rock, 1973). Indeed, inspectors exploited the fact that prosecution was a public event which might bring the full weight of the criminal justice system to bear on offenders. The severity of this sanction was arguably heightened by the sparing use of prosecution by these inspectorates.

The significance of prosecution, of course, meant that it also carried risks for inspectors. As Hawkins (1989) has explained, inspectors calculate the risks of losing a prosecution, and if the risks are too great then they may abandon the idea of prosecution. The reasons are various and include the cost of the resources involved in preparing a case and the risks that may be posed to inspectors' competence and the agency's credibility (*ibid.*, p. 371).

Further light on the issue of compliance and the role of this top layer of the sanctions pyramid may be shed by considering inspectors' reasons for not proceeding with a prosecution. Generally, the inspectors in this research only considered prosecution if they felt that they had a good chance of winning a case. Thus marginal cases would not be considered seriously for prosecution. There were a variety of factors which would increase the probability that inspectors would not proceed with a prosecution. In some cases there were legal factors, and the most obvious of these was having insufficient evidence to proceed with a case. The evidential requirements of the HSW Act 1974 proved to be a particular obstacle to prosecution. If possible, inspectors would try to prosecute under the more specific rules of the Factories Act 1961, where the definition of compliance is much more precise and non-compliance was hence much easier to prove than non-compliance with the general requirements of the more recent legislation (Dawson *et al.*, 1988, p. 15, ch. 9; Hawkins, 1989). Similarly they were more likely to prosecute in the event of an accident (see Chapter 6). In many cases inspectors looked for positive evidence, that is evidence which supported their case (Sanders, 1987), and it could well be that when either a superior officer or solicitor examined the evidence it was found lacking.

There were also 'technical' reasons for not proceeding with a case. One FI I accompanied, for example, visited a garage after receiving a tip-off that an improvement notice which had been served was not being complied with. Basically the garage had been required to install a suitably equipped area for the respraying of cars should it want to undertake this activity. The proper equipment had not been installed, and when we visited the garage cars were being resprayed. Accordingly statements were taken from the employees who were respraying and the FI apparently had clear-cut evidence of non-compliance. A prosecution did not result, however, as the expiry date of the improvement notice had passed and the FI could not prove that there had been respraying within the period of the notice.

A significant reason for not proceeding with a prosecution could be concern that if the case was lost a precedent would be set and the inspectorate would be forced to change its working definitions of compliance to one which was less inclusive or demanded a lower standard of protection. Inspectors were very aware of the dangers of allowing 'once-and-for-all decisions' to be made, especially in relation to new legislation which could be unclear or in cases where they suspected that the working definition of compliance was more demanding than the courts would allow. This reason for not proceeding with legal action highlights the fact that prosecution may also serve to protect the regulated. This was clearly understood by an IAPI who commented that the reluctance of inspectors to prosecute in many respects removed the legal rights of the regulated and their right to appeal. This, of course, was true only to the extent that the regulated were not prepared to call the bluff of the inspectorate. But, that said, one of the features of regulatory control, in Great Britain at least, was the apparent reluctance of the regulated to challenge the authorities. Indeed, it was interesting that where it was believed that the company under consideration of prosecution was well organized with a legal department of its own, and therefore likely to defend the case, scrutiny of the decision to prosecute could be greater than normal, especially in a marginal case. The number of appeals against regulatory action in Britain is low, including the number of appeals against notices issued by HSE inspectorates (see Table 14). This is in direct contrast to the USA where Yeager's (1991, pp. 226–7) discussion of the Environmental Protection Agency describes a regulatory agency besieged by legal challenges to its regulation (Vogel, 1986).

Fear of losing was not the only reason for not pursuing a case through the courts. The perceived attitude of the courts to regulatory cases was also significant. Like many other regulatory agencies HSC/HSE considered the penalties imposed by the courts as derisory and undermining of their efforts (Cranston, 1974; Croall, 1992; Hutter, 1988; Richardson *et al.*, 1983). HSC, HSE, and the individual inspec-

TABLE 14. Appeals Against Enforcement Notices (Improvement and Prohibition) Issued by HSE Inspectorates 1980 and 1985

Year	Enforcement Notices Issued	No. of Appeals	No. Withdrawn	Dismissed Completely	Dismissed with modifications	Upheld
1980	8,637	36	28	2	6	0
1985	8,030	41	31	5	2	3

Source: HSC\HSE Annual Reports; Health and Safety Statistics

torates expressed their dissatisfaction with the courts publicly and regularly. In his 1981 *Annual Report* the Chief IAPI complained about fines and costs of 'little over £2000' imposed for seventeen successful prosecutions (fifteen of which were for illegal cable burning). He considered this 'a derisory figure by comparison with the profits to be made from illegal cable burning' (1982b, p. 2). HSC and HSE made similar remarks in their *Annual Reports* and in evidence to the Select Committee on Employment (HSC, 1990, pp. 119–20). Indeed, no opportunity seems to have been lost, for in 1988 they used the occasion of a 'landmark' fine of £750,000 imposed on British Petroleum to highlight again their grievances about the more typical scenario:

At the other end of the spectrum it is sometimes disappointing for inspectors, and more seriously it gives the wrong signal to management, when serious failures in health and safety attract relatively trivial fines. We realise that this is the prerogative of the courts but we sometimes wonder whether such fines sufficiently reflect the importance which society attaches to the prevention of accidents and ill health. [HSC, 1988, p. 30].

As this quotation reveals, the effects of weak sanctions may also involve a possible lack of deterrence; a negative impact upon victims and their families; and concerns about the effectiveness and the credibility of both the law and the regulatory agency (see HSC, 1990, pp. v, 119). Inspectors identified two main reasons for low fines. The first was a lack of awareness of the seriousness of health and safety and environmental offences amongst magistrates. The second referred to the composition of the bench. Indeed, in its evidence to the Select Committee on Employment (August 1989) HSC referred specifically to agricultural offences in order to highlight this point—'some magistrates' benches, largely composed of farmers, have proved especially reluctant to penalise offences severely' (HSC, 1990, p. 120).

Inspectors felt that the courts did not tend to understand or deal sufficiently harshly with health and safety or environmental cases, and were especially sensitive to the likelihood of the magistrate or jurors being sympathetic to particular types of cases. The most frequently cited example was the prosecution of individuals. Many inspectors voiced the suspicion that they were much more likely to succeed with a prosecution if they targeted the organization (see also Grabosky and Braithwaite, 1986). The reaction of the courts could depress inspectors and it also figured in the legal advice they received. One solicitor's letter to RI advised that while they had a case, it was 'merely a technical offence which would receive a nominal penalty which would detract considerably from the effect of prosecution'. Interestingly the inspectorate did not fully agree that prosecution in these circumstances would be a waste of time. It felt that a successful prosecution would be satisfactory and would have a salutary effect upon a railway department which had repeatedly caused problems.

Weak sanctions have been identified as a characteristic of regulatory enforcement (Snider, 1987) but there is controversy over their effects. Some argue along the same lines as HSC that weak sanctions are ineffective and do not deter (Carson, 1982; Clinard and Yeager, 1980; Pearce, 1976). Others can find no evidence that higher penalties provide more deterrence than lower penalties. Gray and Scholz, for example, claim that 'it appears that any penalty acts as a deterrent. . . . Apparently the penalty itself provides a threshold sufficient to gain the attention of management, while the amount of the penalty is of less consequence' (1991, p. 201). For some authors the arguments are ideological, one view being that those involved in the enforcement process should be 'reasonable' in their use of sanctions (Bardach and Kagan, 1982) and the opposing view being that the concepts of 'reasonable' and 'unreasonable' are always socially negotiated in favour of private capital (Pearce and Tombs, 1990; Yeager, 1991). Whatever the position, the fact that criminal sanctions do form the peak of the sanctions pyramid does mean that they may be used to some effect in the underlying layers of the pyramid. As Rock (1973) explained, sanctions can play a vital symbolic role in a game of threats by enforcement officials. The actual imposition of the penalties may not be their central use.

The sanctions pyramid adhered to by the research inspectorates is portrayed in Figure 4. Different layers of the pyramid were considered appropriate for different offences, people, and circumstances. Enforcement careers could begin at any layer of the pyramid of sanctions, although without a flagrant flouting of the notification or registration requirements most inspectors would start with education and advice and move up through the pyramid in pursuit of compliance. The case of the phurnacite plant at Abercwmboi in Wales is an interesting example.

The 1975 Annual Report of IAPI documents the case of the phurnacite plant at Abercwmboi from the point at which most persuasive sanctions have been exhausted: '[i]n November, the Managing Director of National Smokeless Fuels Limited, and the Chief and Deputy Chief Inspectors visited the works to discuss the programme of improvement

Criminal
Prosecution

Notices
Improvement and
Prohibition

Warnings
Infractions
Written warnings
Verbal warnings

Persuasion
Shaming
Deadlines
Photographic evidence
Dramatic techniques
Education and Advice

FIG. 4. The Sanctions Pyramid

and the future of the existing plant' (HSE, 1977, p. 36). These works, as the *Report* continues to explain, were particularly troublesome, and subsequent *Annual Reports* continued to single out the works and to discuss specifically the state of affairs at the site. In the *Annual Report* for 1978 (1980a, p. 23) the works were described as 'the Inspectorate's most difficult registration in its class and demanding much necessary attention'. The 1979 report explains that the site 'has continued under much local complaint and is a matter of great concern to the local authority and the Inspectorate' (1981, p. 26). Yet another visit is reported by the Chief Inspector in 1979, alongside the comment that 'conditions of plant and operations are considered to be below acceptable standards in various respects and progress appears slow'. Progress evidently remained slow. The 1980 *Annual Report* noted that the inspectorate received persistent complaints about the site, including a petition of 2,000 signatures, and that the site had received frequent visits from IAPI. Eventually in 1980, the inspectorate declared part of the site to be in infraction of the requirement to use best practicable means and fourteen improvement notices were issued under the HSW Act.

This is an interesting case, partly because it shows IAPI employing the strongest informal enforcement techniques available to it before eventually resorting to legal techniques. It also draws attention to the limits of the law. The 1981 *Annual Report* explains that '[t]he design of this process is such that no realisable amount of add-in-pollution abatement equipment is ever likely to reduce emissions to the level where the immediate neighbourhood would not still be subject to loss of amenity' (1982b, p. 8). Part of the explanation for this is to be found in the 1978 *Annual Report*:

> The . . . Phurnacite plant of Abercwmboi continues to present very difficult problems which are aggravated by its increasing age . . . it seems very doubtful to the Inspectorate that the Disticoke process can be made environmentally acceptable without virtually complete redesign and rebuild, particularly in view of the topographical situation of its present location [HSE, 1980a, p. 23].

As may be recalled from Part 2 of this book, the factors identified in this extract are among those IAPI is required to take into account in its definition of compliance. Hence its ability to raise standards substantially was hampered by the law. At the time of my fieldwork this site was still causing enormous problems. Indeed, the miners' strike of 1984–5 confirmed the inspectorate's belief that only a total shutdown of the phurnacite plant would alleviate the environmental problems it caused (HSC, 1987, p. 25).

The pyramid is a particularly useful concept because it takes into account varying company objectives and different types of business, regulated personnel, and inspectors. It also highlights the role of impression management in enforcement, for example, the notion of an enforcement career where non-compliance could lead to something more serious and sinister (Rock, 1973).

Pyramid of Enforcement Strategies: Research Findings

Enforcement careers are also structured by the enforcement strategies pursued by inspectors. The pyramid of strategies is pitched at industry level, and in the case of the inspectorates in this study broadly resembles Figure 5.

The model of *enforced self-regulation* described by Ayres and Braithwaite (1992) is very much the blueprint of regulation laid down by the Robens Committee (1972). So, the government laid down standards which companies were expected to meet by, for example, developing systems and rules to secure compliance. This involved worker co-operation. It also involved regulatory agencies in monitoring whether compliance was being achieved. Generally such a strategy was most suited to large, well-informed, and well-resourced companies. It

Fig. 5. Pyramid of Enforcement Strategies

was less suited to smaller companies which were not fully aware of the requirements and whose regulatory capacity was generally limited. In these cases the *persuasive strategy* was often considered most appropriate. This was essentially an accommodative strategy which relied upon education, advice, and persuasion (see Chapter 1).

The *insistent strategy*, while broadly accommodative, was rather more prone to invoke warnings and notices than the persuasive strategy. This strategy was adopted, for example, when compliance was not readily achieved, especially where inspectorate resources were stretched and frequent visits to a site were not possible. This strategy was also adopted where inspectors judged that a more stringent approach was necessary because of the 'character' of the offender.

The final strategy, *command regulation*, is a sanctioning approach most probably involving legal action. In the case of this sample this strategy was reserved for a minority of cases, notably the most risky industries, so judged because of the activity they were engaged in, or the character of the 'offender', or often both of these.

Debates about the enforcement strategy that should be adopted were a fundamental part of the histories of the inspectorates in this sample (see Chapter 2). In many respects each inspectorate came to HSE with its own traditions and reasons for enforcing the law in a particular way. To a certain extent the Executive has tried to impress its own views about the stringency with which the law should be enforced upon those inspectorates working for it.

HSC's 1989–90 *Annual Report* summarizes the Executive's approach thus:

HSE Inspectors do not approach their task with a view to seeking out legal violations and prosecuting error. They seek to promote reasonable compliance with good standards. Where what they see could be improved, they will so advise; and feedback to HSE is that the advice and experience of its inspectors are greatly valued by employers. An essential part of the inspectorate's armoury is nevertheless the power to take enforcement action, either through the issuing of a statutory notice or, as a last resort, prosecution. This approach accords with the philosophy of the 1974 Act, which first gave inspectors the power to serve legally binding notices [HSC, 1990b, p. 4].

In many respects this statement reflects the position of all of the inspectorates studied, but it particularly reflects the position of FI. This is further emphasized by the following extract from the FI's contribution to the 1987–8 *Annual Report*, which parallels the HSE statement quoted above:

The majority of inspections result in advice being given to employers and workers in oral or written form. But where poor conditions persist in spite of advice, or where there is imminent risk of serious bodily injury or a serious breach of the law, inspectors will consider serving an improvement or prohibition notice and the need to place the matter before the court [HSC 1988, p. 49].

FI was most inclined to adopt the insistent strategy. While the large majority of FIs tended to use informal procedures in the first instance, they would have no hesitation in invoking legal sanctions should they fail to secure compliance. But the statistics do not suggest that inspectors did regularly encounter such failures. The 1985 Chief Inspector's *Report* estimated that '[i]n less than one in every 25 visits does the need for enforcement by prosecution or formal notice arise' (HSE, 1986, p. 8). This accords with my observations. Of the 111 FI visits I accompanied, none resulted in prosecution. In six cases improvement notices were served; in some of these cases more than one notice was served on an employer. The fact that FIs were prepared to consider legal action even this often, however, is in marked contrast to the persuasive strategy.

The position of FIs with regard to the insistent strategy is summed up by the comments of two FIs: '[w]e are policemen of industry. While our primary task is advisory we must never forget that secondary to this, and underlying it, we are still policemen.' Another was more hesitant in approach: '[o]n the one hand they (FIs) are not expected to go around prosecuting everyone, but on the other hand prosecution is regarded as necessary as a public display of activity.'

There was an underlying feeling amongst FIs that they were expected to prosecute at least a few times a year and that if a FI initiated no prosecutions in a year he would be called to account. The underlying assumption seemed to be that everyone must encounter some cases each year warranting prosecution.

The view of FIs may be contrasted with those of IAPIs and REIs.[14] IAPI and RI tended to favour the persuasive strategy. In IAPI's 1981 Annual Report it was explained that 'discussion, persuasion and co-operation leading to mutually agreed solutions, are preferred to coercion. In consequence, the inspectorate has made only limited use of the full enforcement powers' (HSE, 1982b, p. 17).

Persuasion is a key word in describing these inspectorates' enforcement approach, while prosecution does not really form part of their everyday vocabulary. Indeed, one REI quite emphatically told me 'I'm not a policeman', a statement which contrasts quite neatly with the earlier statements of FIs. Legal action of any kind was regarded negatively and as a sign of personal failure. Some inspectors explained their objective as being to make companies regulate themselves rather than catch them out.

These inspectorates valued co-operative relationships with the regulated, and they were concerned that a more legalistic approach would damage these relationships and the information that the inspectorate was privy to as a result, a point which so preoccupied inspectors that it was mentioned by all but a few of the IAPIs and RIs accompanied. One REI explained that he wanted the regulated to take problems to him, not be scared that he was 'waiting around the corner ready to hammer them'. Other disadvantages attaching to legal action, as perceived by these inspectorates, were the time and cost involved in constructing a legal case. As I have discussed elsewhere (Hutter, 1989), contradictory interpretations can be placed upon the relationship between resources and prosecution. On the one hand there were those who considered that they were forced to employ formal legal methods because of a lack of resources which prevented them from making repeated visits to premises to persuade and cajole the regulated to comply (see Hutter,

---

[14] I will consider these two inspectorates together. Their views were so similar that to regard them separately would involve a lot of unnecessary repetition.

1984, 1989; Shover *et al.*, 1982). On the other hand there were those who believed that prosecution costs might lead agencies with insufficient resources to avoid legal action (see in particular the work of e.g. Bartrip and Fenn, 1980; Veljanovski, 1983). While most members of the inspectorates in this sample would have agreed that prosecution was expensive and that it would not be cost-effective to prosecute a large proportion of violators, they differed about the point at which prosecution was cost-inefficient. All would have agreed that there were a number of offenders for whom education and negotiation might not have been cost-effective because they would have required so many visits. Moreover, all understood the idea of general deterrence. It was the extent to which the arguments were adhered to that varied. This suggests that there were other factors in play here (see Chapter 9). It also suggests that there was a relationship between the overall enforcement approach adopted and the explanations used to justify these approaches.

In line with the above, legal action was considered by most IAPIs and RIs as a failure of their own persuasive abilities, but most were also of the opinion that other strategies involving legal action were necessary for the most recalcitrant. The occasional use of the law was deemed useful to the extent that it showed the regulated that these inspectorates had 'teeth'. Exemplary prosecutions were also regarded as useful for their general deterrent effect. But none of this was regarded as inconsistent with the view that prosecution represented their own failure for inspectors were of the opinion that they should be able to persuade even the most obstinate individual to comply. One District Inspector told me that he was proud of the fact that he had never used a notice or prosecuted, indeed he did not know how to do either.

Leaving the Enforcement Career

Leaving the 'career' was only possible with the closure of a site. So long as a firm was in business it was subject to regulation and its enforcement career continued.

There were no procedures to inform inspectorates of the closure of a site. This was of relevance during the period of my fieldwork when the recession was resulting in the closure of numerous works. When large well-known companies were involved inspectors knew well in advance, sometimes before many employees did, that closure was imminent. But inspectors were seldom informed of the many small businesses which suffered closure. This could, of course, involve inspectors in many wasted visits. Sometimes the old businesses had been replaced by new ones and inspectors would hear of these through their visits, but this was not invariably the case. One FI I accompanied in the South of England accomplished the visits planned for a whole day in just a few hours simply because most of the workshops and factories the inspector had intended visiting had closed down since the last FI visit: none had been re-occupied by another business. Sometimes, of course, premises had been reoccupied by another business, and this could be the start of another enforcement career for another firm.

CONCLUSIONS

Compliance is best conceptualized as a process. It involves a negotiated, reflexive, serial, and incremental relationship between regulatory officials and the regulated. Typically this is a long-term, on-going relationship which is well encapsulated in the concept of an enforcement career.

The enforcement career emerges as very complicated. The character and actions of the regulated could do much to control the nature of the career. Inspectors moved from a broad set of assumptions about the nature of compliance and the reasons for compliance and non-compliance (Chapter 7) to form specific judgements about particular sites at particular points in time. Particularistic knowledge could alter inspectors' judgements fairly quickly and the status they accorded the regulated was as much a moral as a legal one.

The strategies and tactics used to achieve compliance and encourage the regulated to move on in their enforcement careers have been analysed through the concept of enforcement pyramids. These comprise a hierarchy of sanctions and a hierarchy of regulatory strategies with the least intrusive interventions at the base of the pyramid and the most intrusive at the pinnacle. The research inspectorates were engaged in responsive regulation to the extent that they employed a range of enforcement sanctions and strategies and they were prepared to move up and down the enforcement pyramids in response to a complex of stimuli. But there were apparently structural differences in the preparedness of these inspectorates to move up the enforcement pyramids and to adopt more stringent enforcement strategies.

In their efforts to achieve compliance through formal legal action it is vital that inspectors consider whether or not they have sufficient evidence to proceed, but there are also *organizational* parameters to the decision to prosecute. These include considerations about the likelihood of success or the possibility of an appeal. Factors such as these are significant for a number of reasons. In part they are perceived to touch upon the credibility of the organization. For example, a high level of failed prosecutions could lead to questions about the definitions of compliance the organization is imposing. More worryingly, from the organizational perspective, this could lead to a higher level of legal action and appeals.

The costs of legal action could be relatively high—putting together a legal case demanded a great deal of inspectorate time and possibly the time of technical and sampling staff. It might even require the additional cost of legal opinion. Inspectorate resources are limited, and what economists refer to as 'opportunity costs' were highly significant, since time spent on a legal case was time lost to other activities. Again the costs and benefits of legal action have to be weighed up at a case level as well as at the macro, legislative, and policy-making levels. And here inspectors, like legislators and policy makers, recognized that it could be to their advantage to have ambiguous laws. One of the risks of legal action is that a precedent will be set and flexibility will be lost. Inspectors were particularly concerned that the courts might accept a standard lower than that they felt able to achieve through more informal means.

All of this could seriously affect agency resources and their deployment. It could also disturb the accommodative approach to enforcement adopted by these agencies, an approach which is to varying extents built upon both bluff and trust. The relationship between regulators and the regulated is vital to our understanding of regulatory control and it is to this topic that we return in the final section.

PART 5

Conclusion

9 Conclusion

Compliance is a complex, flexible, and dynamic concept the definition, assessment, and achievement of which is the product of interaction, the outcome of a series of interpretative judgements. This process of compliance is subject to broad social and institutional constraints. These are embodied in the political, legal, organizational, and cultural spheres of the social context within which these interactions occur.

In attempting to make sense of regulatory control it is important to explore the shared understandings of those involved in regulation as well as of those parts of society which are most obviously of relevance to regulatory issues, such as the law, regulatory traditions, and regulatory work. It is important to be aware of conflicting interpretations of the social world and the political resolution of conflict; as well as of social change. Underpinning all of these are a series of regulatory tensions which inform not just the broader parameters of compliance but also its everyday resolution in the workplace. Moreover, they are tensions which help us to explain how and why regulatory officials come to select particular enforcement styles, especially those which are accommodative and compliance-based. The regulatory community is at the core of the compliance process and the relationship between regulators and the regulated emerges as vital to our understanding of regulatory control.

Kagan (1994, pp. 390 ff.) identified four sets of explanatory factors for variations in regulatory enforcement styles, namely regulatory legal design; the agency's social and economic task environment; its political environment; and its internal leadership. This research lends broad support to these, with support for the fourth being the weakest. This is partly because the focus of this research was not on the work of senior officials[1] and partly because senior British regulatory officials are not subject to the overtly political appointments system which characterizes the United States. The Director General of HSE at the time of this research was a career civil-servant while the Chief Inspectors were all, with one exception, career regulatory officials. The preoccupations of

---

[1] The work of the senior officials at the centre of HSE did not form part of the overall project undertaken by the Centre for Socio-Legal Studies. But some discussion of this important topic is included in the overview of the research undertaken by Keith Hawkins (1992a).

the HSE leadership were to promote and develop health and safety issues and regulation in an essentially hostile economic and political climate (see Chapter 2). It is a tribute to them that HSE remains intact and consolidated in the 1990s and that it has survived repeated attempts to deregulate, cut resources, and privatize its activities.[2] From the viewpoint of field-level inspectors the leadership is both of symbolic importance in their dealings with the regulated and the public and a focal point of criticism. HSE is a federalist organization encompassing a wide range of inspectors with varying skills, professional backgrounds, and regulatory cultures. This creates inherent problems of co-ordination and unification in the face of sometimes fierce inspectorate opposition (see Chapter 2). The extent to which these tensions can be resolved is questionable (Hutter and Manning, 1990). It is certainly a topic worthy of further research and part of a general area which is to date relatively unknown and unresearched (Kagan, 1994, p. 408).

THEORIES OF SOCIAL CONTROL

The findings of this research relate to broader issues of social control, in particular our understanding of legal variation and the circumstances that cause legal actors to select different forms of social control. Social theorists have argued that broad social changes, often characterized as modernity, have profound implications for social control. So such trends as increasing heterogeneity and individualism, the weakening of social ties, and fragmentation are related to changes in patterns of social control. For instance, there has been a decrease in effective informal controls and an expansion of legal forms of control; disputes once settled privately have become public; and new strategies and forms of social control have emerged in response to these changes (Horwitz, 1990). These changes are discussed in some detail by Reiss and in a very general way by Black.

Reiss (1984), for example, takes two broad models of social control,

---

[2] See Ch. 2. Since the research period HSE has continued to be subject to outside scrutiny and intense political pressure to cut costs. For example, in 1992 HSC was asked to undertake a major review of health-and-safety regulations to consider whether or not they could reduce the burdens on industry (HSC, 1994). HSE has also been subject to a review by the National Audit Office on the economy, efficiency, and effectiveness of its use of resources (National Audit Office, 1994). It is also required to market-test its central services to consider whether contracting out could achieve 'efficiency gains' (HSC, 1994, p. 77).

the compliance and deterrence systems, his objective being to understand the conditions under which 'legal agents of control' opt for one system or the other. The two models, which are discussed in Chapter 1, are very general. It is proposed that compliance systems will generally characterize situations when violations are predictable and preventable; conversely, deterrence systems will typify circumstances when violations are unpredictable and preventive actions are not possible. Compliance systems will be preferred where there is a possibility of continuing harm, especially where the process of detecting violations and sanctioning violators is complex, protracted, or costly. These systems will also be preferred when the long-run consequences are more serious than the short-term harms; and when the penalties which may be imposed for non-compliance may be passed on to others and so may be perceived as having no deterrent effect, for example when business can pass on the cost of violations to consumers. Compliance systems will also tend to be selected when the regulators can define a distinct known population of violators who can be monitored and controlled, whilst deterrence systems will predominate when those subject to control are dispersed and unknown.

Reiss (*ibid.*, pp. 30 ff.) believes that systems of control will increasingly be built on compliance rather than deterrence. He relates this to three major changes in modern societies. First, the extension of entitlements. Reiss argues that the individual's position *vis-à-vis* the collectivity has been strengthened. For example, individuals now have strengthened rights to privacy, with respect to both their property and their person. This has implications, it is argued, for detecting and controlling wrong-doing. For instance, the rights to privacy increase the difficulties of observing and collecting evidence of wrong-doing. Thus these rights make it increasingly difficult to detect wrong-doing in deterrence-based systems which are predicated upon securing conformity with the law by detecting violations reactively, determining who is responsible, and penalizing them. Compliance systems, which mobilize resources proactively, are less affected by the growth of entitlements.

The second major change discussed by Reiss is the growth of trust systems which, he argues, is consequent upon the growing inability to observe directly all that goes on around us. Trust, it is argued, has replaced surveillance and the development of trust systems has changed the nature of wrong-doing. 'In modern societies' writes Reiss, 'the prototypical law breaking is a violation of organizational trust' (1984, p. 33). These are fragile relationships, but nevertheless they are the basis of contract which partly rests on the premise that there will be no cause to invoke the enforcement machinery. While Reiss recognizes that trust is an important means of organizing and controlling individual behaviour, he relates its growth very much to the third major change he associates with modern societies, namely the growth of organizations and the complexity of organizational life. The emergence of large-scale organizations creates problems of detection and proof as organizations have greater capacity to avoid detection and the power to bargain. All of this, argues Reiss, has led modern societies to turn increasingly to compliance-based systems.

These very broad trends have emerged as significant in this research. Inspectors clearly used compliance methods more readily when they could potentially have had problems gaining access to information. While inspectors had extensive rights of access to businesses they, nevertheless, relied upon the co-operation of the regulated for information which would enable them to understand fully the activities they regulated. This ranged from technical information about new processes (some of which may have been highly confidential) to gossip about future plans for expenditure or closure. Such information was especially vital in situations where inspectorate resources were organized proactively and where it was difficult to secure evidence of wrong-doing. Similarly, trust was often an important part of inspectorate relationships, partly because of the inability of inspectors to monitor very frequently how compliant or otherwise businesses were. Moreover, these officials spent much, but not all, of their time regulating organizational life. And, as we have seen, the privacy, complexity, and power of organizations could contribute to the adoption of compliance systems.

A number of the factors identified by Reiss are clearly interrelated. For instance, predictability is most likely where there is a known population and fixed location; and where there is a known population it is most likely there is the possibility of continuing harm and long-term consequences if there is non-compliance. To some extent the growth of organizations explains why these factors may be found together, but we need to look more closely at the wider social environment. This is what Black attempts in his model of the relationship between general characteristics of social structure and social control.

Black (1976, 1980, 1989) considers how the various dimensions of social life can be used to predict and explain variations in the use of the law and other types of social control. He regards law as a quantitative variable, which varies across time and space and with 'every aspect of its social environment' (1976, p. 4). Likewise he regards the style of law as something that varies across time, space, and social settings. He identifies four main styles of law—penal, compensatory, therapeutic, and conciliatory. He proposes vertical and horizontal variation in the law. For example, with reference to the vertical dimension (arising from the uneven distribution of wealth), the quantity of law and the style of law are said to vary directly with rank (1976, pp. 17, 28 ff.). Downward law, it is argued, is more penal than upward law, which is more compensatory and conciliatory than downward law. So, where an offender is wealthier than his/her victim compensatory or therapeutic law is most likely, but where an offender's rank is below that of the victim a penal style is more likely.

The horizontal aspects of social life involve 'the distribution of people in relation to one another, including their division of labour, networks of interaction, intimacy, and integration' (*ibid.*, p. 37). Central to Black's discussion of the horizontal dimension is the concept of relational distance which is 'measured by the scope, frequency and duration of interaction between people, and by the nature and number of links between them in a social network' (1980, p. 4). He predicts that the quantity of law will vary directly with relational distance: extra-legal controls will most likely be used in the case of dispute between intimates, with the mobilization of law increasing as people are less intimate. The relational distance between disputing parties, argues Black, affects their willingness to go to law, the willingness of enforcement officials to arrest, the style of law, and even the outcome of legal proceedings. For instance, writing with specific reference to the police, Black (1980, pp. 132, 155 ff.) notes that they alternate between the conciliatory and penal styles of social control, with a tendency to be more conciliatory and neutral in cases where the parties are relatively intimate. This relates to work on the social control of strangers (Ruane and Cerulo, 1990) and, of course, to Reiss's theory of social control.

Black's work has been applied to the work of regulatory agencies. Grabosky and Braithwaite (1986) tested Black's theory in their study of 96 regulatory agencies in Australia. They hypothesised:

1. that an agency with a high percentage of staff drawn from the industries they regulate would prosecute less than those whose staff were recruited from elsewhere;
2. agencies which regulated a relatively small number of companies would use legal action less often than those regulating a large number of companies;

3. the agencies which regulated companies drawn from a single industry would resort to less formal means of achieving compliance than those which regulated a relatively large number of companies from diverse industries; and

4. agencies whose inspectors had frequent contact with the same firms would use less formal sanctions than those characterized by more impersonal contact.

Their data provided strong support for all but the first of these hypotheses. Grabosky and Braithwaite's study found a correlation between the relational distance between the regulator and regulated and the tendency to use formal sanctions. Thus their study added weight to Black's theory. They further suggested (1986, pp. 215 ff.) that the larger the company size the less the probability of prosecution. Again this is consistent with Black's theory of law which suggests that people or organizations of lower rank or inferior status are subject to more punitive sanctions than their wealthier counterparts.

Thus a quantitative study of Australian regulatory agencies, Black's American study of the police, and this qualitative study of British regulatory agencies all come to similar findings about the variations in patterns of social control. The only point over which there is a measure of discrepancy is Black's vertical dimension, which arises from the uneven distribution of wealth. Grabosky and Braithwaite (1986, p. 217) suggest that wealthier people/organizations may be subject to punitive sanctions less often than the less wealthy because of their superior capacity to achieve regulatory ends by means of persuasion. Their overall regulatory capacity—including scientific and technical expertise and fiscal capacity (Baar, 1992)—is often much greater than that of smaller firms. Hence they are more able to achieve regulatory ends and to challenge regulatory controls.

It is therefore possible to reach broad generalizations about the law and the circumstances in which it is mobilized, and the styles of enforcement adopted. Organizational and social factors have been identified as important across a broad range of different cultures. Indeed if Reiss is right and compliance systems are likely to predominate in the future then the nuances of this broad enforcement strategy warrant much more extensive investigation. This is even more vital if Rock is correct in his assertion that 'compliance-based enforcement probably deserves to be taken as the major pattern or archetype of formal social control in Western society' (1995). Such an assertion derives from the extensive use of compliance-based methods by regulatory agencies and an acknowledgement that the police may also routinely use compliance-based approaches.

There is now an extensive body of evidence that regulatory officials in Australia, Britain, the Netherlands, Sweden, and the United States favour compliance-based methods in a variety of areas of social regulation.[3] Moreover there is evidence that these methods are also favoured in financial regulation (Clarke, 1990; Cook, 1989; Gunningham, 1991; Levi, 1987; Shapiro, 1984; cf. Calavita and Pontel, 1994) and certain areas of policing.[4]

Further evidence of a growth of conciliatory and accommodative legal methods is the increasing popularity of mediation and negotiation as methods of dispute resolution. These methods offer alternatives to adversarial, court-based adjudications, and range from direct negotiations between disputing parties to mediation, which is a consensual approach in which neutral persons help disputing parties reach their own resolution. Such conciliatory methods have become popular in family disputes, especially divorce (Dingwall and Eekelaar, 1988; Ingleby, 1992; Rogers and McEwan, 1989); in victim–offender mediation (Coates and Gehm, 1989); small-claims courts (McEwan and Maiman, 1984); personal injury claims (Genn, 1987a); and lawyer–client interactions (Felstiner and Sarat, 1995). Certainly we have enough evidence to warrant further research into the growth of compliance systems and their theoretical and practical significance.

POLICY IMPLICATIONS

The advantages and disadvantages of different enforcement strategies are a controversial matter which causes much debate among enforcement authorities, politicians, and academics. The main arguments have

---

[3] For example, in building regulation (Niemeijer, 1989); consumer regulation (Cranston, 1979; Croall, 1992; Hutter, 1988); environmental control (Aalders, 1993; Gunningham, 1974; Hawkins, 1984; Richardson, 1983; Yeager, 1991); mining (Braithwaite, 1985; Gunningham, 1987; Shover *et al.*, 1982); and occupational health and safety (Carson, 1970; Dawson *et al.*, 1988; Gunningham, 1984; Johnstone, 1994; Kelman, 1981; Rees, 1988; Wilthagen, 1994).

[4] Accommodative and informal enforcement is most likely in connection with minor offences such as traffic or juvenile offences; when the victim is not interested in legal action; when offences are regarded as essentially 'private', for example, gambling and domestic disputes; and in the policing of public order. See Banton, 1964; Cain, 1973; Bittner, 1963; Cummings *et al.*, 1965; La Fave, 1962; Reiss, 1971; Waddington, 1994; Wilson, 1968.

been well and extensively rehearsed elsewhere, and in many respects reflect the theoretical debates about regulation. Basically there is a body of opinion which regards the persuasive or accommodative approach as a 'soft option', a failure to regulate effectively and an approach which places enforcement officials in danger of capture or co-option by the regulated (see especially, Gunningham, 1987; cf. Grabosky and Braithwaite, 1986). This contrasts with accommodative theorists who believe that regulation is managing to curb the activities of the powerful minority in the interests of a less powerful majority, albeit in difficult circumstances (see Chapter 1). In considering the whole question of how 'effective' regulatory officials are it is undoubtedly important to take the view of McBarnet (1981) that front-line enforcers could be the 'fall guys' for the state. Indeed, in considering the role of the law we should pay attention to the laws and legal procedures enacted by the state.

There is no doubt that regulatory legislation can confront regulatory officials with contradictory messages. As we saw in Part 2, the definition of compliance involves balancing competing demands and principles in the implementation of broad statutory standards. Similarly, rather extensive powers of access and inspection and strict liability may be balanced against weak sanctions (Hutter, 1988; Yeager, 1991). But this is not the complete explanation. It still remains the case that regulatory officials who do have strong powers choose conciliatory enforcement techniques even when there is no evidence of capture (Grabosky and Braithwaite, 1986).

There are a number of explanations for this. For example, full enforcement is arguably an impossible and even utopian goal, not least because of insufficient resources. It is also a recognition of the complexity of regulation relating to both the need for discretion and the difficulties in satisfying the evidential requirements of the law (Kagan, 1994). It also relates to evidence that to initiate legal action whenever a violation is detected may be counterproductive and lead to a political backlash in favour of deregulation (Nelken, 1994, p. 381). Establishing whether or not regulatory agencies are effective is bedevilled with difficulties for both regulatory agencies and observers. In particular, it is difficult to arrive at outcomes which will measure effectiveness (Hawkins, 1992a; Wilson, 1985). Statistical data are both poor and unreliable. Moreover, there are serious interpretative difficulties involved in constructing these statistics. Data about occupational ill-health, for instance, are surrounded by the uncertainties of defining and identifying disease (Hawkins, 1992a). Likewise injury figures are social constructs which are influenced by a range of factors such as compensational requirements and payments, the employment rate, and where workers are employed (Wilson, 1985, pp. 163 ff.). In addition, we need to be able to distinguish the effects of regulatory activity from other factors such as changes in industry, the occupational structure, and public expectations.

Assessing the social benefits and economic inefficiencies of regulation is fraught with difficulties. The costs of rules are often easier to estimate than the benefits; indeed cost-benefit analyses may be manipulated to produce desired outcomes (Cheit, 1990). In many respects the way the issue of effectiveness is determined and viewed is heavily influenced by one's theoretical and political views. If one adheres to conflict theory and regards the object of regulation as the curbing of the undesirable activities of the capitalist class and anything less than prosecution of this class for regulatory offences as a 'soft option', then some idea of effectiveness can be gauged from levels of legal activity. Indeed, anything less than regular prosecution may be regarded as indicative of 'capture' and hegemony. If, however, one believes that regulatory activity involves an accommodation of interests then the technical problems of measurement re-emerge to confound the issue of effectiveness.

There are, as several commentators point out, some dangers in considering just the issue of 'effectiveness'. Kagan (1994, pp. 388 ff.) argues that it is 'too simple as a standard of judgement' and that other social values must be taken into consideration. Ayres and Braithwaite (1992, pp. 20 ff.) refer to 'a long history of barren disputation' between 'staunch advocates of deterrence and defenders of the compliance model'.

The important point to recognize is that all enforcement officials use both accommodative and sanctioning techniques. What is at issue is the balance. Many authors have argued for 'responsive regulation' (Ayres and Braithwaite, 1992) or 'flexible enforcement' (Rees, 1988) which can accommodate different styles and techniques. As Braithwaite (1985) so cogently argues, persuasion and prosecution are both needed; indeed it is important to recognize that persuasion is more possible in some situations than others. Moreover, persuasion does not necessarily mean failure. Enforcement is a complex and complicated matter. It is too simplistic to adopt uniformly one approach or the other, or to criticize uniformly one method or another. What is clear is that enforcement is a craft as much as a science—namely, the craft of applying the general to the particular and most especially the craft of getting people who have strong incentives to do otherwise to comply. Inspectors need to be skilled, professional, and sometimes diplomatic (HSE, 1986). They all work, to a greater or lesser extent, with a wide range of people and activities and in a variety of circumstances, and they adapt their knowledge and style to each.

All of this serves to underline the difficulties in using the number of prosecutions initiated or notices served as indicators of 'effectiveness' (Bardach and Kagan, 1982). Moreover, this whole study reveals how difficult it is to evaluate enforcement bureaucracies. As the Chief IAPI pointed out in his 1985 *Annual Report*: '[s]uccess in air pollution control is seldom newsworthy—its invisibility is the very measure of its success—whereas failure and breakdowns lead, quite properly, to complaint, concern and media interest' (1986a, p. 1). Measurements of success or failure are problematic. Thus, the whole bureaucracy is in a vulnerable position, especially in a political climate characterized by deregulatory rhetoric.

This research highlights the complexities of defining, monitoring, and achieving compliance in a 'command-and-control' system of regulation. For example, it underlines the need for flexibility in the face of legal and possibly political ambivalence about regulatory goals. Moreover, it emphasizes that regulation is highly complex, changing, and in many important respects socially constructed. Accordingly there are inevitable difficulties in setting standards, rule-making, policy-making, and enforcement. One implication of this is that effective regulation should involve a mix of styles of regulation. Consideration, for example, of what we know about reasons for compliance and non-compliance with command-and-control types of regulation might, in the context of the regulatory areas which have been researched in this study, suggest the worth of other styles of regulation. For instance, financial reasons for compliance could be addressed by incentive regimes, such as grants for pollution equipment or taxes on pollution. Prior approval procedures, which have been discussed earlier in this study, seem to form a strong regulatory tool as the failure to gain prior approval can prevent the conduct of business at all. Information regulation, such as the mandatory disclosure of risks to employees and the public, could have resonance with the desire for a high-profile, positive corporate image.

It is clear that the study of regulation touches upon areas of vital social importance to our understanding of the relationship between law and society. It is therefore important that detailed empirical work continues so that better theories about regulation, law, organizational deviance, and compliance are developed (cf. Baar, 1992). Our knowledge of regulatory control is growing, but we still have a rudimentary understanding of core areas of regulatory control, notably regulatory policy-making; the impact of regulatory legislation, policies, and enforcement upon those subject to regulation; and the accountability of regulatory officials. We cannot begin to consider the effectiveness of different control strategies until we know much more about the limits of regulatory laws and policies and their impact on business and industry.

Appendix Organization of Data Collection

Data collection was divided into two main stages. The first and major phase comprised a period from December 1983 to March 1985 when I accompanied officials from each inspectorate. Observation was therefore the dominant method of investigation.[1] Members of the Board of Chief Inspectors' Secretariat of HSE and senior members of the inspectorates researched were very helpful in providing information and advice which informed the selection of a research sample.

FACTORY INSPECTORATE

Four FI areas were included in the study, selected according to three criteria. The first was to select offices in *different areas* of England and Wales[2] to include locations with different economic profiles. In particular, it was decided to select areas with different levels of unemployment and different experience of the closure of industries. The second criterion was in some respects related to the first, namely the *type of industry* to be found in each area. Attention was paid to including well-established, 'traditional' industries and the 'new', 'high-tech' industries, as well as incorporating heavy, manual, and light precision industries. So the sample covered industry groups which had responsibility for activities as diverse as iron-and-steel making and construction on the one hand and precision engineering and chemicals on the other. One consequence of this selection procedure was the inclusion of firms of varying size, from the small back-street enterprise employing just one or two people to the large, multi-national corporation, employing thousands.

The third main criterion for the selection of FI areas centred upon their *enforcement activity*, in particular their apparent readiness to resort to legal action. Figures detailing the number of prosecutions initiated

---

[1] For a discussion of the advantages and limitations of this method of investigation see Becker, 1958; Becker and Geer, 1967; Bell and Newby, 1977; Hammersley, 1992; Hammersley and Atkinson, 1983; Silverman, 1985; Whyte, 1984.

[2] Scotland was not included in the sample because of differences in the legal system.

and number of notices served provided crude indicators of the propensity to use formal legal tools, giving rise to four possible scenarios: areas which were low on both prosecutions and notices; those which had high figures for both; and areas which had high figures for one but low figures for the other. Each of these 'types' was represented in the sample.

Once these three dominant criteria had been accounted for, a number of subsidiary factors came into play in the selection of which groups to focus on within each area. These included consideration of the national industry group (NIG) responsibility in each area, with the intention of studying at least two such groups. Attention was also paid to possible sources of interaction with other regulatory agencies: these included areas and sites where FI might be involved in liaison with, or might be visited by, IAPIs, REIs or Environmental Health Officers.

The first stage of fieldwork was devoted entirely to accompanying inspectors during the course of their normal working day. A total of thirty-three inspectors were observed over the course of thirty-four days and 111 premises were visited,[3] encompassing the whole range of types of visit. Following these visits inspectors sent me any paperwork generated, including communications to the business concerned, notices (where appropriate), and the file reports resulting from each visit.

During the second stage of fieldwork some areas were revisited and a number of the cases observed during the first stage were pursued to see what had happened since. This facilitated a longitudinal view of the enforcement process. The other major activity of this stage of fieldwork was a closer examination of the work of the NIGs.

THE INDUSTRIAL AIR POLLUTION INSPECTORATE

Detailed discussions with senior members of the IAPI led to the selection of three districts[4] for incorporation into the sample. Three main selection criteria were used, the objective being to choose a representative sample which would give some idea of the variety of work undertaken by this inspectorate.

The first criterion was to choose areas which would take account of the *range of industries* regulated by IAPIs. The basic aim was to encom-

---

[3] The length of time at each site varied. Large sites could take one or two days to inspect whereas some small businesses could take less than an hour. Check visits took less time than basic inspections. See Ch. 5.

[4] Different inspectorates gave varying names to their administrative divisions; this was very much a matter of agency practice.

pass small and large works; simple and complex situations; new and established premises; private and nationalized organizations; and recently-scheduled works as well as those which had been subject to longer-term control. In many respects these factors were related to the second of the selection criteria, namely the *range of processes* controlled. The inspectorate identified a number of relevant processes which it considered should be incorporated if possible. These included mineral works; asbestos, cement and sulphuric acid works; iron-and-steel works; coke arrestment, petro-chemical, or petroleum works; chemicals; and non-ferrous metal works (that is, lead works).

The third main criterion centred upon the inspectorate rather than industry and aimed to take account of the *range of inspection work* undertaken. This involved consideration of the types of visits undertaken by inspectors such as routine inspection and testing, special investigations, and examinations of new plant. It also incorporated the inspectorate's advisory work with local authorities and its work with the public, namely the investigation of complaints and participation in the local liaison committees which were encouraged in the vicinity of the more troublesome works subject to control.

Attention was also paid to the *geographical location* of the districts selected for examination, in order to take account of the economic health or otherwise of varying areas of the country. This did not need to be a major selection criterion since the other criteria ensured that different geographical areas were chosen because of the location of industries around the country. In addition the type of work undertaken by inspectors was influenced by the economic health of the area: to take a simple example, inspectors working in depressed areas were rarely involved in the approval of new works.

As with FI, the first stage of fieldwork was devoted to accompanying inspectors. Visits to the districts were all arranged through the inspectorate's headquarters. Before embarking on the visits with inspectors I went to each district to explain the nature and purpose of the research to them. A total of fifty-five premises were subsequently visited,[5] with eight inspectors, over the course of twenty-seven days. To all intents and purposes inspectors were observed during the course of their normal working day. However, this inspectorate felt that it should deviate because of my presence from its normal practice of not announcing

---

[5] IAPI visits tended to take more time than FI visits, largely because IAPI regulated a greater proportion of large and complicated sites.

visits in advance.[6] As had been requested, inspectors sent me any reports resulting from the visits I had accompanied them on.

The second stage of fieldwork was devoted largely to examining the work of the inspectorate's headquarters. Time was spent with senior inspectors discussing their role, and documentary sources were studied. There were two main reasons for directing attention to the headquarters activities of this inspectorate, namely the crucial role played by senior inspectors in liaising with industry and in writing and revising notes on Best Practicable Means, and the greater potential for senior officers to become involved in decisions about individual cases in the districts. Meanwhile, the districts included in the first stage of fieldwork were revisited and I was brought up-to-date with the cases observed on my earlier visits to these areas.

THE RAILWAY INSPECTORATE

As with the other inspectorates studied, the first stage of fieldwork with RI concentrated upon observation of its activities. But in contrast to the rest of the sample, this stage included observation of the inspectorate's work at headquarters level. This was at the request of the inspectorate which considered that it would be inappropriate for me merely to concentrate upon its agency work for HSE. Rather, if it was to participate in the study at all, it wanted me to gain a complete picture of its work, which involved following through the work of the Inspecting Officers as well as that of the REIs. Essentially this meant that I was able to follow through work undertaken for the Secretary of State for Transport under the 1871 railway legislation, notably accident investigations and the approval of new works. This was of relevance to the overall study, not least because these activities were part of the compliance process and paralleled the work undertaken by the other inspectorates in the sample.

The first weeks of fieldwork were spent with the Inspecting Officer responsible for the enforcement of health and safety legislation and accident investigation. During this period I was able to discuss the nature of his work, observe him at work, including accompanying him

---

[6] Most inspectors announced most of the visits undertaken with me in advance when it was possible to do so. It is interesting that this practice was used as a 'test' for companies to see how many would have attempted to 'tidy things up' because of the prior warning. It transpired that few bothered to do so.

on meetings with railway representatives, and attend a meeting of Principal REIs. Once I had an understanding of the breadth of the work undertaken a programme of visits was arranged. This was designed to cover the inspectorate's activities with several regions of British Railways and with the minor railways, including London Transport. REIs from four regional offices were accompanied and their work observed. These inspectors, like the others in the sample, sent me any written reports which followed visits on which I had accompanied them.

In accordance with the initial agreement with this inspectorate, a variety of accident investigations were followed through, some conducted by REIs and others by Inspecting Officers.[7] Included in this aspect of the work was the observation of a major accident inquiry from its early stages through to the publication of the Inspecting Officer's official report. The work of other Inspecting Officers was also observed, notably their inspection and statutory approval of new railway works.

The second stage of fieldwork was devoted entirely to an examination of the work of the headquarters organization. In particular, the inspectorate's relationship with the hierarchy of British Railways was examined. This involved a detailed documentary survey, discussions with Inspecting Officers, and several meetings between these officers and members of British Railways Board.

COMMON POINTS

The first stage of fieldwork with the IAPIs and RI included my attending their annual meetings of all inspectors.[8] This enabled me to meet most members of these agencies and sit in on their discussions, thus gaining a wider perspective on topical issues. FI did not hold an annual meeting, but I was invited to talk to a Chief Factory Inspector's meeting of area directors and one of the area directors in the sample invited me to several meetings of his Principal Inspectors (as did the RI). Thus I was able to meet a cross-section of staff from this inspectorate. It is worth commenting that none of these more general meetings indicated that the inspectors included in the sample were in any way unrepresentative or exceptional.

[7] See Ch. 6 for discussion of accident investigation.
[8] In the case of RI all REIs and the Inspecting Officer responsible for the enforcement of health and safety legislation attended.

Observation with all inspectorates followed a common pattern. Those accompanied were asked to continue working as normal and I joined them for the course of their working day (or night in some cases). During visits my presence was minimized as much as possible and the main interactions included only the inspector and the regulated. I did not take notes during visits for the simple reason that it drew undue attention to my presence. Instead, brief prompting notes were scribbled when the opportunity arose and extensive field-notes were either dictated or written out in the evenings.

No attempts were made to analyse the data as they were collected. Apart from a desire not to influence subsequent observations, there was a practical reason for this, namely the intensity of the first stage of field-work. Once the data had been collected and field-notes written up there was little time or energy to spare for analysis. Rather this stage of the research was undertaken once the first stage of fieldwork with all three inspectorates was complete. A preliminary analysis of the data collected in the field with inspectors informed data collection in the second stage of fieldwork. For example, it indicated further areas for inclusion in the documentary survey and for discussion with senior inspectors. Another source of data collection, which was contemporaneous with the second stage of fieldwork or followed it, was inspectors' reactions to written papers resulting from the research and their discussions and questions at conferences and seminars during this period.

THE RESEARCH ENVIRONMENT

Research does not, of course, take place in a vacuum, irrespective of the wider environment and pressures upon the subjects of research.[9] Some of the pressures upon HSE at the time of this study have been discussed elsewhere (Hutter and Manning, 1990), but a number of points are worth repeating. Perhaps one of the most outstanding environmental factors, given the remit of the agencies studied, was the economic recession (some might add social depression) of the late 1970s and early 1980s. It has already been noted that the economic health of various geographical areas was a selection criterion for the fieldwork sample, but it should be remembered that redundancies and closures were phenomena encountered by all inspectors, albeit to varying

---

[9] Nor, of course, of the researcher's environment.

degrees (cf. Richardson, 1983). This influenced inspectors on both a professional and a personal level.

Another feature of this period was government attempts to rationalize the Civil Service. Not only did this have a detrimental effect on the morale of those concerned but it also had implications for the research. At the time of the pilot study and early days of fieldwork, the Government was in the throes of scrutinizing the Civil Service. Various studies were in progress to root out wastage. Inspectors were in little doubt that the main purpose of these studies was to legitimate cuts in resources, and hence they were understandably suspicious of any study. In particular my early days of fieldwork overlapped with a Raynor Efficiency Study of HSE, so FIs and IAPIs were understandably deeply suspicious of my motives and intentions.[10] It took time and the development of a degree of trust before these suspicions were allayed.[11]

The degree of initial acceptance of the study was also related to different experiences of being researched previously. Within my sample, IAPI was the most sensitive in this respect. In the 1970s this inspectorate had been subject to some criticism of its work and it was worried by the prospects of laying itself open to what it was concerned might be further 'misrepresentation'.[12] Another relevant factor here may have been that this inspectorate was not entirely happy in its relationship with HSE at this time and feared that this study could generate data which could be used against it.

Access agreements made by senior officials may be met with suspicion by their staff. As Burgess (1984, p. 45) notes, gaining access involves negotiation and renegotiation with individuals at different levels in an organization. Certainly research agreements reached with senior personnel do not guarantee automatic acceptance at field level, particularly when the researcher's method of study is unfamiliar to the participants, as was observation. While most inspectors did not feel especially threatened by the prospect of sitting in an office and being subject to an interview of some hours, having a shadow accompanying them for several days was an altogether different proposition. Taken at face value, the prospect of someone you do not know following you around for your entire working day and asking questions was perhaps

---

[10] RI, it will be remembered, undertook work for HSE on an agency basis. As it was not an integral part of the organization it was not subject to this particular Raynor study.

[11] Inspectorate 'grapevines' emerged as significant here.

[12] The main vehicle of criticism at this time was *The Social Audit Report* (Frankel, 1974).

intimidating. Given this, it was surprising how quickly inspectors over-
came their initial diffidence.

It was interesting that RI was the most relaxed about the research
and apparently the least threatened. Observation was immediately
understood as an appropriate research technique, and from the outset
the research was regarded as genuine and not the tool of organizational
connivance. This inspectorate's major consideration in agreeing to the
research was whether or not it had sufficient resources to cope with a
researcher. Once it had decided that the resource demand would not
be too great I was given every co-operation.

RI was not an integral part of HSE in the way that the FI and IAPI
were, and this may explain the initial differences in reaction to the
research. The pressures upon the relatively 'new' Executive to legitimate its resources in a climate of deregulation led to consequent effects
and uncertainty among its staff (see Hutter and Manning, 1990). All of
this served to underline the importance of understanding the environment within which the subjects of research operated. Nevertheless, once
I had spent some time with inspectors from each of the selected areas,
all of the selected inspectorates 'relaxed' and no significant problems
were encountered. Indeed, it is important to record that the data upon
which the following analysis is based were collected during a period of
fieldwork which was not only instructive but enjoyable.

Bibliography

AALDERS, M. (1993), 'Regulation and In-Company Environmental Management in the Netherlands', *Law and Policy* 15, 2, 75–94.

ADLER, M., and ASQUITH, S. (eds.) (1981), *Discretion and Welfare* (London: Heinemann).

ALDERMAN, G. (1973), *The Railway Interest* (Leicester: Leicester University Press).

ASHBY, E., and ANDERSON, M. (1981), *The Politics of Clean Air* (Oxford: Clarendon Press).

AUSTIN, R. (1989), 'Freedom of Information: The Constitutional Impact' in Jowell, J., and Oliver, D., *The Changing Constitution* (2nd edn., Oxford: Clarendon Press).

AYRES, I., and BRAITHWAITE, J. (1992), *Responsive Regulation* (New York: Oxford University Press).

BAAR, E. (1992), 'Partnerships in the Development and Implementation of Canadian Air Quality Regulation', *Law and Policy* 14, 1, 1–43.

BALDWIN, R. (1985), *Regulating the Airlines: Administrative Justice and Agency Discretion* (Oxford: Clarendon Press).

—— (1990), 'Why Rules Don't Work?', *Modern Law Review* 53, 321–36.

—— (1995), *Rules and Government* (Oxford: Clarendon Press).

—— and HAWKINS, K. H. (1984), 'Discretionary Justice: Davis Reconsidered', *Public Law*, 570–99.

BANTON, M. (1964), *The Policeman in the Community* (London: Tavistock).

BARDACH, E., and KAGAN, R. (1982), *Going by the Book: The Problem of Regulatory Unreasonableness* (Philadelphia, Penn.: Temple University Press).

BARTRIP, P. W. J., and BURMAN, S. (1983), *The Wounded Soldiers of Industry* (Oxford: Clarendon Press).

—— and FENN, P. T. (1980), 'The Administration of Safety: The Enforcement Policy of the Early Factory Inspectorate, 1844–1864', *Public Administration* 58, 87–102.

—— and —— (1983), 'The Evolution of Regulatory Style in the Nineteenth Century British Factory Inspectorate', *Journal of Law and Society* 10, 2, 201–22.

BAUCUS, M., and DWORKIN, T. M. (1991), 'What is Corporate Crime? It is not Illegal Corporate Behaviour', *Law and Policy* 13, 3, 231–44.

BECKER, H. S. (1958), 'Problems of Inference and Proof in Participant Observation', *American Sociological Review* 23, 652–60.

—— (1963), *Outsiders* (New York: The Free Press of Glencoe).

—— (1982), 'Culture: A Sociological View', *Yale Review* 71, 513–27.

—— and GEER, B. (1967), 'Participant Observation and Interviewing: A Comparison' in Manis, J. G., and Meltzer, B. N. (eds.), *Symbolic Interaction* (Boston: Allyn and Bacon).

BELL, C., and NEWBY, H. (eds.) (1977), *Doing Sociological Research* (London: Allen and Unwin).

BERNSTEIN, M. H. (1955), *Regulating Business by Independent Commission* (Princeton, N.J.: Princeton University Press).

BITTNER, E. (1967), 'The Police on Skid-Row: A Study of Peace Keeping', *American Sociological Review* 32, 699–715.

BLACK, D. J. (1971), 'The Social Organization of Arrest', *Stanford Law Review* 23, 1087–111.

—— (1973), 'The Mobilisation of Law', *Journal of Legal Studies* 2, 125–49.

—— (1976), *The Behaviour of Law* (New York: Academic Press).

—— (1980), *The Manners and Customs of the Police* (New York: Academic Press).

—— (1989), *Sociological Justice* (New York: Oxford University Press).

BLAU, P. M. (1963), *The Dynamics of Bureaucracy* (Chicago, Ill.: University of Chicago Press).

BOX, S. (1983), *Power, Crime and Mystification* (London: Routledge).

BRAITHWAITE, J. (1984), *Corporate Crime in the Pharmaceutical Industry* (London: Routledge & Kegan Paul).

—— (1985), *To Punish or Persuade: Enforcement of Coal Mine Safety* (Albany: New York Press).

—— (1989), *Crime, Shame and Reintegration* (Cambridge: Cambridge University Press).

—— and FISSE, B. (1985), 'Varieties of Responsibility and Organizational Crime', *Law and Policy* 7, 3, 315–43.

—— GRABOSKY, P., and WALKER, J. (1987), 'An Enforcement Taxonomy of Regulatory Agencies', *Law and Policy* 9, 323–51.

BRIMBLECOMBE, P. (1987), *The Big Smoke: A History of Air Pollution in London* (London: Routledge).

BRITTAN, Y. (1984), *The Impact of Water Pollution Control on Industry* (Oxford: Centre for Socio-Legal Studies).

BURGESS, R. G. (1984), *In the Field* (London: Routledge (1991 Reprint)).

BUGLER, J. (1972), *Polluting Britain* (Harmondsworth: Penguin).

BUTLER, R. (1993), 'The Evolution of the Civil Service—A Progress Report', *Public Administration* 71, 395–406.

CAIN, M. (1973), *Society and the Policeman's Role* (London: Routledge and Kegan Paul).

CALAVITA, K., and PONTELL, H. N. (1994), 'The State and White-Collar Crime: Saving the Savings and Loans', *Law and Society Review* 28, 2, 297–324.

CARSON, W. G. (1970), 'Some Sociological Aspects of Strict Liability and the Enforcement of Factory Legislation', *Modern Law Review* 33, 396–412.

—— (1974), 'Symbolic and Instrumental Dimensions of Early Factory Legislation: A Case Study in the Social Origins of Criminal Law', in Hood, R. (ed), *Crime, Criminology and Public Policy* (London: Heineman).

—— (1980), 'The Institutionalization of Ambiguity: Early British Factory Acts', in G. Geis and E. Stotland (eds.), *White Collar Crime: Theory and Research* (Beverley Hills, Cal.: Sage).

—— (1982), *The Other Price of Britain's Oil* (Oxford: Martin Robertson).

—— and JOHNSTONE, R. (1990), 'The Dupes of Hazard: Occupational Health and Safety and the Victorian Sanctions Debate', *Australian and New Zealand Journal of Sociology* 26, 126–41.

CENTRE FOR SOCIO-LEGAL STUDIES (1983), *An Agenda for Socio-Legal Research into the Regulation of Health and Safety at Work* (Oxford: Centre for Socio-Legal Studies).

CHEIT, R. E. (1990), *Setting Safety Standards: Regulation in the Public and Private Sectors* (Berkeley, Cal.: University of California Press).

CLARKE, M. (1990), *Business Crime: Its Nature and Control* (Cambridge: Polity Press).

CLINARD, M. B., and YEAGER, P.C. (1980), *Corporate Crime* (New York: Free Press).

COATES, R. B., and GEHM, J. (1989), 'An Empirical Assessment' in Wright, M., and Galaway, B. (eds.), *Mediation and Criminal Justice: Victims, Offenders and Community* (London: Sage).

COHEN, S. (1980), *Folk Devils and Moral Panics* (New York: St. Martins).

COOK, D. (1989), *Rich Laws Poor Law* (Milton Keynes: Open University Press).

COTTERRELL, R. (1992), *The Sociology of Law* (2nd edn., London: Butterworths).

COUNCIL OF THE LAW SOCIETY (1967), 'First Memorandum to the Royal Commission on the Penal System in England and Wales', in *Written Evidence from Government Departments, Miscellaneous Bodies and Individual Witnesses* (London: HMSO), ii.

CRANSTON, R. (1978), *Consumers and the Law* (London: Weidenfeld and Nicolson).

—— (1979), *Regulatory Business: Law and Consumer Agencies* (London: Macmillan).

CROALL, H. (1988), 'Mistakes, Accidents and Someone Else's Fault: The Trading Offender in Court', *Journal of Law and Society* 15, 293–315.

—— (1992), *White-Collar Crime* (Buckingham: Open University Press).

CULLEN REPORT (1990), *The Public Inquiry into the Piper Alpha Disaster* (Cm 1310, London: HMSO).

CUMMING, E., CUMMING, I., and EDELL, E. (1965), 'Policeman as Philosopher, Guide and Friend', *Social Problems* 12, 276–86.

DAVIS, K. C. (1969), *Discretionary Justice* (Baton Rouge, Louisiana: Louisiana State University Press).

DAWSON, S., WILLMAN, P., BAMFORD, M., and CLINTON, A. (1988), *Safety at Work: The Limits of Self-Regulation* (Cambridge: Cambridge University Press).

DEPARTMENT OF TRANSPORT (1981), *Report on the Derailment that Occurred on 16th February 1980 at Bushey* (London: HMSO).

—— (1981a), *Railways Construction and Operation Requirements for Level-Crossings* (London: HMSO).

—— (1982), *Report on the Safety Record of the Railways in Great Britain during the Year 1981* (London: HMSO).

DEPARTMENT OF TRANSPORT (1983), *Report on the Safety Record of the Railways in Great Britain during the year 1982* (London: HMSO).

DEPARTMENT OF TRANSPORT (1984), *Railway Safety: Report on the Safety Record of the Railways in Great Britain during 1983* (London: HMSO).

—— (1985), *Railway Safety: Report on the Safety Record of the Railways in Great Britain during 1984* (London: HMSO).

—— (1985a), *Report on the Derailment that Occurred on 30th July 1984 near Polmont* (London: HMSO).

—— (1989), *Railway Safety: Report on the Safety Record of the Railways in Great Britain During 1988* (London: HMSO).

DINGWALL, R., and EEKELAAR, J. (eds.) (1988), *Divorce Mediation and the Legal Process* (Oxford: Oxford University Press).

DI MENTO, J. F. (1986), *Environmental Law and American Business: Dilemmas of Compliance* (New York: Plenum Press).

DOUGLAS, M. (1985), *Risk: Accountability According to the Social Sciences* (London: Routledge and Kegan Paul).

—— and WILDAVSKY, A. (1982), *Risk and Culture* (Berkeley, Cal.: University of California Press).

EDELMAN, L. E., PETTERSON, S., CHAMBLISS, E., and HOWARD, S. E. (1991), 'Legal Ambiguity and the Politics of Compliance: Affirmative Action Officers' Dilemma', *Law and Policy* 13, 1, 73–97.

ENDS Report, 247 (1995) (London: Environmental Data Services).

FELSTINER, W. L. F., and SARAT, A. (1995), *The Process of Negotiation* (New York: Oxford University Press).

FENNELL, P. (1988), *Investigation into the King's Cross Underground Fire* (Cm 499 London: HMSO).

FISSE, W. B., and BRAITHWAITE, J. (1983), *The Impact of Publicity on Corporate Offenses* (Albany, N.Y.: State University of New York).

FRANK, N. (1984), 'Assaults Against Inspectors: The Dangers in Enforcing Corporate Crime', *Law and Policy* 6, 361–77.

FRANKEL, M. (1974), *The Alkali Inspectorate: The Control of Industrial Air Pollution* (London: Social Audit).

FRIEDLAND, M. L. (ed.) (1990), *Securing Compliance: Seven Case Studies* (Toronto: University of Toronto Press).

GALANTER, M. (1974), 'Why the "Haves" Come Out Ahead: Speculations on the Limits of Legal Change', *Law and Society Review* 9, 95–160.

GALLIGAN, D. J. (1986), *Discretionary Powers* (Oxford: Clarendon Press).

GENN, H. (1987), *Great Expectations: The Robens' Legacy and Employer Self-Regulation*, unpublished paper presented to HSE, Centre for Socio-Legal Studies, Oxford University.

—— (1987a), *Hard Bargaining: Out of Court Settlement in Personal Injury Actions* (Oxford: Clarendon Press).

—— (1993), 'Business Responses to the Regulation of Health and Safety in England', *Law and Policy* 15, 3, 219–34.

GERBER, J., and SHORT, J. F. (forthcoming), 'Publicity and the Control of Corporate Behaviour. The Case of Infant Formula', *Deviant Behaviour*.

GRÄBE, S. (1991), 'Regulatory Agencies and Interest Groups in Occupational Health and Science in Great Britain and West Germany: A Perspective from West Germany', *Law and Policy* 13, 1, 55–72.

GRABOSKY, P. (1994), 'Green Markets: Environmental Regulation by the Private Sector', *Law and Policy* 16, 4, 419–48.

—— and BRAITHWAITE, J. (1986), *Of Manners Gentle* (Melbourne: Oxford University Press).

GRAY, W. B., and SCHOLZ, J. T. (1991), 'Analyzing the Equity and Efficiency of OSHA Enforcement', *Law and Policy* 13, 3, 185–213.

GUNNINGHAM, N. (1974), *Pollution, Social Interest and the Law* (London: Martin Robertson).

—— (1984), *Safeguarding The Worker* (Sydney: The Law Book Company).

—— (1987), 'Negotiated Non-Compliance: A Case Study of Regulatory Failure', *Law and Policy* 9, 1, 69–95.

—— (1991), 'Private Ordering, Self-regulation and Futures Markets: A Comparative Study of Informal Social Control', *Law and Policy* 13, 4, 297–326.

GUSFIELD, J. (1981), *The Culture of Public Problems: Drinking, Driving and the Symbolic Order* (Chicago, Ill.: University of Chicago Press).

HAMMERSLEY, M. (1992), *What's Wrong with Ethnography?* (London: Routledge).

—— and ATKINSON, P. (1983), *Ethnography: Principles in Practice* (London: Tavistock).

HARTUNG, F. E. (1950), 'White-Collar Offences in the Wholesale Meat Industry in Detroit' and 'Rejoinder' to Burgess, *American Journal of Sociology* 56, 35–73.

HAWKINS, K. (1983), 'Bargain and Bluff: Compliance Strategy and Deterrence in the Enforcement of Regulation', *Law and Policy Quarterly* 95, 35–73.

—— (1984), *Environment and Enforcement: Regulation and Social Definition of Pollution* (Oxford: Clarendon Press).

—— (1989), 'FATCATS and Prosecution in a Regulatory Agency: A Footnote on the Social Construction of Risk', *Law and Policy* 11, 3, 370–91.

—— (1990), 'Compliance Strategy, Prosecution Policy, and Aunt Sally', *British Journal of Criminology* 30, 444–66.

—— (ed.) (1992), *The Uses of Discretion* (Oxford: Clarendon Press).

—— (1992a), *The Regulation of Occupational Health and Safety: A Socio-Legal Perspective*, Report to the Health and Safety Executive, unpublished report.

—— and HUTTER, B. M. (1993), 'The Response of Business to Social Regulation in England and Wales: An Enforcement Perspective', *Law and Policy* 15, 3, 199–218.

—— and THOMAS, J. M. (eds.) (1984), *Enforcing Regulation* (Boston, Mass.: Kluwer–Nijhoff).

HM INSPECTORATE OF POLLUTION (1983), *Report of the District Industrial Air Pollution Inspector, District G, to the Health and Safety Executive*

HEALTH AND SAFETY COMMISSION (1980), *Health and Safety Commission Report 1979–80* (London: HMSO).

HEALTH AND SAFETY COMMISSION (1981), *Control of Lead at Work: Approved Code of Practice* (London: HMSO).

—— (1983), *Plan of Work 1983–84 and Onwards* (London: HMSO).

—— (1985), *Plan of Work 1985/86* (London: HMSO).

—— (1985a), *Work with Asbestos Insulation and Asbestos Coating: Approved Code of Practice* (London: HMSO).

—— (1985b), *Annual Report 1984/85* (London: HMSO).

—— (1987), *Annual Report 1986/87* (London:HMSO).

—— (1988), *Annual Report 1987/88* (London: HMSO).

—— (1990a), *Annual Report 1988/89* (London: HMSO).

—— (1990b), *Annual Report 1989/90* (London: HMSO).

—— (1991), *Annual Report 1990/91* (London: HMSO).

—— (1994), *Annual Report 1993/94* (London: HMSO).

—— (1974), *A Guide to Woodworking Machines Regulations 1974* (London: HMSO).

—— (1975), *Asbestos: Health Precautions in Industry* (Health and Safety at Work Booklet 44, London: HMSO).

—— (1977), *Industrial Air Pollution 1975* (London: HMSO).

—— (1978), *Industrial Air Pollution 1976* (London: HMSO).

—— (1979), *BPM1/79: Best Practicable Means: An Introduction* (London: HMSO).

—— (1979a), *Industrial Air Pollution 1977* (London: HMSO).

—— (1980), *Foundries: Health and Safety 1975–78* (London: HMSO).

—— (1980a), *Industrial Air Pollution 1978* (London: HMSO).

—— (1981), *Industrial Air Pollution 1979* (London: HMSO).

—— (1981a), *Managing Safety* (London: HMSO).

—— (1981b), *Guidance Note ETMI: Sampling and Analysis of Emissions to the Air from Scheduled Works* (London: HMSO).

—— (1981c), *Guidance Note EH28: Control of Lead: Air Sampling Techniques and Strategies* (London: HMSO).

—— (1981d), *Guidance Note MS18: Health Surveillance by Routine Procedures* (London: HMSO).

—— (1981e), *Guidance Note MDHS5: On-site Validation of Sampling Methods* (London: HMSO).

—— (1982), *Best Practicable Means: An Introduction (BPM/82)* (London: HMSO)

—— (1982a), *Industrial Air Pollution 1980* (London: HMSO).

—— (1982b), *Industrial Air Pollution 1981* (London: HMSO).

—— (1983), *Construction: Health and Safety 1981–82* (London: HMSO).

—— (1983a), *Guidance Note MS8 Isocyanates—Medical Surveillance* (London: HMSO).

—— (1984), *Guidance Note EH10 Asbestos—Hygiene Standards and Measurements of Airborne Dust Concentrations* (London: HMSO).

—— (1984a), *The Report on a Petroleum Spillage at Micheldever Oil Terminal, Hampshire 2 February 1983* (London: HMSO).

—— (1985), *General Access Scaffolds: Guidance Note GS 15* (London: HMSO).

—— (1985a), *BPM 16: Notes on Best Practicable Means: Lead Works* (London: HMSO).

—— (1986), *Report by HM Chief Inspector of Factories 1985* (London: HMSO).

—— (1986a), *Industrial Air Pollution 1985* (London: HMSO).

—— (1987), *Report by HM Chief Inspector of Factories 1986–87* (London: HMSO).

—— (1991), *Research and Technological Services 1990/91* (London: HMSO).

HIDDEN, A. (1989), *Investigation into the Clapham Junction Railway Accident* (Cm 820, London: HMSO).

HILL, M. J. (1972), *The Sociology of Public Administration* (London: Weidenfeld and Nicolson).

HORWITZ, A. V. (1990), *The Logic of Social Control* (New York and London: Plenum Press).

HUTTER, B. M. (1986), 'An Inspector Calls: The Importance of Proactive Enforcement in the Regulatory Context', *British Journal of Criminology* 26, 114–28.

—— (1988), *The Reasonable Arm of the Law?: The Law Enforcement Procedures of Environmental Health Officers* (Oxford: Clarendon Press).

—— (1989), 'Variations in Regulatory Enforcement Styles', *Law and Policy* 11, 2, 153–74.

—— (1992), 'Public Accident Inquiries: The Case of the Railway Inspectorate', *Public Administration* 70, 2, 177–92.

—— (1993), 'Regulating Employers and Employees: Health and Safety in the Workplace', *Journal of Law and Society* 20, 4, 452–70.

—— (forthcoming), *On the Right Tracks? Regulating Health and Safety on the Railway.*

—— and LLOYD-BOSTOCK, S. (1990), 'The Power of Accidents: The Social and Psychological Impact of Accidents and the Enforcement of Safety Regulations', *British Journal of Criminology* 30, 4, 409–22.

—— and —— (1992), 'Field-Level Perceptions of Risk in Regulatory Agencies', in Short, J. F., and Clarke, L.

—— and MANNING, P. K. (1990), 'The Contexts of Regulation: The Impact Upon Health and Safety Inspectorates in Britain', *Law and Policy* 12, 2, 103–36.

—— and SORENSON, P. (1993), 'Business Adaptation to Legal Regulation', *Law and Policy* 15, 3, 169–78.

INGLEBY, R. (1992), *Solicitors and Divorce* (Oxford: Clarendon Press).

IRELAND, F. E., and BRYCE, D. J. (1979), 'The Philosophy of Control of Air Pollution in the United Kingdom', *Royal Society Transcript*, London A.290, 625–37.

JACKSON, R. M. (1967), *Enforcing the Law* (London: Macmillan).

JAMES, C. (1993), 'Social Processes and Reporting or Non-reporting' in Quinlan, M. (ed.).

JAMIESON, H. (1985), 'Persuasion or Punishment: The Enforcement of Health and Safety at Work Legislation by the British Factory Inspectorate', M. Litt. dissertation, University of Oxford.

JASANOFF, S. (1986), *Risk Management and Political Culture* (New York: Russell Sage Foundation).

JOHNSTONE, R. (1994), *The Court and the Factory: The Legal Construction of Occupational Health and Safety Offences in Victoria*, unpublished PhD thesis, University of Melbourne.

JOWELL, J. (1973), 'The Legal Control of Administrative Discretion?', *Public Law*, Autumn, 178–220.

—— (1975), *Law and Bureaucracy* (New York: Dunallen).

JUSTICE (1980), *Breaking the Rules* (London: Justice).

KADISH, M. and KADISH, S. (1973), *Discretion to Disobey: A Study of Lawful Departures from Legal Rules* (Stanford, Calif.: Stanford University Press).

KAGAN, R. A. (1978), *Regulatory Justice* (New York: Russell Sage Foundation).

—— (ed.) (1989), 'Understanding Regulatory Enforcement', *Law and Policy* 11, 2, 89–119.

—— (1994), 'Regulatory Enforcement' in Rosenbloom, D. H., and Schwartz, R. D. (eds.), *Handbook of Regulation and Administrative Law* (New York: Marcel Dekker).

—— and SCHOLZ, J. T. (1984), 'The "Criminology of the Corporation" and Regulatory Enforcement Strategies', in Hawkins, K., and Thomas, J. M. (eds.), *Enforcing Regulation* (Boston, Mass.: Kluwer–Nijhoff).

KAUFMANN, H. (1960), *The Forest Ranger. A Study in Administrative Behaviour* (Baltimore, Maryland: Johns Hopkins University Press).

KELMAN, S. (1981), *Regulating America, Regulating Sweden: a Comparative Study of Occupational Safety and Health Policy* (Cambridge, Mass.: MIT Press).

LA FAVE, W. R. (1962), 'The Police and Non-enforcement of the Law' [1962] *Wisconsin Law Review* 104–37, 179–239.

LEMERT, E. (1967), *Human Deviance, Social Problems and Social Control* (Englewood Cliffs, New Jersey: Prentice Hall).

LEVI, M. (1991), 'Regulating Money Laundering', *British Journal of Criminology* 31, 109–25.

LEWIS, N., and BIRKINSHAW, P. (1993), *When Citizens Complain* (Buckingham: Open University Press).

LLOYD-BOSTOCK, S. (1988), *Legalism and Discretion: A Study of Responses to Accidents and Accident Information Systems in the Occupational Safety and Health Administration, USA* (Oxford: Centre for Socio-Legal Studies).

—— (1992), 'The Psychology of Routine Discretion: Accident Screening by British Factory Inspectors', *Law and Policy* 14, 45–76.

LOWI, T. J. (1972), 'Four Systems of Policy, Politics and Choice', *Public Administration Review* 32 (4).

LYNXWILER, J., SHOVER, N., and CLELLAND, D. A. (1983), 'The Organization and Impact of Inspector Discretion in a Regulatory Bureaucracy', *Social Problems* 30, 4, 425–36.

MCLEAN, I., and FOSTER, C. (1992), 'The Political Economy of Regulation: Interest, Ideology, Voters, and the UK Regulation of Railways Act 1844', *Public Administration* 70, 313–31.

MANNING, P. K. (1977), *Police Work: The Social Organisation of Policing* (Cambridge, Mass.: MIT Press).

—— (1988), Review of Braithwaite, J., *To Punish or Persuade*, *British Journal of Criminology* 28, 4, 559–61.

—— (1988), *Symbolic Communication: Signifying Calls and the Police Response* (Cambridge, Mass.: MIT Press).

—— (1992), 'Technological Dramas and the Police: Statement and Counterstatement in Organisational Analysis', *Criminology* 30, 3, 327–46.

MARTIN, B. (1983), 'The Development of the Factory Office up to 1878: Administrative Evolution and the Establishment of a Regulatory Style in the Early Factory Inspectorate', paper presented to 'Regulation in Britain: A Conference', Trinity College, Oxford University, September 1983.

MASHAW, J. L. (1983), *Bureaucratic Justice* (New Haven, Conn.: Yale University Press).

—— and HARFST, D. L. (1990), *The Struggle for Auto Safety* (Cambridge, Mass.: Harvard University Press).

MCBARNET, D. J. (1981), *Conviction: Law, the State and the Construction of Justice* (London: Macmillan).

MCCABE, S., and SUTCLIFFE, F. (1978), *Defining Crime* (Oxford: Blackwells).

MCEWAN, C., and MAIMAN, R. (1984), 'Mediation in Small Claims Court: Achieving Compliance Through Consent', *Law and Society Review* 18, 1.

MEIDINGER, E. (1987), 'Regulatory Culture: A Theoretical Outline', *Law and Policy* 9, 4, 355–87.

MINISTER WITHOUT PORTFOLIO (1986), *Lifting the Burden* (Cmnd. 9571 London: HMSO).

MINISTRY OF TRANSPORT (1968), *Report of the Public Inquiry into the Accident at Hixon Level-Crossing on January 6th, 1968* (Cmnd 3706, HMSO: London).

NADER, L. (ed.) (1980), *No Access to Law: Alternatives to the American Judicial System* (New York: Academic Press).

NATIONAL AUDIT OFFICE (1991), *Control and Monitoring of Pollution: Review of the Pollution Inspectorate* (London: HMSO).

—— (1994), *Enforcing Health and Safety Legislation in the Workplace* (London: HMSO).

NELKEN, D. (1994), 'White-Collar Crime' in Maguire, M., Morgan, R., and Reiner, R. (eds.), *The Oxford Handbook of Criminology* (Oxford: Oxford University Press).

NELKIN, D. (1992), 'Genetic Screening in the Workplace' in Short, J.F. and Clarke, L.

NIEMEIJER, B. (1989), 'Urban Land-use and Building Control in the Netherlands: Flexible Decisions in a Rigid System', *Law and Policy* 11, 121–52.

OGUS, A. (1994), *Regulation: Legal Form and Economic Theory* (Oxford: Clarendon Press).

OLSEN, P. (1992), *Six Cultures of Regulation* (Copenhagen: Handelshøjskolen).

PARRIS, H. (1965), *Government and the Railways in the Nineteenth Century* (London: Routledge and Kegan Paul).

PAULUS, I. (1974), *The Search for Pure Food* (London: Martin Robertson).

PEARCE, F. (1976), *Crimes of the Powerful* (London: Pluto Press).

—— and TOMBS, S. (1990), 'Ideology, Hegemony, and Empiricism', *British Journal of Criminology* 30, 4, 423–43.

PERROW, C. (1984), *Normal Accidents* (New York: Basic Books).

PILIAVIN, T., and BRIAR, S. (1964), 'Police Encounters with Juveniles', *American Sociological Review* 70, 206–14.

PONSFORD, B. (1988), 'Logic and Practice in Environmental Pollution Control', *Annual Occupational Hygiene* 32, 3, 261–70.

POSNER, R. (1981), *The Economics of Justice* (Cambridge, Mass.: Harvard University Press).

QUINLAN, M. (ed.) (1993), *Work and Health* (South Melbourne: Macmillan).

REES, J. (1988), *Reforming the Workplace: a Study of Self-Regulation in Occupational Safety* (Philadelphia, Penn.: University of Pennsylvania Press).

REINER, R. (1991), *Chief Constables* (Oxford: Oxford University Press).

REISS, A. (1971), *The Police and the Public* (New Haven, Conn.: Yale University Press).

—— (1984), 'Selecting Strategies of Social Control over Organisational Life' in Hawkins, K., and Thomas, J.

—— (1992), 'The Institutionalization of Risk' in Short, J.F. and Clarke, L.

Report of the Committee of Inquiry into an Outbreak of Food Poisoning at Stanley Royd Hospital (1986) (London: HMSO).

Report of the House of Representatives Standing Committee on Aboriginal Affairs (1984), *The Effects of Asbestos Mining on the Baryugil Community* (Canberra: Australian Government Publishing Service).

RICHARDSON, G. M., with OGUS, A. I., BURROWS, P. (1983), *Policing Pollution: A Study of Regulation and Enforcement* (Oxford: Clarendon).

ROBENS COMMITTEE (1972), *Safety and Health at Work* (London: HMSO).

ROCK, P. (1973), *Making People Pay* (London: Routledge & Kegan Paul).

—— (1983), 'Law, Order and Power in Late Seventeenth- and Early Eighteenth-century England' in Cohen, S. and Scull, A. (eds.) *Social Control and the State* (Oxford: Blackwell).

—— (1986), *A View from the Shadows* (Oxford: Clarendon Press).

—— (1990), *Helping Victims of Crime* (Oxford: Clarendon Press).

—— (1995), 'Sociology and the Stereotype of the Police', *Journal of Law and Society* 22, 1, 17–25.

ROGERS, N. M., and MCEWAN, C. A. (1989), *Mediation: Law, Policy and Practice* (Rochester N.Y.: Lawyers' Co-Operative).

ROLT, L. T. C. (1986), *Red for Danger* (London: Pan Books).

ROYAL COMMISSION ON ENVIRONMENTAL POLLUTION (1976), *Fifth Report: Air Pollution Control: An Integrated Approach* (Cmnd. 6371, London: HMSO).

—— (1983), *Ninth Report: Lead in the Environment* (Cmnd. 8852, London: HMSO).

—— (1984), *Tenth Report: Tackling Pollution—Experience and Prospects* (Cmnd. 9149, London: HMSO).

RUANE, J. M., and CERULO, K. A. (1990), 'The Police and CMHCs: The Transition from Penal to Therapeutic Control', *Law and Policy* 12, 2, 137–54.

SANDERS, A. (1987), 'Constructing the Case for the Prosecution', *Journal of Law and Society* 14, 2, 229–53.

SCHNEIDER, C. E. (1992), 'Discretion and Rules: A Lawyer's View' in Hawkins.

SCHOLZ, J. T. (1983), 'Co-operation, Regulatory Compliance, and the Enforcement Dilemma', paper presented at the annual meeting of the American Political Science Association, 1-4 September, Chicago, cited in AXELROD, R (1984), *The Evolution of Co-operation* (New York: Basic Books).

SHAPIRO, S. (1984), *Wayward Capitalists* (New Haven, Conn.: Yale University Press).

—— (1987), 'The Social Control of Impersonal Trust', *American Journal of Sociology* 93, 3, 623–58.

SHEEN COMMITTEE (1987), *MV Herald of Free Enterprise: Report of the Court No. 8074 Dept. of Transport* (London: HMSO).

SHORT, J. F. (1992), 'Defining, Explaining, and Managing Risks' in Short, J. F., and Clarke, L. (eds.), *Organizations, Uncertainties and Risk* (Boulder, Colo.: Westview Press).

—— and CLARKE, L. (eds.) (1992), *Organizations, Uncertainties and Risk* (Boulder, Colo.: Westview Press).

SHOVER, N., CLELLAND, D., and LYNXWILER, J. (1982), *Constructing a Regulatory Bureaucracy: The Office of Surface Mining Reclamation and Enforcement* (Washington, DC: National Institute of Justice).

SILVERMAN, D. (1985), *Qualitative Methodology and Sociology* (Aldershot: Gower).

SKOLNICK, J. (1975), *Justice Without Trial* (2nd edn., New York: John Wiley & Sons).

SMITH, J. C., and HOGAN, B. (1978), *Criminal Law* (4th edn., London: Butterworths).

SNIDER, L. (1987), 'Towards a Political Economy of Reform, Regulation and Corporate Crime', *Law and Policy* 9, 1, 37–68.

STEWART, J., and WALSH, K. (1992), 'Change in the Management of Public Services', *Public Administration* 70, 499–518.

TAPPAN, P. (1947), 'Who is the Criminal?', *American Sociological Review* 12, 1, 96–102.

TURNER, K. (1989), 'Safety, Discipline and the Manager: Building a Higher Class of Men', *Sociology* 23, 4, 611–28.

VAUGHAN, D. (1982), 'Transaction Systems and Unlawful Organizational Behaviour', *Social Problems* 29, 4, 373–79.

VELJANOVSKI, C. G. (1983), 'Regulatory Enforcement: An Economic Study of the British Factory Inspectorate', *Law and Policy Quarterly* 5, 75–96.

VOGEL, D. (1986), *National Styles of Regulation: Environmental Policy in Great Britain and the United States* (Ithaca: Cornell University Press).

WADDINGTON, P. A. J. (1994), *The Strong Arm of the Law?: Public Order and Policing in the Capital City* (London: UCL Press).

WEAIT, M. (1989), 'The Letter of the Law? An Enquiry into Reasoning and Formal Enforcement in the Industrial Air Polluting Inspectorate', *British Journal of Criminology* 29, 57–70.

WELLS, C. (1992), *Corporations and Criminal Responsibility* (Oxford: Clarendon Press).

Whyte, W. F. (1984), *Learning from The Field* (London: Sage).

Wilson, G. K. (1985), *The Politics of Safety and Health* (Oxford: Clarendon Press).

Wilson, J. Q. (1968), *Varieties of Police Behaviour* (Cambridge, Mass.: Harvard University Press).

—— (1980), *The Politics of Regulation* (New York: Basic Books).

Wilthagen, T. (1994), 'Reflexive Rationality in the Regulation of Occupational Health and Safety' in Rogowski, R., and Wilthagen, T., *Reflexive Labour Law* (Boston, Mass.: Kluwer–Nijhoff).

Winter, G. (1985), 'Bartering Rationality in Regulation', *Law and Society Review* 19, 219–50.

Yeager, P. C. (1991), *The Limits of the Law: The Public Regulation of Private Pollution* (Cambridge: Cambridge University Press).

Author Index

Aalders, M., 243
Adler, M., 12
Alderman, G., 34
Anderson, M., 32, 33, 34
Ashby, E., 32, 33, 34
Asquith, S., 12
Atkinson, P., 249
Axelrod, 189
Ayres, L., 206–7, 215, 228, 245

Baar, E., 242, 247
Baldwin, R., 12, 67, 72, 157
Bamford, M., 70, 163, 243
Banton, M., 10, 12, 19, 243
Bardach, E., 6, 13, 16, 77, 86, 94, 160, 166, 183, 185, 189, 195, 226, 246
Bartrip, P.W.J., 32, 33–4, 232
Baucus, M., 8
Becker, H.S. and Geer, B., 19, 30, 249
Bell, C. and Newby, H., 249
Bernstein, M.H., 5, 6
Birkinshaw, P., 135
Bittner, E., 10, 243
Black, D.J., 239–42
Blau, P.M., 51
Box, S., 5, 86
Briar, S., 10
Braithwaite, J., 6, 16, 18, 152, 165, 187, 206–7, 214, 215, 222, 225, 228, 241, 242, 243, 244, 245
Braithwaite, J., Grabosky, P. and Walker, J., 16
Brimblecombe, P., 32
Brittan, Y., 9
Bryce, D. J., 86
Bugler, J., 70, 86
Burgess, R.G., 19, 255
Burman, 34
Burrows, P., 9
Butler, R., 45, 61, 135

Cain, M., 10, 12, 19, 243
Calavita, K. and Pontell, H.N., 243
Carson, W.G, 5, 6, 9, 14, 27, 32, 45, 61, 70, 118, 165, 212, 214, 226, 243

Cerulo, K.A., 241
Charnbliss, E., 12–13, 18
Cheit, R.E., 10, 11, 18, 78, 87, 93, 95, 102, 150, 245
Clarke, M., 243
Clinard, M.B., 5, 226
Clinton, A., 70, 163, 243
Coates, R.B., 243
Cohen, S., 11
Cook, D., 243
Cotterell, R., 12
Council of the Law Society, 8
Cranston, R., 5, 10, 14, 107, 116, 185, 187, 215, 224, 243
Croall, H., 8, 224, 243
Cumming, E., Cumming, I., and Edell, E., 243

Davis, K.C., 12, 67
Dawson, S., 70, 163, 243
Di Mento, J.F., 4, 12, 13, 18, 152, 165, 182, 184
Dingwall, R., 243
Douglas, M., 95, 150
Dworkin, T.M., 8

Edell, E., 243
Edelman, L.E., 12–13, 18
Eekelaar, J., 243
ENDS Report, 58

Felstiner, W.L.F., 243
Fenn, P.T., 32, 33–4, 232
Fennell, P., 134
Fisse, W.B., 215, 222
Frank, N., 130
Frankel, M., 32, 33, 48, 255
Friedland, M.L., 4

Galanter, M., 17
Galligan, D.J., 12
Geer, B., 259
Gehm, J., 243
Genn, H., 9, 158, 182, 243
Gerber, J., 215, 222

Gräbe, S., 24
Grabosky, P., 6, 16, 18, 134, 165, 187,
    225, 241, 242, 244
Gray, W.B., 226
Gunningham, N., 5, 6, 9, 18, 70, 83,
    183, 243, 244
Gusfield, J., 150

Hammersley, M. and Atkinson, P., 249
Harfst, D.L, 10, 93
Hartung, F.E., 9
Hawkins, K., 6, 7, 9, 10, 12, 14, 15, 17,
    19, 24, 29, 46, 51, 67, 86, 96, 120,
    125–6, 168, 185, 187, 192, 195, 196,
    214, 216, 222, 223–4, 236, 244
Hidden, A., 197
Hill, M.J., 51
Hogan, B., 8
Horwitz, A,V., 238
Howard, S.E., 12–13, 18
Hutter, B.M., 4, 5, 6, 7, 9, 11, 14, 16, 18,
    27–8, 29, 45, 47, 46, 47, 51, 53, 59, 62,
    70, 94, 96, 117, 126, 138, 141, 142,
    147, 148, 150, 160, 168, 172, 185, 187,
    195, 214, 224, 231–2, 238, 243, 244
Hutter, B.M. and Lloyd-Bostock, S., 29
Hutter, B.M. and Manning, P.K., 11, 27,
    45, 47, 62, 100
Hutter, B.M. and Sorenson, P., 4

Ingleby, R., 243
Ireland, F.E. and Bryce, D.J., 86

Jackson, R.M., 8
Jamieson, H., 10, 45, 47
Jasanoff, S., 75, 95
Johnstone, R., 243
Jowell, S., 12, 67
Justice, 8, 9

Kadish, M. and Kadish, S., 12
Kagan, R.A., 6, 13, 16, 77, 86, 94, 160,
    169, 183, 185, 187, 189, 195, 226,
    237, 238, 244, 245, 246
Kaufmann, H., 12, 51
Kelman, S., 6, 11, 15, 18, 243

La Fave, W.R., 243
Lemert, E., 19
Levi, M., 243
Lewis, N. and Birkinshaw, P., 135
Lloyd-Bostock, S., 29, 94, 96, 139, 142,
    147, 148, 150

Lowi, T., 4
Lynxwiler, J., Shover, N. and Clelland,
    D.A., 165

Maiman, R., 243
Manning, P.K., 4, 11, 12, 13, 19, 27, 45,
    47, 61, 172, 238
Martin, B., 32–3
Mashaw, J.L. and Harfst, D.L., 10, 12
McBarnet, D.J., 244
McEwan, C., 243
Meidinger, E., 19, 20, 193

Nader, L., 6
Nelkin, D., 94, 244
Newby, H., 249
Niemeijer, B., 243

Ogus, A., 5–6, 7, 9
Olsen, P., 11, 182, 222

Parris, H., 32, 34
Paulus, I., 5, 9, 70
Pearce, F., 86, 226
Perrow, C., 150
Petterson, S., 12–13, 18
Piliavin, T. and Briar, S., 10
Posner, R., 87

Rees, J., 243, 245
Reiner, R., 38
Reiss, A., 14, 15, 29, 93, 94, 105, 150,
    238–9, 241, 243
Richardson, G.M., 5, 51, 212
Richardson, G.M. with Ogus, A.I.,
    Burrows, P., 9, 14, 19, 29, 115, 187,
    196, 224
Rock, P., 10, 13, 14, 19, 194, 195, 215,
    223, 226, 228, 242
Rogers, N.M., 243
Rolt, L.T.C., 32
Ruane, J.M., 241

Sanders, A., 223
Sarat, A., 243
Schneider, C.E., 71
Scholz, J.T., 28, 187, 189, 226
Shapiro, S., 193 243
Short, J.F., 75, 93, 95, 215, 222
Shover, N., 15, 18, 28, 29, 232, 243
Silverman, D., 249
Skolnick, J., 10, 12, 19
Smith, J.C. and Hogan, B., 8